D0227382

Great Brand Blunders

The Worst Marketing and Social Media Meltdowns of All Time . . . and How to Avoid Your Own

Rob Gray

crimson

Great Brand Blunders: The Worst Marketing and Social Media Meltdowns of All Time ... and How to Avoid Your Own

This edition first published in Great Britain in 2014 by Crimson Publishing Ltd, The Tramshed, Walcot Street, Bath BA1 5BB

© Rob Gray, 2014

The right of Rob Gray to be identified as the author of this work has been asserted by him in accordance with the Copyright, Designs and Patents Act 1988.

All rights reserved. This book is sold subject to the condition that it shall not, by way of trade or otherwise, be lent, resold, hired out or otherwise circulated without the publisher's prior written consent in any form of binding or cover other than that in which it is published and without a similar condition including this condition being imposed on the subsequent purchaser. No part of this publication may be reproduced, stored in a retrieval system or transmitted in any form or by any means, electronic and mechanical, photocopying, recording or otherwise without prior permission of Crimson Publishing.

British Library Cataloguing in Publication Data
A catalogue record for this book is available from the British Library.

ISBN 978 1 78059 229 9

Typeset by IDSUK (DataConnection) Ltd
Printed and bound in the UK by Bell & Bain Ltd, Glasgow

For my wife Ginny, whose loveliness, loyalty, willingness to indulge me and crazily infectious sense of fun offer some degree of proof that there's more to me than blundering.

Contents

About the author

Rob Gray has written about marketing and brands for over two decades. He is a long-standing, regular contributor to the Chartered Institute of Marketing's magazine *The Marketer*, and since 2000 he has worked in a freelance capacity as head of editorial content at the International Public Relations Association, where he is responsible for commissioning and editing the highly respected *IPRA Thought Leadership* series of essays.

His insightful journalism on brands, marketing and communications has appeared in a wide variety of publications, from leading newspapers such as the *Financial Times* and the *Guardian* to business titles including *Marketing, Campaign, Broadcast, PR Week, HR Magazine, The Grocer* and *Management Today*. He also works as a copywriter and marketing consultant.

Rob lives with his wife and children in a village on the border of Northamptonshire and Oxfordshire. He is renowned for the relish with which he winkles out the lessons to be learned from a good blunder. Go to @RobGrayWriter to follow him on Twitter.

Introduction

It's said that the best way to learn is through our own mistakes. If that were always true, the incompetent and reckless would be the wisest among us, and lurching ostentatiously from one awful error to another would hold the key to success. Follow such flawed logic to its conclusion and we'd entrust vital assignments to people known to have frequently screwed up. Reassured by that? No, nor me. Better, surely, to keep our own mistakes to a minimum by learning from those made by our rivals and contemporaries, with insight gained from historic disasters thrown in for good measure.

Even the greatest brands make a mess of their marketing from time to time. The roll-call in this book includes Coca-Cola, McDonald's, Apple, Starbucks, Virgin, Nestlé, Qantas, Mattel, Sony, Danone, Microsoft, Colgate, Wal-Mart, Bic and many others on the global A-list. I've also drawn on plenty of instances of flops and calamities from across the world featuring smaller brands. All told, *Great Brand Blunders* covers more than 175 examples of marketing misadventures, major and minor, spanning Europe, North America, South America, Asia, Africa and Australasia.

Yet although the book is predominantly about those occasions when things went awry, I have purposely leavened it with some inspiring examples of getting it majestically right. It doesn't do to be relentlessly negative. And while there are passages where I may be a trifle acerbic in tone, I have aimed also to be upbeat, balanced and instructive – without,

I hope, being preachy. In addition to scrutinising stupid decisions and dissecting cadaverous campaigns, I offer some helpful marketing tips. By marching expectantly down blind alleys, others pinpoint for us directions to rule out.

A high proportion of examples in this book are drawn from the last few years. On the one hand, that's a deliberate effort on my part to be relevant, but on the other it also reflects the fact that more brand blunders than ever are occurring and being magnified because of the phenomenon that is social media platforms such as Twitter and Facebook. However, no comprehensive book on marketing disasters would be complete without 'classic' failures such as the Ford Edsel, New Coke and Hoover's infamously out-of-control free flights debacle. Through new research and analysis and some first-hand interviews with those involved, I like to think I've brought a fresh perspective to bear on such famous fiascos. At the same time, I hope my take on many of the lesser known *faux pas* that feature on the following pages will be equally entertaining and illuminating, if not more so.

Blunders from previous generations provide timeless insights and valuable lessons even today. But at the same time it's important to acknowledge how much the world has changed. We now live in the age of 'conversational brands'. While without question interacting with a target audience through social media channels is a good thing, it has made marketing more immediate and infinitely more perilous. In the rush to exploit digital opportunities, a lot of the old checks and balances have been swept away. Sometimes relatively junior team members who 'get' social media are left to make decisions that can have huge implications for a brand reputation nurtured over decades. Moreover, the loss of message control that is inherent in social media opens the door to all manner of unintended consequences. Today's consumers expect their voices to be heard. They are passionate in support of their favourite brands. But they also have a sense of ownership that often manifests itself in holding brands to account. The world isn't populated by unaware, constantly sunny characters like Forrest Gump or Ned Flanders who see good in everyone, everywhere. Real people have strong opinions and take great pleasure in pointing out shortcomings and faults. And when there's a bona fide balls-up, they may relish the role they play in criticising the brand that's to blame, helping bad news spread like wildfire – the nightmarish flipside of a successful viral marketing campaign packed with rigorously pre-agreed messages.

Brands that should know better have dropped some terrible social media clangers. Some have opened themselves up to abuse by posting insulting or offensive content – dissing President Obama, joking with young teenagers about hardcore pornography and making light of natural disasters being just a few choice examples of errant behaviour – or by unleashing hashtags that are wildly inappropriate or carelessly present an open invitation to mischief makers. Social media has an insatiable appetite for content, and it is in trying to feed this appetite that brands can come unstuck.

Just as marketing itself has many facets, this book considers numerous aspects of failure, from crass ads that are offensive to their target audience (and in one case a campaign so misjudged it drove a brand to extinction) to publicity stunts so ill-conceived and chaotic that they required the intervention of the emergency services, and in a couple of extreme instances even caused the deaths of participants and bystanders. Brands have unwittingly or incompetently found themselves embroiled in unpalatable controversies about sexism, racism, violence and child abuse. Marketers have blown huge sums of money by pursuing misguided strategies, launching laughable new products such as the Sinclair C5, misunderstanding their customers and running badly devised promotions. There have been fateful product reformulations, like Unilever's development of a washing powder potent enough to shred clothes, which despite being a bruising, expensive experience was not even close to being the most disastrous product revamp the company had ever undertaken. And there have been bizarre brand extensions (hats off in particular to Kraft in Australia – the oddness of the Vegemite iSnack 2.0 story takes some beating). We can also throw into the mix panicked U-turns, baffling cross-cultural miscommunication, ridiculous rebrandings, devious dishonesty, rogue creative teams and so much more.

Read on, to be amused and amazed. This isn't a book about taking delight in the foolhardiness of others (well, maybe sometimes a little – when people have done something that is truly, jaw-droppingly, *what-were-they-thinking?* idiotic) but about understanding why marketing mistakes were made and how to avoid repeating them. It's about context and insight as much as it's about comedy and ineptitude. It's a book not just for marketers, academics, students and business owners but for anyone curious about the complicated issues brands and the people behind them must deal with in order to thrive. When poor choices are made, as with bad architecture the results are there for all to judge – as obtrusive as a giant digital billboard. It's perhaps of little consolation to those involved in marketing mishaps, but their errors provide a wonderful learning opportunity.

Let's hear it for the f-word that no advertiser thinks is sexy: failure.

Chapter 1
Awful advertising
The worst campaigns in history

Great advertising has the power to surprise, to change perceptions and, at its best, to sear itself into the memory and take root in popular culture. Think of the Smash Martians, Coke teaching the world to sing, the intense art-house beauty of surfers and horses riding the crashing waves for Guinness, the adorable scampering Andrex puppy in all its cuddly incarnations. These are unforgettable examples of campaigns that delivered brand messages by connecting with their target audience. Sometimes, through the cleverness of the creative idea, the technical brilliance of its execution or the sheer ambition of what the advertiser is trying to achieve, advertising can become a landmark event. The Apple Macintosh was a ground-breaking product, but would it have succeeded to the same degree without the excitement of the much-vaunted *1984* commercial by ad agency Chiat/Day? This big-budget dystopian epic, directed by renowned filmmaker Ridley Scott, fresh from critical and imaginative success with movies *Blade Runner* and *Alien*, not only got people talking about the product but positioned Apple as the smart and daring underdog with the interests of the public at heart, while rival IBM was implicitly cast in the role of a totalitarian 'techie' Big Brother imposing drudgery and conformity.

Yet in order to be great, advertising need not be lavish in scale. Often it is the simple idea unfussily told that is most effective of all. Doyle Dane Bernbach's insightful and brave work for clients VW and Avis in the 1950s and 1960s – the *Mad Men*-era heyday of Madison Avenue – worked by turning conventional wisdom on its head. At a time when bigger was generally regarded as better, DDB urged drivers to reconsider what is important in a vehicle by promoting the nimbleness and efficiency of the Beetle with the tagline 'Think Small'; while for car hire company Avis, DDB flaunted what had been perceived as a weakness – lagging behind Hertz – with a campaign asserting that because it was in second place it had to try harder. By making a virtue of a market position that might otherwise be seen as a negative, Avis gained respect for its honesty and presented itself winningly as a challenger brand prepared to go the extra mile (a good attribute in the car business) because it was steeped in customer service. On the back of the campaign, over a four-year period in the 1960s Avis saw its market share leap from 11% to 35%. The 'We Try Harder' tagline proved so compelling that it became the mainstay of Avis's marketing communications for half a century.

More recently, the multi-award winning *Three Little Pigs* commercial for the *Guardian* dramatically reimagined the classic fairy tale as it would be told in today's social media-influenced, fast-moving 24-hour news cycle and positioned the newspaper as the authoritative choice for anyone looking for the whole picture. Meanwhile, piggybacking – for want of a better expression – on the London 2012 Olympics were a pair of campaigns from different sides of the Atlantic that packed a powerful emotional punch. Channel 4's *Meet the Superhumans* work to promote its Paralympics coverage and Procter & Gamble's (P&G's) 'Thank You, Mom' campaign shared a focus on sacrifice, determination and athletic endeavour that celebrated humanity at its best and most diverse and did so in a way that, considering the limitations of such a short form, was both filmic and exceptionally moving.

When it works, advertising can help brands achieve fantastic results. But when it's bad . . .

How to upset a billionaire – Virgin Mobile's knock-out idea

Sir Richard Branson knows a thing or two about marketing. The Virgin founder is one of the great contemporary entrepreneurs and his sharp eye for business opportunities, mastery of brand building and flair for self-publicity have helped him amass a huge personal fortune. Part of Branson's considerable charm comes from the boyish gusto with which he throws himself into promotional set pieces. As well as his death-defying long-distance hot air ballooning exploits, classic Branson marketing stunts include shaving off his beard, applying make-up and donning a wedding dress for the launch of Virgin Brides, in the process achieving a passing resemblance to transvestite comedian Eddie Izzard; driving a heavily branded tank down New York City's Fifth Avenue to draw attention to his cola; and promoting routes for Virgin Atlantic by dressing as a Zulu warrior in South Africa and exposing his bare bottom in Canada to reveal part of his beloved airline's name. It may appear that he is a man immune to embarrassment, the billionaire who doesn't blush.

Nevertheless, it *is* possible to embarrass Richard Branson. How? Through the bizarre move of creating an ad that associates his cherished Virgin brand with date rape. That's exactly what happened in December 2012 as part of an online Advent calendar campaign for Virgin Mobile USA. The image for the 8th December 'surprise' showed a man standing behind a woman in a living room, covering her eyes with one hand while holding a nicely wrapped bijou gift in the other. All very homely, festive and innocent − until we come to the caption. This read: 'The Gift of Christmas Surprise. Necklace? Or chloroform?'

Needless to say, when the ad appeared online it provoked instant criticism. The condemnation fanned out via social media and soon came to Branson's attention. As it happens, the Virgin Mobile USA business is owned by Sprint Nextel Corporation, which licenses the right to use the Virgin name from Branson, having bought out the entrepreneur in 2009. Although no longer the owner of the mobile business in the USA, Branson was immediately aware of the damage that could be done to his wider Virgin empire, a tangled web of about four hundred different companies around the globe.

Swiftly putting out a statement on his Virgin Group website, Branson wrote: 'Having just seen, for the first time, the Virgin Mobile US advert which has upset many today, I agree it is ill-judged. Although I don't own the company, it carries our brand. I will speak to the team there, make my thoughts clear and see what can be done about it. Virgin

Mobile US usually get these things right, although on this occasion it is clear they have gone too far.' After contacting the team in the States, Branson updated his post to say: 'Having spoken with them just now they acknowledge a dreadful mistake was made, the advert will be withdrawn within the hour, never to be seen again.' Once the ad had been taken down, Virgin Mobile USA apologised deeply for any offence it had caused and claimed that it had not approved the image.

Branson's prompt and prudent intervention took the heat out of the situation. The Everyday Sexism Project, set up to catalogue instances of sexism experienced by women day to day, was among those tweeting appreciation of Branson for listening to their concerns and taking decisive action. Had the controversy not been addressed in this way, the outcome would have been far worse. It's safe to assume that Virgin Mobile USA has tightened up its advertising authorisation procedures – and that future festive campaigns will feature more traditional and innocuous Christmas images.

PETA's vegan violence – shock tactics don't work if you trivialise serious issues

While Virgin was caught completely off guard, the same cannot be said of pressure group People for the Ethical Treatment of Animals (PETA), which has a long history of employing shock tactics in its campaigning. PETA's use of nudity and graphic images relating to animal cruelty in advertising has generally served it well, attracting attention and amplifying its voice in the animal welfare debate. Criticism from its opponents is to be expected, but a groundswell of criticism from people who would otherwise support the aims and methods of the organisation is something else entirely. And that's what PETA faced when it unleashed its *Boyfriend Went Vegan* commercial on Valentine's Day 2012.

The supposedly tongue-in-cheek ad features the return home of an injured young woman wearing a neck brace who looks as though she has been the victim of domestic violence. Its punch line, for want of a better expression, is that she is suffering from BWVAKTBOOM: 'Boyfriend Went Vegan And Knocked The Bottom Out Of Me'. Over the strains of doleful piano music, a male narrator explains that this is a 'painful condition that occurs when boyfriends go vegan and can suddenly bring it like a tantric porn star'. At the end of the commercial the woman smiles at her boyfriend, presumably to reassure him that she likes the rough sex that's been triggered by the libido-enhancing change in his diet. Together with the ridiculous name given to the fictional condition, this is clearly meant to bring some levity to the ad. The big problem here is that by appropriating the mood and tropes of a domestic abuse awareness campaign run by a shelter, the advertising reinforces a mindset in the viewer that is not remotely amusing.

You have to ask, what is the message PETA wants its audience to aspire to? That battered and bruised equals great sex? That eating cheese is bad but hurting people is aspirational? Apart from casting Chris Brown and Rihanna, PETA could hardly have got it more wrong.

Not as smooth as Belvedere would like – when vodka advertising goes down badly

Was there something in the water in 2012 that impaired the judgement of several creative teams? Perhaps their drinks were spiked – with vodka. I pick that particular spirit because upmarket Polish vodka brand Belvedere sits alongside Virgin Mobile and PETA on the shameful list of advertising that, in heavy-handedly attempting to be both risqué and humorous, could easily be construed as portraying sexual assault as a laughing matter. Belvedere, which is distributed globally by French luxury goods group LVMH, is named after the Polish presidential palace and is positioned as a premium product quadruple-distilled from the finest rye. The LVMH website describes it as a privileged treat to satisfy the most discriminating taste. All the more inexplicable, then, that such a 'classy' brand should take a cheap shot and lower itself with some disturbing innuendo.

In March 2012 Belvedere posted an ad to its official Facebook and Twitter accounts. The ad showed a startled-looking woman grappling to escape the clutches of a leering young man. Its accompanying text read: 'Unlike Some People, Belvedere Always Goes Down Smoothly.' Maybe the drink does, but this time its advertising didn't. Consumers couldn't see how a woman being pressurised into performing oral favours might be either funny or a fitting way to market a liquor brand. Previous Belvedere ads had also gone for the 'sex sells' approach, one, for example, featuring a man blindfolding a woman and the line 'Trust Your Instincts'. While an open-minded audience would perceive this earlier ad as playful, sensual and unthreatening, the implicit coercion in the 'Unlike Some People, Belvedere Always Goes Down Smoothly' execution provoked a very different reaction.

Considering that alcohol can often be a contributory factor in sexual assaults, Belvedere had taken itself into dangerous territory. Consumers immediately voiced their outrage on social media at this 'shameful' and 'horrifying emblem of rape culture' using hashtags such as #rapeisnotfunny. Just an hour after it first went up, Belvedere pulled the ad and hastily issued the following apology: 'We sincerely apologize to any of our fans who were offended by our recent post and related comments. As always, we continue to be an advocate of safe and responsible drinking.' That initial apology didn't cut much ice and criticism persisted, forcing the president of Belvedere Vodka, Charles Gibb, to issue his own personal apology in which he undertook to investigate how the offensive ad had appeared and to make sure that such an error was never repeated. 'The content is contrary to our values and we deeply regret this lapse,' he wrote. As a further expression of contrition over the matter, Gibb announced that Belvedere was making a donation to America's largest anti-sexual violence organisation, the Rape, Abuse and Incest National Network (RAINN). The charity thanked Belvedere for its 'generous' donation, adding in a statement on its own Facebook page: 'Nice to see a company that not only undoes its mistake but looks for a way to do good afterwards.'

This could well have been enough to defuse the situation had another problem not surfaced. Not only was the wording of the ad a terrible mistake, it soon came to light that Belvedere had not bothered to secure copyright to reproduce the image. The still was in fact lifted from a short online comedy video, *Awkward Moments: The Baby Picture*, in which an overbearing mother embarrasses her grown-up daughter by persuading her to recreate a family photo from her childhood. The daughter is played by the actress Alicyn Packard, known for her work as a voiceover artist on computer games and for the kids' TV series *The Mr Men Show*. Strictly Viral Productions, a digital media production company co-owned by Packard, made the video. The week after the ad made its fleeting appearance, Packard filed a lawsuit in Los Angeles seeking compensation from the drinks company for emotional distress and for misappropriating her likeness in contravention of Californian law, which prohibits the unauthorised use of a person's picture for advertising purposes.

According to *The Hollywood Reporter*, the lawsuit stated:

> *'While Defendants have apologized to nearly everyone else, and admitted the offensiveness of the advertisement they have yet to apologize to the plaintiff, whose image she says they used without permission to sell vodka, and who has now been unwillingly made the face of the Belvedere advertising campaign that jokes about rape, and has been put front and center in the worldwide controversy created by Defendants.'*

Belvedere's online calamity was by no means the first time advertisers have tried to shift product by making blow job puns. Another member of this odd little club is a 2006 campaign in Singapore for Danish skincare brand Imedeen. One of Singapore's biggest stars, the actress Zoe Tay was the face of the campaign to push pills said to be beneficial to the skin. The print ad was dominated by an alluring image of Tay in which she appeared to be recumbent on white sheets. Its headline contained a double entendre that had all the subtlety of Miley Cyrus on a wrecking ball: 'My Secret to Beautiful Skin? I Swallow.' Cue a small furore, plenty of giggling and lots of quips about the precise nature of what Tay was doing to nourish her skin from within. The campaign was quickly toned down. An interesting footnote is that pharmaceutical giant Pfizer bought Imedeen in a 2011 acquisition. Now that the brand is part of a vast corporation, its days of smutty advertising belong firmly in the past – but then again, as one of Pfizer's most famous products is Viagra, perhaps the opposite will be true.

Dale Wurfel and the used Ford - repeating BMW's misogynist mistake

If Dale Wurfel, a Chrysler car dealership in Ontario, Canada, had known how the Imedeen campaign was received it's doubtful it would have made a similar blunder with its press advertising in early 2011. Like the skincare brand, Dale Wurfel opted to use an image of an attractive young woman in an alluring pose. In this instance, though, the aim of the campaign was to sell used vehicles. What caught the attention wasn't the finance package on offer from the dealership; it was the woman's coquettish manner, pristine make-up and skimpy black dress. But most of all it was the headline text on her arm: 'You know you're not the first. But do you really care?' Complaints began pouring in. From Chrysler to crisis in an impressive 0–60 time. Many people felt that the dealership was objectifying women by comparing them to used cars. As for the allusion to previous sexual partners ... well, the headline would hardly have worked for Branson's Virgin brand, would it? Strangely enough, Dale Wurfel's campaign mirrored a 2008 ad run in Greece by BMW for its premium used cars, which didn't receive nearly as much flak. Mind you, Twitter was still in its infancy back then. The rise of social media has unquestionably made it easier for anyone offended by an ad to share their displeasure or concerns with a receptive, often judgemental audience. While cultural differences between Greece and the USA go some way towards explaining why there was less fall-out from BMW's advertising, if the luxury car maker were foolish enough to run the same advertising copy again today it would guarantee itself a greater level of criticism, with opinionated social media users fanning the flames of the controversy.

In what had the whiff of a damage limitation exercise, on 9th April, the day after the original Dale Wurfel ad ran in the *London Free Press*, another full-page ad from the dealership appeared in the Canadian newspaper. This ad had the same headline as the last. Only this time the image was of a good-looking man, bow tie loosened, crisp white shirt unbuttoned far enough to reveal some chest hair. Could the dealership now claim it was even-handed to the sexes? There was a suspicion that this second ad may have been hastily cobbled together. There was also something very familiar about the guy in the ad. Wait a minute, people started wondering, isn't that Tom Ford? *The* Tom Ford? Handsome, multi-talented saviour of Gucci, founder of the glamorous fashion label bearing his own name and director of an Oscar-nominated movie starring Colin Firth? *The* Tom Ford flogging second-hand autos in provincial Canada?

Yes, astonishingly, it really was. Dale Wurfel had made use of an image of Ford from an old photo shoot, perhaps without any idea who it was, and certainly without authorisation. Showing the same lack of rigour as Belvedere, this sort of lapse has derailed many more campaigns than might at first be imagined and is an issue I explore at greater length in Chapter 7, Can You Believe It? Ford, though an apt name for a car salesman, was reportedly far from amused at this déclassé turn of events and Dale Wurfel abandoned the campaign at top speed. Ironically, while this time Ford was involved inadvertently, he is no stranger to controversial marketing. In his days at Gucci he oversaw some much complained-about advertising and faced claims of sexism himself for an infamous 2002 campaign shot by A-list photographer Mario Testino in which supermodel Louise Pedersen had her pubic hair shaved into the shape of the Gucci G.

Shaking up the marketing of milk – CMPB annoys its target audience

Of course it's impossible to determine precisely where the line between sexy and sexist lies – it varies depending on an individual's point of view. What's clearer is that even advertising that is in no way intended to be sexy can be pilloried as sexist. A seemingly innocuous drink like milk, more commonly in hot water as part of tea or coffee, can find itself in the sort of trouble that may be more usually associated with beverages such as vodka. This is what happened in July 2011 when the California Milk Processor Board (CMPB) launched a campaign with a radical new approach to increasing milk sales. CMPB is the marketing body for milk processors in the state of California and is behind the popular 'Got Milk?' brand, which it also licenses for use by other dairy businesses outside the state. A small levy on each gallon of milk sold by CMPB members is used to fund marketing activity that promotes milk consumption.

One of the biggest challenges in marketing milk is its very pervasiveness. It's a dietary staple. People already know to pour it on their cereal or add it to their coffee. They know whether they prefer full fat, semi-skimmed or skimmed. Consequently, it's far from easy to find a fresh angle with which to promote milk. But in summer 2011 CMPB thought it had hit upon something a little bit out of the ordinary – by using the findings of several academic studies which concluded that taking calcium could be a simple and effective way to reduce the symptoms of PMS. One of these was a 1998 study published in the *American Journal of Obstetrics and Gynecology* called 'Calcium carbonate and the premenstrual syndrome: Effects on premenstrual and menstrual symptoms' (by Susan Thys-Jacobs MD, Paul Starkey MD, Debra Bernstein PhD, Jason Tian PhD and the Premenstrual Syndrome Study Group). At this point it should be noted that this and other studies focused on the use of calcium supplements, not on the consumption of milk. However, armed with the knowledge that milk is a good source of calcium (though incidentally not as high in calcium as some other foods, such as sesame seeds and almonds), CMPB and its well respected San Francisco-based ad agency Goodby Silverstein & Partners set about developing a campaign to highlight how milk could treat the symptoms of PMS.

Rather than pursuing a stale, scientific approach (well, they were on shaky scientific ground) the team opted for humour, putting the focus on downtrodden male partners cowed by the irrational and unreasonable behaviour of women afflicted by PMS symptoms. A series of online and billboard ads featured pictures of quivering, apologetic males holding cartons of milk as peace offerings to unseen, implicitly fierce women. Among the headlines were: 'I'm sorry I listened to what you said … and not what you meant'; 'We can both blame myself; I'm sorry for the thing – or things – I did or didn't do'; 'I apologize for letting you misinterpret what I was saying.' To further drive home the message of the male partner as hapless victim of the curse of PMS, the ads displayed a URL to a website called Everything I do is Wrong.

Visitors to the website, positioned as 'your home for PMS management', were treated to tools for defusing women's anger such as a Puppy Dog-Eye-Zer that would enable men to master a facial expression that's 'hard to stay mad at'. As well as providing advice on placatory words for men to use – for example substituting 'irrational' for 'passionate', the site had an emergency milk locator, tracked the global PMS level and boasted a Whose Fault It Is chart, which showed that men were to blame an overwhelming 99.97% of the time. Undeniably, a lot of hard work and creative flair went into putting the campaign together. Yet by portraying men as cringing wimps and women as hormonal and shrewish, this endeavour was undermined by the accusations of sexism it would provoke.

In an interview with the *New York Times* at the outset of the campaign, CMPB executive director Steve James expressed 'a little trepidation' about how it would be received. The strategy of focusing on men when addressing PMS was intended to surprise, get attention and trigger social media debate, he confirmed. 'Everything I do is Wrong' certainly met its targets in this regard. Unfortunately, the reaction to the advertising was far less favourable than CMPB had bargained for. Within days of the launch, a groundswell of criticism was building across social and traditional media. There was more to this than random sniping. Comment pieces denouncing the campaign appeared in publications as diverse as *AdWeek* and the country's oldest continuously published newspaper, the *Hartford Courant*. In the latter, a scathing piece was headlined 'Wrong: Milk Ad Campaign Blames PMS, Insults Women'. The campaign was turning sour. With criticism showing no sign of abating, CMPB pulled the plug on the advertising after a mere two weeks. The 'Everything I do is Wrong' website was replaced by an online forum for discussing the issues raised by the campaign. Unsurprisingly, this new site also contained some words of apology: 'Over the past couple of weeks, regrettably, some people found our campaign about milk and PMS to be outrageous and misguided — and we apologize to those we offended. Others thought it funny and educational. It has opened up a topic that affects women, of course, but also relationships.'

The trepidation James expressed at the beginning of the campaign turned out to be well founded. Although the advertising was intended to be edgy, James concedes that he and the rest of the marketing team miscalculated the ferocity of the reaction it would provoke. James is not the first man, nor will he be the last, to rue making jokes about PMS. But while TV comedy shows may be allowed the leeway to address such a touchy subject amusingly, it's a much riskier route for advertisers to take. Annoying or offending people you are selling to is never a great idea.

Energy Watch and Popchips offend with stereotypes

Let's move on ... from unappealing sexism to unacceptable racism. In August 2011 a TV commercial by Australia's leading energy broker Energy Watch was banned by the Advertising Standards Bureau for stereotypically portraying Indian people as dishonest 'door knockers'. Here's a quick summary of the 'plot', although that must be too grand a word to describe the derisory script. A young man in a suit is canvassing house to house. As soon as his ring on a doorbell is answered by an Aussie bloke, the door knocker launches into his spiel about saving money on electricity bills in a heavy, caricatured Indian accent. Offered a 25% discount on his bill, the householder agrees – only to be stopped in his tracks by a shrill referee's whistle and the appearance on his doorstep of a young lady with long blonde hair who is dressed in sports gear. She admonishes the householder for being about to sign up without looking at alternative offers and advises him that even if something sounds like a good deal it's best to check with the 'energy umpire' Energy Watch first. After that, she blows her whistle a second time and gives the crestfallen door knocker his marching orders by pointing to the metaphorical touchline. His pitch is deemed so untrustworthy that he is sent off the pitch, as it were.

Among the complaints received by the ASB was one from an Australian with Indian roots, who wrote: 'I find the ad racist and given that there are hardly any Indians or Asians in ads on Australian TV it merely is pandering to a stereotypical depiction of my heritage.' Another complainant was more acerbic: 'If it is acceptable for blue-eyed white people to blow a whistle and show Asians a red card then Hitler will indeed be proud.'

The commercial was directly overseen by Energy Watch's opinionated, maverick founder and CEO, Ben Polis. In a fascinating turn of events, it soon emerged that racism wasn't the sole concern about the company's advertising. Two weeks after the ASB ban, the Australian Competition and Consumer Commission instituted Federal Court proceedings against Energy Watch and Polis on the basis of misleading claims in a number of its ads about how much consumers had saved, or stood to save, by using the service provided by the energy broker. On 5th April 2012, it was fate that came knocking at Polis's door. The three sports clubs sponsored by Energy Watch – Melbourne Victory (football), Melbourne Rebels (rugby) and Melbourne Football Club (Australian rules football) – all announced that they were pulling out of their sponsorship deals in response to racist comments made by Polis on Facebook. Polis was forced to resign that same day from the company he had founded. Before long, Energy Watch was in liquidation. That didn't prevent the Federal Court from taking action once it had found the company guilty of misleading advertising, however. On 13th July 2012 the court slapped a AUS$1.95m fine on the company formerly known as Energy Watch. Additionally, Polis was personally fined AUS$65,000 for his voiceover work in misleading radio ads.

Summing up why the penalties were awarded, Justice Marshall said:

> *'Energy Watch deceived the Australian public in a very serious way. Mr Polis did likewise in radio broadcasts in Brisbane. He did so as the figurehead of Energy Watch, thereby giving greater gravitas to the false and misleading conduct than if the radio advertisements had been spoken by a voiceover actor. The Australian people have been misled and deceived by the sharp business practices engaged in by Energy Watch and Mr Polis and they would rightly expect that such conduct not be treated lightly by this Court.'*

As a minor point in defence of Energy Watch's patronising and predominantly indefensible advertising, at least the TV commercial didn't have a white person 'black up' or wear 'brownface' in a throwback to a less enlightened era. How far back from Energy Watch's ad do we need to rewind to find an example of something that crass? Sadly, we actually need to fast *forward* a year from 2011 to 2012. In May 2012 snack brand Popchips thought it a good idea to permit its 'president of pop culture', the actor and producer Ashton Kutcher, to do just that. The *Two and a Half Men* star appeared in an internet campaign called 'World Wide Lovers', which parodied lonely hearts videos. He played four separate bachelors hungry for romance, including one obviously based on a famous fashion designer – no, not Tom Ford again; Kutcher's creation

Darl could only be a 'tribute' to flamboyant couturier Karl Lagerfeld. But it was Kutcher's portrayal of 39-year-old Bollywood producer Raj that provoked outrage. Kutcher played Raj in 'brownface' make-up and gave him a stereotypical Indian accent. The Raj video quickly went viral and just as quickly triggered a wave of negative commentary on Twitter. New York-based technology entrepreneur, investor and prominent 'blogging pioneer' Anil Dash wrote a scathing, widely noticed piece on his Dashes blog under the pull-no-punches headline 'How to fix Popchips' racist ad campaign' in which he accused the marketers behind the video of making the world worse by hurting and demeaning people. 'I know it's old-fashioned,' Dash continued, 'but *sell your product on the virtues of being a good product*! I promise that'll work, and be more sustainable long term than hitching your brand to the public's knowledge of the dating life of a recently-divorced celebrity who's willing to perform in brownface.'

As the critical clamour intensified, Popchips founder and CEO Keith Belling issued an apology and the Raj video was taken down. The planned use of the Raj character in a billboard campaign was also abandoned. Beyond the idiocy of its racial stereotyping, the campaign was also a failure in that it strayed too far from product relevance. Humour is a wonderful component of an advertising campaign, but not when it alienates or lacks focus.

The smoking gun – how Strand was killed by the friendless fire of its own advertising

In extreme cases, ill-judged advertising can kill a brand stone dead – even if the ad is well-made and memorable. Such was the fate of cigarette brand Strand back in the long-ago days when tobacco products could be advertised on UK television. In 1959 Imperial Tobacco's subsidiary W.D. & H. O. Wills, a firm able to trace its roots in the business back to a tobacconist's shop in Bristol in the 1780s, launched Strand with a high-profile TV advertising campaign supported by posters, press advertising and coupons that could be redeemed for free packs. The TV commercial, devised by copywriter John May at British agency S. H. Benson, saw actor Terence Brook smoking while roaming the rain-drenched streets of London in stylish trench coat and trilby hat. Brook was cast due to his resemblance to crooner-cum-movie star Frank Sinatra, at the time the epitome of cool. Atmospheric black and white cinematography was coupled with a pensive, slightly melancholy tune by composer Cliff Adams. A male voiceover was limited to a couple of lines: 'You're never alone with a Strand. The cigarette of the moment.' While the lines may have been delivered as a pair, the Sinatra doppelgänger was most certainly a solitary figure.

The style of the protagonist and soundtrack to the commercial appealed to the public. Once it went on air people began getting in touch to find out if the theme tune was available to buy as a record. Sensing an opportunity, Cliff Adams and His Orchestra booked some recording studio time and laid down the track, *The Lonely Man Theme*, for release as a single. In 1960 *The Lonely Man Theme* broke into the Top 40. Further evidence of the commercial's success at tapping into popular culture came when it was lampooned by one of the leading comics of the era, Tony Hancock. In Hancock's TV sketch, Strand became the prosaic-sounding food brand Grimsby Pilchards and its now famous slogan was tweaked to the absurd, 'You're never alone with a pilchard.'

Undeniably, the advertising campaign earned Strand tremendous recognition. As Winston Fletcher writes in his book *Powers of Persuasion: The Inside Story of British Advertising 1951–2000*, 'Public awareness of the brand and its advertising rocketed to over 90% within weeks. This was unprecedented and has rarely if ever been surpassed.' It was a brilliant achievement, but one with a fatal flaw. Despite the high awareness levels delivered by the campaign, hardly anyone was buying the product. The reasons why revolved around how the Lonely Man was perceived. Many viewers found the focus on loneliness uncomfortable. If the man was reliant on a packet of smokes for company, did this mean he was a bit of an oddball unable to sustain friendships? Was he an addictive personality, craving nicotine above human company? Could he be on his own because of a failed relationship or even due to bereavement? Might he be depressed? Powerful as they were, the imagery and approach of the campaign would have been far better suited to advertising something altogether different from cigarettes. Imagine the tagline slightly recast again, albeit not with tinned fish this time: 'You're never alone with … Samaritans/Befrienders Worldwide/Lifeline.' For an emotional support helpline, this could have been very effective. But trying to position a new tobacco brand around loneliness – rather than something much more positive and aspirational, such as individuality – was doomed to failure. With sales failing to take off despite the high level of standout the advertising achieved, Strand was soon withdrawn from the market.

In a macabre parallel for those who read a degree of existential despair into the character of the Lonely Man, comic genius Hancock, who parodied the ad so drolly with his pilchards, saw his own career and personal life disintegrate in the following years as he became heavily dependent on alcohol. In 1968, shortly after the breakdown of his marriage, Hancock was found dead from an overdose of amphetamines and booze, an empty vodka bottle by his side. A sad end to the story of a lonely man.

More bad ads in brief

- An ad for sunglasses company Sky Optic that appeared on a large billboard on Highway 101, in Encinitas, California was taken down after just one week in September 2012. Clear Channel Outdoor, the company managing the billboard space, removed the ad and deemed it 'inappropriate' after hearing complaints about the headline: 'Happy to sit on your face'.
- Online deals company Groupon had big hopes for its 2011 TV commercial that debuted in one of the expensive, high-profile Superbowl Sunday slots. Unfortunately, the ad, starring Timothy Hutton, was slammed for belittling the plight of people in Tibet. Hutton informed viewers sombrely that the people of Tibet were in trouble, their culture in jeopardy, before continuing in a more jaunty tone: 'But they still whip up an amazing fish curry. And since 200 of us bought on Groupon.com, we're each getting $30 of Tibetan

food for just $15.' The idea was to spoof celebrity do-gooders, but the outcome stank like a fish dish left to stand in the sun.

- In 2007 Mars also found itself in trouble over a Superbowl ad that sparked allegations of homophobia. The commercial for the food group's Snickers bar featured two male mechanics accidentally kissing. Additional online content included sports stars jeering at the kiss. Gay rights organisations accused Mars of anti-gay bullying. The ad was swiftly shelved.
- Singapore broadband provider M1 ran an ad in the *Straits Times* including a customer care number . . . that belonged to its rival StarHub.
- A Washington DC billboard ad for Amazon Kindle was accused of being a spoiler. The poster showed the opening page of *Mockingjay*, the final book in the *Hunger Games* trilogy by Suzanne Collins. The extract revealed key plot twists from the first two novels in the series, potentially spoiling things for anyone planning to read those earlier books. Oops!
- More than a thousand disgruntled fathers signed a petition called 'We're Dads, Huggies, Not Dummies' in protest at a 2012 ad from the Kimberly-Clark nappies and baby wipe brand, which portrayed men as incompetent at looking after children. Like a soiled nappy, the ad was changed.
- A German poster campaign promoting Tchibo coffee at 700 Esso service stations had to be abandoned in 2009 after complaints that the slogan '*Jedem den Seinem*' ('To each his own') was almost identical to the chilling sign at the entrance to Nazi concentration camp Buchenwald, which implied that the prisoners taken there were getting what they deserved. The Central Council of Jews in Germany told the *Frankfurter Rundschau* newspaper that the posters were either 'unsurpassable tastelessness' or reflected a 'total ignorance of history'. Nokia, Burger King, REWE and Merkur Bank have all previously been censured for using the controversial phrase in advertising material.

- In 2010 VW pulled a US TV commercial for its Jetta model after complaints that it encouraged dangerous driving. A married couple who describe themselves as normally 'conservative' drivers lose their heads with the excitement of taking a Jetta for a test drive on the highway. Suddenly overwhelmed, the wife yells at her husband to 'shoot the gap'. He then recklessly accelerates to overtake in the small space between two huge trucks. Professional truck drivers and road safety campaigners were appalled.
- A carefree shot of four kids in beachwear had to be hastily taken down from French fashion retailer La Redoute's website once people noticed and began commenting on the presence of a naked man emerging from the sea behind them...
- ... which begs the question, is it worse to not wear any pants or to wet them? For a definitive answer to that we'd better ask another fashion retailer, Harvey Nichols. Its 2012 efforts to generate excitement about its sale centred on images of fashionably dressed models with wet patches around their groins. The tagline read: 'Try to contain your excitement.' Yuck! The *Financial Times* scored the campaign a zero.

Tips and lessons

- Humour can make an ad memorable and create affection for a brand. But it can also offend. Consider very carefully what you say and how you say it.
- Don't entrust 'sign off' to a junior team member, even for small or low-budget campaigns. Remember that ads intended for a small audience can become a big problem if reported on by mainstream media or spread virally with negative intent.
- Always make sure you have proper copyright permission for everything you use in a campaign.
- Make sure the claims you make in your ads can be substantiated. Advertising in most major markets is well policed by regulators whose job it is to ensure ads are legal, decent, honest and truthful.

- Check, check and check again. There's no excuse for factual errors or typos, even when deadlines are tight.
- Have a PR plan in place to help amplify your advertising, and so that you can react quickly to any negative comments on social media. If an apology is called for, it should be comprehensive, speedy and sincere.

Chapter 2

What's the deal?

Out-of-control promotions

From collectible toys to branded cereal bowls, from mini Xbox games to a tie-in with Major League Baseball, Kellogg's has for decades stayed at the forefront of sales promotion by moving with the times. Trawl through eBay today and you'll find all manner of promotional items connected with the brand. Maybe some plastic Snap, Crackle and Pop figures are what you need to make your workspace or kitchen complete? If not, worry not – for they and countless other sales promotion devices have done their job, underpinning the success of Kellogg's and its sub-brands. As tastes, regulations and technology have moved on, so too has sales promotion. Coca-Cola's recent 'Share a Coke' promotion brought personalisation into the mass market by replacing its brand name on bottles with a choice of hundreds of popular first names, rendered in the style of the iconic Coke logo. Still quintessentially Coke, but also Emma or Josh or Abdul. In the age of QR (Quick Response) codes, digital printing and online communities, there's greater scope than ever for brands to run inventive sales promotions. Unfortunately, that also means there's the potential for far more to go wrong. And the risk is at its greatest when a promotion is built on a faulty premise.

Olympian blunder - McDonald's miscalculates the medal haul

Geopolitically speaking, the world was a very different place back in 1984. There was not yet a thaw in the Cold War. Ronald Reagan occupied the White House, while the Soviet Union, under the short-lived leadership of Konstantin Chernenko, was still a year away from the presidency of Mikhail Gorbachev and the beginnings of *glasnost*. The relationship between the superpowers was strained. After the Soviet Union's invasion of Afghanistan in 1979, the USA led a boycott of the 1980 Summer Olympics in Moscow. Now, four years later, the Games were being held in Los Angeles and the USA was in thrall to the ballyhoo of the International Olympic Committee's sporting extravaganza. McDonald's was one of the main sponsors of the Games and even covered the $3m cost of building a new outdoor Olympic swimming stadium. To leverage its sponsorship and ride the wave of patriotic fervour building behind American athletes, it decided to run a massive sales promotion called 'When the US wins, you win.'

McDonald's supported the promotion with TV commercials in which it invited consumers to be 'part of the US Olympic team' by playing a scratch card game. Each 'game piece' card featured an Olympic event and the promotion's mechanics were fairly simple: if a US competitor won a medal in that event, the lucky consumer was entitled to a free menu item; and if that medal was gold, the free item would be a Big Mac, the burger on which McDonald's built its global reputation. From McDonald's point of view, the ideal scenario was to drive footfall to its restaurants and boost sales, while presenting itself as an enthusiastic supporter of the US Olympic team – without having to give away too many menu items; particularly its culinary main attraction, the Big Mac, honoured in the commercial with a place at the top of the podium as if it were the dietary equivalent of track and field superstar Carl Lewis.

Given that the USA had not competed in the previous Games, McDonald's needed to look back eight years to the 1976 Montreal Olympics for medal tally data. It found that the US team had won 94 medals, 34 of them gold. Armed with this information, McDonald's was able to make a rough calculation as to how many free menu items it would have to give away and factored that in to the cost of the promotion. Had the US team competing in Los Angeles achieved a similar medal haul to that of its predecessor in Montreal, McDonald's would have been able to congratulate itself on a successful promotion. But the value of the data from 1976 was undermined when the Soviet Union announced it would not be taking part in the Los Angeles Games in a tit-for-tat reprisal for the US boycott of Moscow. One by one, its Communist allies followed suit. On the one hand, this was an unwanted blow to the prestige of the Games; on the other, it boosted the medal prospects of American athletes. In Montreal, the USA had finished third in the medals table – behind the Soviet Union and East Germany. With these and other Eastern bloc countries out of the way, the distribution of medals would not resemble the pattern seen in Montreal.

Amid great rejoicing, US athletes won 83 gold medals at their home Olympics, far eclipsing the 34 of eight years earlier. To add to the party atmosphere, many consumers playing 'When the US wins, you win' were picking up prizes. McDonald's gave away substantially more food than it had envisaged, at a cost to the business running into millions of dollars. From its standpoint, the promotion would have been better named, 'When the US wins so often, we lose . . . big time!'

The promotion turned out to be a disaster of such epic proportions that it has found its way into popular culture. In an episode of *The Simpsons* entitled *Lisa's First Word*, McDonald's painful setback is lampooned as an Olympic promotion by Krusty the Clown for his Krusty Burger chain. In this fictional case, the game cards are rigged so that they only relate to events that 'Communists never lose'. When the Soviets pull out of the Games, Krusty discovers he stands to make a $44m loss. Enraged, he tells his viewers: 'I personally am going to spit in every 50th burger.' Homer Simpson, true to character, responds: 'I like those odds.'

It's a classic slice of funny *Simpsons* dialogue, but Homer's joke about odds is also relevant in a marketing context. When sales promotions go disastrously wrong it is often because marketers haven't properly worked out the odds or understood their implications. Thorough risk assessment and cost planning should be a fundamental aspect of any sales promotion campaign. Over the years, quite a few brands have been caught out by far higher than anticipated redemption rates. Not only can this prove expensive, but it may also be the case that there is simply not enough product available to meet the demand generated by the promotion – a state of affairs that makes brands look bad and antagonises consumers.

In the case of the Olympics promotion, McDonald's, rather than its customers, took the hit. But for a 2006 promotion in Japan, the company had to make a humbling public apology and swing into crisis management mode after a potentially damaging problem with its prizes emerged. Japanese consumers were able to claim McDonald's branded mp3 players pre-loaded with 10 songs if they found a winning code number on cups of Coca-Cola. There were 10,000 mp3 players on offer, supplied to McDonald's by a marketing company in Hong Kong. In theory, this was a nice idea for a promotion. However, things turned nasty once consumers took their prizes home with them and connected them to their computers. Some of the music players were infected with malware which began stealing sensitive information such as passwords and user names, putting consumers at risk of fraud. McDonald's rushed out instructions, via a link on its website, telling people how to download anti-virus software to deal with the Trojan spyware, opened a consumer helpline and replaced all the mp3 players with new, uninfected devices. It added that it was 'very sorry' and launched an investigation into the cause of the infection.

Wake up and smell the coffee – Timothy's slow response when technical problems arose

Online promotions, which may be spread virally, carry obvious risks. If clear limits are not built into their terms and conditions, or those limitations are in place but are not properly communicated to consumers, there is the chance that they will take off to such a degree that demand cannot be met and it hurts rather than helps a brand. This was the case for Canadian coffee business Timothy's Coffees of the World, which was confronted by a situation far less palatable than its Arabica beans when a Facebook promotion got out of hand. In December 2011, in an act of festive season generosity, Timothy's decided to reward its fans by giving them some left-over seasonal coffee. On 16th December it offered to send consumers four 24-pack boxes of single-serve Perfectly Pumpkin coffee just for Liking Timothy's on Facebook. Now, as each box would normally retail at around C$17, offering to give away four just for hitting a Like button was gifting at a level that might make even Santa break into a sweat.

Bearing in mind people's love of a good freebie, it's not hard to predict what happened next. The Likes began stacking up on Facebook, as did comments from fans applauding the brand for its largesse. A handful of the more cynical wondered if it was too good to be true. But as the offer came from a reputable brand and seemed legitimate, word spread like wildfire and people from outside Timothy's core fan base flocked to its Facebook page in the hunt for something for more or less nothing – Facebook Likes are all well and good, but try paying a supplier's bill with one. The offer even found its way onto competition and deal websites. Within three days, the entire stock was depleted. But as people signed up, due to what Timothy's describes as 'an unfortunate technical issue' they continued to receive an email telling them that their coffee was on its way.

The situation was worsening as Christmas loomed and it seemed that the team at Timothy's wasn't giving the promotion much attention. Even though it was obviously not in a position to honour the offer with everyone who signed up, there was no comment from the company until the New Year.

Eventually, on 4th January, Timothy's clarified that the promotion was 'first come, first served' and added that those who missed out would receive an email offer. The reaction to this on Facebook was decidedly mixed; while some fans thanked the company for its generous intentions, others were seething that they had supplied it with their personal details under what amounted to false pretences. Another week passed by before Timothy's apologised for its mistake in a video. Marketing Services Director Marie-Claude Dessureault said that those who had signed up for the promotion would receive a coupon entitling them to a 12-pack of single-serve coffee and pledged that all private information captured in the botched exercise would be deleted.

With the passage of time and the chance to reflect on the affair, what do the marketers behind the promotion believe they learned from this bruising experience? Laetitia Sorribes, director of marketing and innovation at Timothy's parent company Green Mountain Coffee Roasters in Quebec, told me that she and her colleagues now have a far keener appreciation of the potential pitfalls of marketing via social media channels in comparison to the more controlled environment of traditional forms of marketing communications.

'It was very much of a learning experience for us because obviously we were not expecting that reaction. It was the beginning of our social network communication, and what we learned is that information spreads out very rapidly. You have to stay alert and be responsive to your customers. It is a very rapid and direct way to interact and consumers are expecting you to be honest and really to go beyond their expectations.'

Timothy's made the apology video after listening to advice from social media experts, and Sorribes is utterly certain that saying sorry and explaining why things have gone wrong is absolutely essential in maintaining customer faith when social media marketing activity backfires. These days, according to Sorribes, the company is far more cautious and thorough when planning a promotion. A technical issue was a major contributor to the problems of December 2011: there was supposed to be a 'counter' counting down to zero to show when all of the stock allocated for the promotion was used up; this failed to work. Consequently, now the technological aspects of a promotion are rigorously beta-tested before being taken live. In addition, said Sorribes, the company has upped the quantities of product it uses in promotions to minimise the chances of causing disappointment and, having seen its reputation take a pummelling over the holiday season when there was no one around to respond decisively to criticism, now gives far greater thought to the timing of promotions. Typically these are now launched on a Monday to make sure the whole team is there to monitor what's going on through the week and respond to any problems should they arise.

Underestimating demand can lead to deep consumer disenchantment, with ramifications for brand image. Timothy's is not by any stretch of the imagination the only brand to get its Facebook projections entirely wrong; it's not even the only brand to foul up in this way in Canada. L'Oréal also botched its take-up forecast when it ran a product giveaway promotion for new scent Trésor Midnight Rose. The plan was to give away 2,000 free samples of the perfume, the public face of which is *Harry Potter* star Emma Watson, in a promotion running for five nights and beginning at midnight. By two minutes after midnight on the first night of the promotion, 3,000 people had gone onto the Facebook page to request samples, crashing L'Oréal's servers and exhausting its supply of free product. 'We created a huge disappointment for those consumers [who missed out] and we had to readjust our thinking,' Marie Josee Lamothe, Chief Marketing Officer at L'Oréal Canada confessed to the *National Post*. 'We didn't anticipate the traffic. Now when we market on Facebook we try to overestimate what the response will be because consumers get very vocal once they're disappointed.'

They certainly do. And as the following example shows, consumers have long been adept at expressing their disappointment and could do so potently, with terrible consequences for a brand, even in those benighted twentieth-century years before social media.

The Hoover flights fiasco – probably the worst sales promotion of all time

What an evocative brand name Hoover is; and it's unusual for being doubly synonymous. At one point its domestic appliances had such a strong hold on the home cleaning market that vacuuming was widely referred to as hoovering; and still is by many today, even if they are wielding a Dyson as they go about their chores. But in the field of sales promotion, Hoover is a synonym for something else entirely. Its name has become a byword for unmitigated marketing catastrophe.

The seeds of the sales promotion disaster were sown in South Wales in summer 1992. Top executives at Hoover's UK headquarters were brainstorming ways to boost sales and shift surplus stock in a tough recession. It was noted that air miles schemes and other promotions involving flights were popular, so Hoover was instructed by its US parent company Maytag to contact a firm of travel agents and set to work on shaping a promotion of its own. The idea behind the promotion was startlingly simple: anyone paying over £100 for Hoover products such as vacuum cleaners and washing machines would be entitled to two free flights to a choice of six European destinations. Hoover was warned by several sales promotion risk management companies that its plans had some potentially serious drawbacks. Mark Kimber, managing director of PIMS-SCA, was one of the risk experts sounded out by Hoover. The high-value offer to the consumer for a relatively low cost made absolutely no sense to him. 'I told them you can't afford to run it,' Kimber recalls. Undaunted, marketers at Hoover pressed on with the promotion.

More often than not, vacuum cleaners and washing machines are 'distress purchases' – they are bought to replace older models that have stopped working. To its initial delight, Hoover enjoyed a massive spike in sales as consumers – most of them in no kind of domestic distress – were drawn to the offer. In fact, demand was so strong that Hoover decided to launch a second version of the promotion, this time offering flights to the USA. It supported this with TV advertising bearing the tag line, 'Two return seats: unbelievable.'

What was truly unbelievable was the scale of the calamity Hoover was bringing on itself. Its travel agent was already struggling to secure enough tickets for the European offer; the ads encouraged more people to try to redeem their coupons for European flights as well as opening the floodgates as prospective transatlantic travellers leaped at the opportunity to secure tickets at a price lower than they would normally pay. Hoover's factory was at full capacity, working seven days a week, and had to hire 75 extra staff. But it wasn't as if consumers were desperate for Hoover appliances. As most were buying just to get their hands on the flight tickets, they sought out the cheapest products available and soon the second-hand market was awash with bargain Hoover washing machines and vacuum cleaners, many still in their packaging. Rival manufacturers looked on aghast as their own sales plummeted. However, their problems were insignificant compared to those now faced by Hoover.

Instead of the 50,000 or so applications for tickets Hoover had forecast, it was inundated with over 300,000. Its travel agent had to take on more staff but was floundering, unable to get its hands on enough cut-price tickets. Suddenly Hoover was in the crazy situation of buying pairs of flight tickets at prices that were often higher than the retail price of the products they were selling while giving the flights away. 'The airlines soon cottoned on to the fact that if someone was calling about Hoover flights to America and they wanted bulk numbers, they could charge whatever they liked because they were desperate,' says Kimber. Hoover's management had to scratch around for millions of pounds to cover rapidly escalating costs. Its approach to marketing couldn't have been any more mixed up if it had thrown its plans into a tumble dryer. The company had hoped that consumers would buy its products but neglect to take advantage of the offer, hiding hurdles to redemption in the small print. But this failed to take into account the determination of the public, who were only buying in the first place because of the tempting offer and were disinclined to be denied. Hoover had also hoped that its retailers would be able to do a better upselling job in store. But customers didn't want more expensive models or accessories. They wanted to pay as little as possible, because what they were in the market for was flights, not appliances. Additionally, Hoover was banking on its travel agents being able to sell profitable extras such as travel insurance, car hire and hotel bookings to consumers trying to redeem the offer, but as this was a very price-conscious group there were few takers.

In a desperate bid to keep costs under control, Hoover deliberately put obstacles in the path of redemption – consumers found it hard to get through on the company's phone lines and if they did, they frequently discovered that the flights they wanted were unavailable. Many began to feel conned and started airing their grievances with the media.

Hoover's reputation was becoming tarnished and despite its sometimes underhand efforts to stem the flow, losses from the promotion were mounting fast. Consumers were genuinely furious at the way they were being treated. None more so than the imposing figure of Sandy Jack, a former headmaster and one-time commando in the Royal Marines during World War II – when he was twice wounded in action – who became the first person to take Hoover to court over the promotion (Hoover v. Jack, Sheriff Court, Kircaldy, Fife 1993). The legal precedent Jack set with the action and the news coverage of his grit and tenacity had a galvanising effect, encouraging many others to take up the fight against Hoover.

Together with Harry Cichy, Jack formed the Hoover Holiday Pressure Group in 1993 as a rallying point for irate consumers and set about trying to persuade the company to meet its obligations. Jack and Cichy contacted the Office of Fair Trading and BBC consumer affairs programme *Watchdog*, asking them to investigate Hoover, and even made an approach to Her Majesty the Queen, requesting the removal of Hoover's Royal Warrant. *Watchdog* investigated customer complaints and sent an undercover researcher to produce an exposé on Hoover's slipperiness. The matter was even addressed in the House of Commons. In March 1993, the company conceded that the ill-starred promotion would cost it at least £20m and fired the three senior executives responsible for the debacle. If Hoover thought this would draw a line under events, it was utterly mistaken.

Two months later, an exasperated horse trainer from Cumbria briefly became a national hero when he hit upon a highly effective way to vent his anger. David Dixon had been repeatedly frustrated in his efforts to secure free flights to take his family to Florida. Adding insult to injury, the Hoover washing machine he had bought developed a fault. The engineer sent out to fix the problem unwisely commented that anyone who believed they'd get two free tickets to the USA by buying a washing machine was an idiot. Seeing red, Dixon moved his lorry and blocked in the Hoover van on his drive. He would hold the vehicle hostage, he told journalists, until Hoover came good on the flights.

The media lapped it up. One newspaper offered him a holiday to the USA, another said it would cover any legal fees he incurred. The police were called to Dixon's home but refused to intervene, judging the dispute to be a civil matter. Within a few days, Dixon had received around eighty phone calls from other consumers who had been given the run-around when trying to claim their free flights. The scale of the fiasco was becoming clearer by the day and consumers, seeing the advantages of banding together, contacted the Hoover Holiday Pressure Group in growing numbers.

Cichy and Jack made the smart decision to buy a small number of shares in Hoover's US parent company Maytag and flew out to attend the company's AGM in Newton, Iowa. Jack made a speech to a packed room of Maytag shareholders and gave interviews to newspaper and

TV journalists. The story even made the front page of the main Iowa local newspaper, the *Des Moines Register*, as well as gaining significant coverage on national TV stations and in leading newspapers such as *USA Today* and the *Washington Post*. Prior to the AGM, Jack and Cichy headed to Maytag headquarters for a rendezvous with company CEO Len Hadley. However, Hadley backed out at the last minute, leaving Maytag Head of Communication Jim Powell to take the meeting. 'He had heavies ready to eject us from Maytag HQ,' Cichy tells me. 'However, with the TV and media keeping a watchful eye they decide against this action, bearing in mind that the heavies were actually gun-wielding local police from Newton on the Maytag payroll!' Cichy adds that a team of private detectives followed his every move in Newton and continued to dog his steps on his return to the UK. 'I was advised by a top lawyer "not to mess with the Corporation", something I will always remember being told.'

But Cichy and Jack were not to be intimidated. At its height, the pressure group had almost eight thousand members and was overseeing a class action campaign. It helped hundreds of consumers take Hoover to small claims courts across the UK. 'Hoover had a full legal team flying up and down the country to fight legal cases, brought throughout the small claims court system,' says Cichy. 'At one point there were more writs flying than Hoover flights. In addition, Hoover was settling many more cases with out of court settlements, making people sign confidentiality clauses, so they could not disclose these settlements.'

Legal cases against Hoover carried on being heard until 1998, a full six years after the promotion took place. By the end of it all, Hoover Europe was £50m out of pocket – and now under new ownership, after Maytag washed its hands of the business by selling it to Italian company Candy. All told, around 220,000 people flew with Hoover – but that still left around 380,000 people who were disappointed.

'A disgruntled customer may well go away,' concludes Cichy. 'However, a well-oiled media-savvy group, with the help of the internet and the speed at which a complaint can grow, are not going to give up or stop. We did not, and it really did see Hoover sales dwindle and the reputation of the brand flounder.'

Scavenging in the cemetery - Dr Pepper's disrespectful treasure hunt

The soft drink Dr Pepper is made up of 23 different flavours – a piece of trivia that you will be forever grateful I shared with you. In early 2007, the brand ran an advertising campaign around this message and decided to generate extra excitement with a promotion offering $1.7m in cash prizes. 'The Hunt for More' saw 23 prize coins hidden at physical locations in cities across the USA and Canada. Each coin was assigned a different monetary value – the highest could be traded in for a cool $1m – and consumers were encouraged to track down the coins in what amounted to an elaborate scavenger hunt. There were 30 clues to find each coin. Clues went live on the competition website nightly at midnight Pacific Time and consumers needed a new code from a bottle of Dr Pepper to unlock every step – thereby encouraging daily purchase of the drink. With each coin, the starting point for the hunt would always be a great distance from the hiding place. Every clue took competitors a geographical step closer with the use of compass directions from famous landmarks. Competitors didn't need to actually go out to hunt for the coins until the very last clue, at which point the race was well and truly on to be the one to retrieve the prize. At the time, the hobby of geo-caching was gaining lots of attention and growing in popularity as access to GPS technology became widespread. Based on the ZIP codes they entered when registering on the site, competitors were given clues pertaining to the coin concealed in their region.

The $1m coin was found in a Houston park by a 23-year-old recent graduate and avid geo-cacher, Laura Janisch. Ironically, however, it was the hunt for one of the $10,000 coins that caused a greater stir. In its wisdom, the marketing agency working with Dr Pepper on the promotion had hired a private detective to hide this particular coin in the Granary Burying Ground, a 350-year-old cemetery in Boston that is of tremendous historical significance, not least because it is the resting place of some of the founding fathers of the US republic. Paul Revere, the patriotic silversmith who famously rode through the night to warn of approaching British forces during the Revolutionary War, is buried in the cemetery, as are three signatories of the Declaration of Independence: Samuel Adams, John Hancock and Robert Treat Paine.

All told, the remains of around five thousand Boston citizens have been interred at Granary, many of them notable local and national figures, and there are nearly 2,500 gravestones, tombs and monuments at the cemetery, some of them in a fragile condition, plus a 25-foot tall obelisk marking the tomb of Benjamin Franklin's parents.

As with all the other clues, the final clue for the Boston coin was published on the website at midnight Pacific Time, 3a.m. in Massachusetts. Desperate to get their hands on the treasure, competitors headed for the cemetery as soon as they had solved the riddle pointing to its hiding place, some converging on the graveyard in the early hours like spectres, undeterred by the darkness and the wintry weather. On arrival they found Granary's gates locked. And they stayed locked, even after sunrise. The Boston Parks and Recreation Department, which had not heard from Dr Pepper and was totally unaware of the promotion, had closed the cemetery the previous day on public safety grounds because its paths had become treacherous due to the icy conditions. As the new working day began, the Department's phones started ringing. Dozens of angry treasure hunters were demanding to know when they could get into the cemetery to complete their search for the coin. Wisely, given the danger of damage posed to important monuments and the risk of over-eager competitors injuring themselves while dashing around on slippery ice, the Parks Department decided to keep the cemetery shut. 'I think the fact that the gates were closed was almost like an act of God,' said relieved Parks Department spokesperson Mary Hines. 'It kept them out.' A police guard was sent to the cemetery to make sure it stayed that way.

Dr Pepper abandoned the Boston portion of its promotion, awarding the $10,000 prize money by drawing the name of a participant at random. Timothy L. Sullivan, the private detective who planted the coin, was brought in to retrieve it from where it lay secreted in a black leather pouch at the entrance to a 200-year-old crypt. Cadbury Schweppes, owner of the Dr Pepper brand, apologised to the city of Boston and admitted the coin should never have been stashed on hallowed ground. 'It absolutely is disrespectful,' said Boston Parks Commissioner Toni Pollak in an interview with the *Boston Globe*. 'It's an affront to the people who are buried there, our nation's ancestors.'

City officials were especially touchy as this promotional foul-up took place less than a month after another marketing mishap – this time involving Cartoon Network (see page 100) – caused a major terrorist alert in downtown Boston. Cadbury Schweppes sought to smooth ruffled feathers at city hall by making a $10,000 donation to Granary Burying Ground and offering to cover the cost of the policing operation.

Why can't I have an ice cream? Trade partners land D'Onofrio in trouble

It's time to switch from ice to ices, from American late winter to Peruvian late summer. In March 2009, Nestlé-owned D'Onofrio launched a promotion called 'Gracias Peru' to thank Peruvians for buying its ice creams during the summer months. D'Onofrio is the dominant ice cream brand in the market and has a rich heritage. The bright yellow tricycle carts of its vendors are a familiar and cherished sight on Peru's urban streets. In the 'Gracias Peru' promotion, all ice creams bought from tricycles on Friday 27th March and Saturday 28th March were to cost just one Peruvian sol (around 30 US cents), a massive reduction on the usual price for many D'Onofrio products of 3.5 soles. Word spread quickly and there was huge public expectation.

Unfortunately, when the promotion began, problems on the ground soon materialised. Vendors and their tricycles were harder to find than usual. Not all of those who were on street corners were sticking to the terms of the promotion. Some claimed to have sold out of all D'Onofrio premium products; others tried to persuade customers that they could only sell them an ice cream for one sol if they bought another at the normal full price. Public confidence in the promotion melted faster than a choc ice in the sun. Feeling cheated, angry Peruvians vented their displeasure on social media and contacted newspapers and radio phone-ins to complain. The ice cream maker was taking a licking.

How did things go so badly wrong from idea to execution? The reason for the shambles is that D'Onofrio does not own or control its trade channel. *Heladeros* – as the vendors are known – are independent businesses, buying product from the food maker at trade prices and then selling it on to the public at a higher retail price. Some of the *heladeros* couldn't resist the temptation to hold back stock during the 'Gracias Peru' promotion with the goal of making a far larger profit margin by selling it at the full retail price afterwards. D'Onofrio simply had not nailed down its ice cream vendors to abide by the promotion.

Public anger at D'Onofrio failing to deliver on its promise was so strong that the Peruvian consumers' association ASPEC brought a complaint against Nestlé before Indecopi, Peru's national competition and consumer protection institute. Nestlé argued that the promotion had given poor children who could not usually afford its premium products the opportunity to try them at a heavily discounted price. Indecopi was unimpressed and in March 2011 handed the company a fine of 1.4m soles, equivalent to around half a million US dollars, for advertising deception. A promotion designed to thank consumers had annoyed them instead by failing to comply with the promises it made. The lesson to emerge from this affair is that all trade partners must be fully on board with a promotion.

Too hard, too easy . . . and too much fat – New Covent Garden, Walkers and Cadbury

Any sales promotion offering prizes to the consumer has to walk the line between being too easy and too hard. If winning is too easy, the chances are this will be a costly exercise for the brand. If winning is too difficult, participants will feel they are being swindled and will probably kick up a fuss. New Covent Garden Soup and crisp brand Walkers provide examples from opposite ends of the spectrum. In October 2011 the premium soup and its sister brand Farmhouse Fair launched the 'Win a Farm' promotion, which offered a first prize of £500,000 and 50 pairs of Joules designer wellies as runner-up prizes.

Code numbers were printed on the tops of soup cartons and puddings. Anybody wishing to take part could enter their code into a special competition website. 'The winner will get to pick their very own farm or fill their (welly) boots with cash,' the website trumpeted. All told, more than 260,000 people entered. Yet nobody won the top prize. And most of the wellies went unclaimed too. The carton with the winning code was probably thrown away. Many purchasers were too busy to enter, were not the kind of people inclined to enter competitions, did not notice the competition or noticed it only after opening the product, after which the idea of handling packaging covered in sloppy soup or sticky dessert may have put them off.

The campaign was vetted in advance by the Institute of Promotional Marketing, which found its terms and conditions to be entirely legal and within the rules for such promotions. That didn't change the fact that over a quarter of a million people entered and many were now aggrieved that no one had won. Negative comments began appearing on the brands' websites and Facebook pages. Consumers felt they had been the victim of a scam. The media swiftly picked up on the story, dragging New Covent Garden Soup's brand name through the mud. 'Soup firm's win-a-farm competition leaves a sour taste,' ran a headline in the *Telegraph*, while the *Mail* opted for a headline almost long enough to be a whole news story in its own right: 'Win-a-farm competition where everyone is a loser: Soup firm faces fury after 260,000 enter – but no one gets £500,000 prize.' There's a lot of muck on your average farm, and by running a promotion set up in this way the soup marketers found themselves up to their necks in it.

'When people saw that one person maybe won a pair of wellies, they thought it was the biggest rip-off ever,' says promotions risk expert Mark Kimber. 'What New Covent Garden should have done is put together a proper prize pyramid with lots of secondary prizes. If the chance is only one in 50 that the main prize will go, you've got to give your promotion credibility with lots of secondary and tertiary prizes. It's a classic example of somebody being a bit foolish.'

I forecast the chances of PepsiCo-owned crisps brand Walkers reprising its 'Win £10 Every Time it Rains' promotion as being round about zero. In this 2010 promotion, Walkers divided a map of the UK into a grid of 21,000 spaces. After keying codes found on packs of crisps into the Walkers website, competitors could pick a grid spot on the map and predict when it would rain in that part of the country. If they were correct, they won £10. The Met Office provided daily rainfall data to keep things impartial. Anyone with even the vaguest knowledge of the UK climate will divine the danger here straightaway. We're not talking the Atacama Desert here: in the UK it rains ... a lot. There were 128,000 winners, leaving the crisp maker to pay out around £1.3m in prize money. Not ruinous for a brand as large as Walkers, but without doubt that money could have been better spent. Maybe it should have handed out branded umbrellas instead.

How a promotion works, its 'mechanic', needs to make sense for brand and consumer alike. There is also the vital matter of brand fit. A mechanic that sits well with one kind of product or brand might be jarring if applied to another. Sainsbury's has been successfully running its 'Active Kids' scheme annually since 2005, issuing vouchers to shoppers that schools and other organisations can redeem for sports equipment and experiences. David Beckham and Paralympian Ellie Simmonds were the faces of its 2013 campaign – and as part of 'Active Kids', the supermarket group has donated over £120m worth of equipment and experiences to around 50,000 different organisations.

Yet when chocolate maker Cadbury introduced a similar scheme, 'Cadbury Get Active', in 2003 it immediately came in for heavy criticism. Independent watchdog the Food Commission issued a scathing press release stating: 'To earn the most expensive item Cadbury has to offer (a set of posts for a volleyball net), secondary school children would need to eat 5,440 chocolate bars containing over 33kg of fat, and nearly one-and-a-quarter million calories.' The British Dietetic Association reproached Cadbury for making a link between activity and chocolate, while in an interview with the *Guardian*, government adviser and founder of the International Obesity Taskforce Professor Philip James said: 'This is a classic example of how the food and soft drinks industry are failing to take on board that they are major contributors to obesity problems throughout the world. They always try to divert attention to physical activity. Independent analysts have found that Cadbury Schweppes has one of the worst portfolios for products in terms of children's wellbeing.' Cadbury was out of the blocks with its promotion two years before Sainsbury's, but the simple fact is that somewhere you can buy fruit and vegetables is more easily accepted as a promoter of healthy living than the company behind chocolate brands such as Dairy Milk, Flake and Crunchie.

More bad promotions

- A New York outlet of gourmet grocery store Balducci's ran a 'delicious for Chanukah' special offer on meat for the Jewish holiday in 2007. The problem with the promotion? The meat in question was ham – which Jewish people are not supposed to eat because it is non-kosher.

- American Apparel was lambasted for insensitivity by consumers and media commentators when it launched a Hurricane Sandy Sale as the devastating storm bore down on the US east coast in October 2012. In a promotional email blast to customers, the clothing retailer offered a 20% discount on all its stock for 36 hours 'in case you're bored during the storm'.

- During the 1994 World Cup in the USA, Heineken produced beer bottles with the flags of all the finalists printed on the underside of the bottle caps. Unfortunately, the brewer did not take into account the fact that one of the nations to qualify was the strictly Islamic state of Saudi Arabia. The Saudi flag features the *shahada*, the Islamic declaration of faith, and its use in association with any kind of product marketing is frowned upon. Using it to promote alcohol was completely unacceptable to devout Muslims. When the error came to light, Heineken had no option but to recall the bottles and abandon the promotion.

- Small British baking business Need a Cake ran a promotion on money-saving website Groupon in 2011 that created so much demand that the company was nearly crushed beneath a cupcake Kilimanjaro. The loss-leading 75% discount sparked orders for 102,000 handmade cupcakes, rather more than the 100 it baked in a typical month. After frantically recruiting 25 agency staff to assist with mixing, baking and decorating, the SME (small to medium sized enterprise), which had fewer than 10 full-time employees, saw its profits for the year wiped out. Company founder Rachel Brown said the promotion was the worst business decision she had ever made.

- In December 2011 the *New York Times* sent out an email with the aim of luring back recently lapsed subscribers by offering a 50% discount for 16 weeks. But instead of going out to the intended group of around 300 people who had cancelled their subscriptions, the email was despatched in error to the more than eight million email addresses on the paper's marketing list, including existing subscribers. Some recipients began speculating on Twitter as to whether the *Times*'s email system had been hacked by spammers, while existing subscribers contacted the paper asking for a reduction in their full price subscription rate in line with the terms of the promotion. For a few hours the paper honoured the offer, but as the requests kept rolling in it became apparent that continuing to abide by it could damage subscription revenue. So the paper changed its position and issued an apology. It's a good job there's more rigour behind the stories it runs on its front page.

- Colgate encouraged consumers to exchange their battered old electric toothbrushes for its new high-end ProClinical A1500. The offer proved so attractive that at 5a.m. on the morning of 9th July 2013, two hours before it was due to open, people began queuing at its promotional stall at London Waterloo station. The stall only had around 150 toothbrushes to give away and soon ran out of product. Fearing chaos on the concourse, Network Rail closed it down, leaving Colgate to apologise on social media. The company took a further kick in the teeth the next day when rival Philips ran tactical advertising pointedly celebrating its own Sonicare toothbrush with the headline 'The best things in life aren't free' in newspapers and on a digital billboard at Waterloo station, the scene of Colgate's embarrassment. Philips also leaped on Colgate's #brushswap hashtag, but Colgate hit back by taking its promotion online and increasing its scale. Ah, the buzz on social media — of battling electric toothbrushes!

Tips and lessons

- Make sure you have a realistic estimate of consumer take-up.
- Check the legality of a promotion before running it.
- Build in controls to prevent retail/restaurant staff simply handing out vouchers to friends.
- Bear in mind that if you put codes on the outside of packaging it's easy for people to capture these on smartphones without buying any product.
- Using the phrase 'while stocks last' in your terms and conditions may not save you from public anger or a media grilling if consumers are disappointed.
- Trade partners must be fully on board.

Chapter 3

Provoking a social media backlash

Indiscreet tweets, Facebook foul-ups and hashtag horror stories

---

Social media can make or break a campaign. It can fuel a buzz or spread condemnation. In Brazil, beer brand Heineken brought a smile to people's faces with a simple but visually smart idea: every time someone Liked its Facebook page, a guy in an office blew up a green balloon. As the Likes mounted up, so too did the balloons, providing enjoyable images to share online of the man being swamped as his office became a sea of inflated rubber.

A balloon, this time a red one, also features in one of the most successful viral marketing videos to date, Metro Trains' 'Dumb Ways to Die' campaign. Using humour in the form of animated jellybean-style people meeting their brutal end in a variety of brainless ways, described with unflinching jollity in an incredibly catchy song, the Melbourne transit company succeeded in turning a potentially dry public safety campaign into a social media smash. Rightly garlanded with awards internationally, 'Dumb Ways to Die' has been seen over 50 million times on YouTube, retweeted more than 100,000 times and drawn well over three million Likes on Facebook. It's a shining example of the upside, a demonstration of what's possible when messages are delivered in a tone that is spot on for the target audience. Sadly, Australia has also produced the odd social media marketing disaster.

Not the best time to talk of luxury – Qantas and its Twitter Hindenburg

Qantas planes may criss-cross the world, but in terms of joined-up thinking Australia's national carrier has at times been found wanting. In 2011 the airline, which sells itself as 'The Spirit of Australia', was mired in a bitter industrial dispute. A disagreement over pay and conditions between Qantas and three unions representing pilots, engineers and other staff escalated as the year progressed. In July, pilots flying internationally undertook their first industrial action since the 1960s – making in-flight announcements to tell passengers about their grievances. At the same time, quick-fire strikes by engineers caused service disruptions and passenger delays as uninspected planes were grounded. The relationship between the two sides soured further in August when Qantas unveiled restructuring plans that would involve 1,000 job losses and a greater focus on Asia.

When news of the plans broke, Qantas pilot Nathan Safe – a spokesman for the AIPA pilots' union, whose surname must be reassuring for passengers nervous of air travel – told the *Australian* newspaper: 'There's a saying in the flying industry, "If you think safety is expensive, try having an accident." Why would you flush down the toilet 90 years of safety excellence just in search of saving a few dollars?' Amid growing animosity and with no sign of a resolution in sight, strike action rumbled on through September and October, sapping revenue of about AUS$15m a week and damaging the credibility of the airline. With neither side showing any inclination to back down, an impasse had been reached. Then at the end of October Qantas made a bold and unexpected move to break the deadlock. Chief Executive Alan Joyce took an unprecedented step to 'lock out' staff and ground all aircraft until an agreement was reached, accusing the unions of trashing the airline's strategy and brand – a move that affected 70,000 passengers, leaving many of them stranded around the globe. Australian Prime Minister Julia Gillard expressed her concern about the impact the grounding of the fleet would have on Australia's national economy. To minimise further damage to tourism and Australia's business community, Gillard instructed industrial tribunal Fair Work Australia to put an end to the dispute in the interests of the country. In the early hours of 31st October, Fair Work Australia ordered that all industrial action be terminated immediately.

So we move into November 2011 with Qantas struggling to deal with disgruntled passengers while getting its services back to normal and facing continuing employee relations acrimony, typified on 11th November by pilots' union AIPA initiating Federal Court proceedings with the goal of seeing the Fair Work Australia ruling overturned. At this nightmarish point in the airline's existence it could hardly be the perfect moment to launch a promotional campaign about a dream flying experience, especially one on social media, with its huge scope for negative comments. Yet that is precisely what Qantas did. In a breathtaking example of marketing tunnel vision, the Qantas promotions folk ignored the bigger picture of recent passenger inconvenience and fractured stakeholder relationships, taking to Twitter to ask people to name their dream luxury in-flight experience and embellish it with the hashtag #QantasLuxury. Unquestionably Qantas opened the departure gate on a campaign of this nature way too early, inviting derision from customers it had let down and criticism from others who sympathised with the position of the unionised workforce.

For anyone on the promotions team who assumed that the airline's travails would be overlooked, the first tweet in response to the promotion didn't bode well. Axel Bruns summed up his dream luxury experience as, 'Planes that arrive intact and on time because they're staffed and maintained by properly-paid, Australia-based personnel.' Another Twitter user, Stephen Dann, chipped in with: 'Flights that leave on schedule because Management doesn't arbitrarily shut down the airline,' while yet another wrote poignantly of being stranded on the other side of the world when wanting to get home to see his 10-month-old daughter. Qantas had unwittingly provided aggrieved customers with the perfect stage on which to vent their displeasure. As the criticism mounted, more people warmed to the task. There was much more interest in giving the airline a hard time than in claiming the Qantas goody bag competition prizes up for grabs. The prizes, incidentally, included first-class pyjamas – maybe symbolic of an airline sleepwalking into a marketing fiasco.

There was some amusing and probably quite accurate conjecture in certain tweets. 'Somewhere in Qantas HQ a middle-aged manager is yelling at a Gen Y social media "expert" to make it all stop. LOL,' tweeted Kiwi Kali. Jeremy Sear, meanwhile, offered some sensible advice, 'Quick note to corporate Australia: when you're in the middle of crushing your workforce, don't start a Twitter promotion.' Elsewhere the promotion was described cuttingly as 'the Hindenburg of social media strategies' and TV reporter Sally Sara, at the time covering the conflict in Afghanistan for Australian broadcaster ABC, was sardonically 'wondering if #QantasLuxury PR execs may be deployed for first Sydney–Kabul flight'. The social media turkey shoot continued in this vein, with Qantas itself eventually responding with the rueful-sounding quip that, 'At this rate our #QantasLuxury competition is going to take years to judge.' Hardly! Anyone with any common sense had already judged it a terrible failure.

Briefly, #QantasLuxury became the top-trending topic on Twitter in Australia. Had the comments been predominantly favourable, this would have been quite a coup for the social media team. Instead, as people jumped on the airline-trashing bandwagon in droves, it pointed to a business that had utterly lost touch with consumer sentiment. As one of the oldest airline brands in the world and a powerful symbol of Australian identity – from the kangaroo livery on its aircraft tailfins to its historic full name dating back to 1920, Queensland and Northern Territory Aerial Services – Qantas had garnered plenty of respect and affection over the best part of a century. Yet a great brand history brings with it the burden of expectation. Australians expected better from their flag carrier. Let down by service disruption, wary of the decisions the airline was taking, people's trust in Qantas had been eroded. This truly was a bad time to run a Twitter promotion.

A big #McMess – hashtag choice lays McDonald's open to criticism

Asking consumers to share their views on your brand or service via a social media network carries an obvious risk. Fast food chain McDonald's found itself eating humble pie after it unintentionally paved the way for consumers to do just that with a couple of tweets on its official Twitter account on the same day in January 2012. Both tweets praised McDonald's suppliers of ingredients such as beef, potatoes and lettuce and incorporated the hashtag #McDstories. One read: 'Meet some of the hard-working people dedicated to supplying McDs with quality food every day' and bore a link for curious customers to follow that led to video content about farmers on McDonald's corporate website. By using #McDstories more than once, the restaurant chain put some momentum behind the hashtag. It also gave the campaign greater prominence by using a paid-for service to boost the visibility of its tweets. All too quickly, like a burger dropped at a drive-through window, the campaign rolled out of control. Earlier tweets in McDonald's promotional campaign to 'big up' its suppliers had used the definitive phrase #MeetTheFarmers. The far more open nature of #McDstories was interpreted by people as an invitation to share their own experiences and deliver their opinions about the purveyor of Big Macs.

In short order, those with a negative tale to tell or with an axe to grind against the Golden Arches were making their feelings known with the assistance of #McDstories. There were tweets on everything from a fingernail found in a burger to customers throwing up. Some detractors showed great skill in keeping their barbs short yet brutal, such as the pithy and memorable: 'McDialysis? I'm Loving it!'

Watching the feeding frenzy of criticism unfold from the corporation's Oak Brook, Illinois headquarters, McDonald's social media director Rick Wion was quick to appreciate that the campaign was not proceeding as planned. Within an hour he had pulled it and McDonald's changed course, re-introducing the original #MeetTheFarmers promotional hashtag. It's been said by McDonald's that there were more harmless mentions of Egg McMuffins on Twitter that January day than there were hostile #McDstories tweets. There's no reason to doubt this – a business of the scale and nature of McDonald's attracts lots of attention from happy customers and is typically referenced in more than 20,000 tweets every day. Even so, it would be wrong to dismiss the social media blunder as inconsequential. When a campaign misfires in this way it's inevitable that it will make news beyond the media platform where it began. Websites and newspapers around the world reported on the #McFail with relish – some also opting for extra cheese. *Forbes* headlined its story 'When a hashtag becomes a bashtag' while Canada's *Globe and Mail* preferred 'McDonald's not lovin' out of control hashtag campaign.'

After returning to the original hashtag, the torrent of scathing tweets soon slowed to a trickle. The fast food chain decided not to engage directly with any of its #McDstories detractors, although at the same time it took issue with animal rights pressure group PETA, which had claimed on its own Twitter feed that McNuggets are made from mechanically separated white meat. Dismissing this assertion as absolutely false in a tweet addressed to PETA, McDonald's insisted that its popular product was made from white meat inspected by the US Department of Agriculture. For a while it felt as if McDonald's the brand was receiving the kind of grilling normally reserved for its burgers. It certainly opened itself up for an onslaught, but it might have avoided it altogether if it had paid closer attention to the experience of rival fast food chain Wendy's, which caught some flak in 2011 when it served up #HeresTheBeef. If a hashtag can be easily interpreted as a cue for put-downs, there's a good chance people will amuse themselves at the brand owner's expense. So devote more time to weighing up how a hashtag might be perceived or abused than it takes to put a burger and fries in a paper bag.

Uptown put-downs - Waitrose and Coles rue unfinished sentences

British supermarket chain Waitrose — which has a considerably more upmarket positioning than its rivals Tesco, ASDA, Sainsbury's and Morrisons — found itself the target of some humorous digs when asking the Twitterati to complete the sentence 'I shop at Waitrose because . . .'. Here are a few witty responses:

- 'I shop at Waitrose because Clarissa's pony just will not eat ASDA Value straw.'
- 'I shop at Waitrose because, darling, Harrods is just too much of a trek mid-week.'
- 'I shop at Waitrose because their colour scheme matches my Range Rover.'
- 'I shop at Waitrose because I once heard a 6yr old boy in the shop say "Daddy does Lego have a 't' on the end like Merlot?" '
- 'I shop at Waitrose because if you buy a full tank of helicopter fuel you get 10% off Champagne. It is a recession after all.'
- 'I shop at Waitrose because you say "Ten items or fewer" not "Ten items or less", which is important.'
- 'I shop at Waitrose but re-pack it in Tesco bags so the rest of the estate doesn't know I won the EuroMillions.'

The saving grace for Waitrose was that the tone of much of the badinage was good natured and polite – in keeping with the store's own values and positioning, one might say – and may even have cemented its appeal among those middle-class shoppers attracted to the aspirational elements of the brand. On the downside, though, it completely detracted from the supermarket's efforts at the time to appeal to a broader market by price-matching some of its products with rivals such as Tesco.

Waitrose took the mickey-taking on the chin, responding on Twitter: 'Thanks for all the genuine and funny #WaitroseReasons tweets. We always like to hear what you think and enjoyed reading most of them.' Naturally (a Waitrose word if ever there was one!) the campaign went viral and while it may not have played out quite as Waitrose had hoped, as blunders go it was civilised and largely benign. Any egg on the face was probably of sufficient quality to meet the exacting standards of Waitrose brand ambassador Heston Blumenthal, Michelin-starred chef and esteemed molecular gastronomy innovator.

Similarly, Australian supermarket group Coles also laid itself open to jibes in 2012 when using its @Coles Twitter handle to ask people to finish the sentence, 'In my house it's a crime not to buy ...' In a flash, knocking comments began to appear. One took issue with Coles' treatment of its suppliers, completing the sentence '... bread and milk at prices that allow primary producers to survive.' Within an hour the supermarket had backtracked. A disarming follow-up tweet read: 'It's a social media crime not to ... finish a sentence yourself. Sorry guys that post was not meant for Twitter!'

Turning human tragedy into marketing disaster - Kenneth Cole, Habitat, Microsoft and Gap

Piggybacking on the news agenda can be a very cost-effective form of marketing and allows brands to appear up-to-the-minute and in tune with the times. Doing so by riding the trending waves of Twitter carries risks, however. Picking the wrong story with which to associate your brand or misjudging the tone or timing of a tweet could trigger accusations of callousness, cynical exploitation and insensitive opportunism. Latching on to sporting or cultural stories, or exploiting celebrity froth – if such things are a good fit for a brand – tend to be safer options than seeking a cheap boost from hard news or potentially divisive political stories. Interpolating your brand into the midst of discussion on a disaster or crisis without good reason is a very bad idea indeed. Human suffering is not an appropriate context for brand promotion. You'd think everybody would know that ... and you'd be wrong.

The popular protests of the Arab Spring brought turmoil and bloodshed to large parts of the Middle East. Old regimes were toppled, swept away by civil unrest, much of it co-ordinated via social media. In Egypt, demonstrators took to the streets of Cairo in force during January and February 2011 in a concerted effort to overthrow the country's long-time authoritarian ruler, President Hosni Mubarak. Violent clashes exacted a terrible toll. In the weeks leading up to Mubarak's resignation on 11th February 2011, 846 people were killed in the revolutionary struggle and more than 6,400 others injured. These were dangerous, volatile, frightening times.

As concerned people around the world monitored the progress of the conflict, wondering what course it would take, fashion designer Kenneth Cole, in an act of breathtaking imbecility, decided these were ideal circumstances in which to plug his latest collection. On 3rd February 2011 Cole tweeted: 'Millions are in uproar in #Cairo. Rumor is they heard our new spring collection is now available online.'

The backlash against the designer's attempt to capitalise on this serious topic began at once. Outraged responses sprang up across Twitter and there were plenty of stories about the tasteless tweet in popular media titles. Showing remarkable speed out of the blocks, a social media satirist set up a spoof @KennethColePR Twitter account to poke fun at the designer's gift for the gaffe. 'People of New Orleans are flooding into Kenneth Cole stores!' read one parody tweet. 'Our new looks are dropping faster than the World Trade Center,' went another brutal lampoon. Attempting to inveigle the Kenneth Cole brand into the conversation about the momentous protests in Cairo gave detractors tacit permission to paint the fashion label and the man behind it as heartless, grasping and oblivious to the pain of those affected by traumatic events.

Ignoring the outrage was not an option. Cole tweeted his regret and soon afterwards removed the offending tweet. To further dampen the flames of controversy, he posted a more comprehensive apology to his Facebook page:

> '*I apologize to everyone who was offended by my insensitive tweet about the situation in Egypt. I've dedicated my life to raising awareness about serious social issues, and in hindsight my attempt at humor regarding a nation liberating themselves against oppression was poorly timed and absolutely inappropriate. Kenneth Cole, Chairman and Chief Creative Officer.*'

Anyone who has ever seen the hilarious Ben Stiller movie *Zoolander* may now be wondering if its depiction of the vanity and vacuity of the fashion world is far more accurate than they originally supposed. Nevertheless, before we get too judgemental of couturiers, it should be pointed out that Kenneth Cole is not the only brand that has attempted to make hay from online discussion of the political situation in the Middle East. Back in 2009, British furniture retailer Habitat used Twitter to encourage people to join its database for the chance to win a £1,000 gift card. To draw attention to the promotion, Habitat sprinkled its tweets with totally irrelevant trending keywords including #Iranelection and #Mousavi – the latter referring to Iranian opposition leader Mir Hossein Mousavi, who was standing against President Mahmoud Ahmadinejad. Other trending topics that Habitat shamelessly annexed for its tweets included the Apple iPhone and the name of a contestant appearing on TV show *MasterChef Australia*. Habitat's inept efforts to muscle in on subjects of online conversation irrelevant to its business drew scorn and accusations that it was spamming Twitter users, who were perplexed or irritated to find the decor store popping up when they searched trending topics that had nothing in common with fancy rugs and mood lighting.

Once the level of disquiet at the hashtag hijacking became clear, Habitat apologised and blamed an over-enthusiastic intern for the trend-plundering.

Habitat is not the only brand that has hit trouble by entrusting social media duties to a team junior – on the mistaken assumption that it is unimportant or simply because older members of the marketing team don't 'get' this new-fangled Twitter stuff. There's no excuse for this, on either score. Habitat's blatant Twitter spam-fest will for years to come be held up as a glaring example of how not to use social media. At least the brand seems to have learned its lesson. In recent times its Twitter feed has focused on far more sensible topics such as product news, interior design tips and addressing customer service issues.

For another example of riding the coat tails of disaster we must return to 2011. A few short weeks after the Kenneth Cole debacle, Japan faced its biggest crisis since World War II when its Tohoku Pacific coast was hit by a 9.0 magnitude earthquake and devastating tsunami that claimed more than 19,000 lives, wrought havoc with infrastructure and caused nuclear catastrophe at the Fukushima Daiichi power plant. Technology colossus Microsoft was commendably quick to pledge $2m in cash and in-kind support for the urgent relief efforts. Then it went and did something stupid. On the Twitter account for its search engine Bing, Microsoft tweeted the following: 'How you can #SupportJapan – http://binged. it/fEh7iT. For every retweet, @bing will give $1 to Japan quake victims, up to $100K.'

Some people saw no reason to take exception to this and happily retweeted, taking the view that an initiative to raise money for the victims of the earthquake had to be a positive thing. But others perceived the tweet as a marketing ploy in which misfortune on an epic scale was being used to promote Bing – as part of Microsoft's determined efforts to close the gap on the dominant player in the search engine market, Google. Awareness of the tweet did indeed spread fast, though not at all in a way that was comfortable for Microsoft. Critics who considered the tech company had been disingenuous and opportunistic rallied around a blunt new hashtag that left little doubt as to their opinions on the matter: #fuckyoubing. Feelings were running high. Here are just a few of the many scathing tweets directed at Bing:

- 'Coming soon! Microsoft branded Tsunami commemorative mugs and T-shirts. 20% of every sale goes to good causes!'

- 'Hey, remember how Google set up a people finder to help Japanese find loved ones and didn't brag about it?'
- 'Dear Microsoft, that's not how it works, you're supposed to do something good first, then you get good publicity from it.'
- 'Soon the word bing will become a verb for exploiting a disaster.'

Although Microsoft probably had good intentions, people clearly resented even a hint of self-promotion in the context of a major tragedy. Why, consumers wondered, should they be asked to help promote the Bing brand when Microsoft clearly had the means to just donate the money, without receiving a quid pro quo for an action that should be purely altruistic? Seven hours after the offending tweet, Microsoft followed it up with an apology on Twitter: 'We apologize the tweet was negatively perceived. Intent was to provide an easy way for people to help Japan. We have donated $100K.'

Hurricane Sandy may not have been a disaster on the same apocalyptic scale, but it nevertheless affected the entire eastern US seaboard when it hit with terrible force in October 2012, causing damage estimated at $32.8bn in New York State alone. Clothing retailer Gap brainlessly treated the natural disaster as an opportunity to plug its e-commerce website, tweeting: 'All impacted by #Sandy, stay safe. We'll be doing lots of Gap.com shopping today. How about you?'

Only if you kit your social media idiots out with sou'westers and make them dance in the storm! Gap's 'Be Bright' campaign has never seemed more heavily ironic.

When jokes fall flat - KitchenAid and Durex cause offence

Facing Mitt Romney in an election debate televised live on NBC in October 2012, President Barack Obama was well prepared for slights and barbs from the Republican candidate. In attempting to cover all the bases, communications guru David Axelrod and other members of the incumbent's slick and thorough re-election team may well have anticipated a variety of allusions to the President's beloved grandmother

Madelyn Lee Payne Dunham, a formative presence in Obama's childhood who unfortunately died less than a week before he swept to power in his historic 2008 election victory and whom Obama proudly referred to live on air four years later. But even the most accomplished political strategist could not have foreseen that a tasteless quip about the President's grandmother delivered during the debate would come not from the challenger but would arise instead on the Twitter feed of a well-known manufacturer of kitchen appliances.

So it was that KitchenAid entered the political fray with the following indiscreet tweet: 'Obamas gma even knew it was going 2 b bad! She died 3 days b4 he became president.' Not much of a joke. In fact, not at all the sort of thing you'd expect from a brand identified with products such as its classic stand mixer. Why was this icon of cake-making mixing it up by joining a bruising political bun fight?

It soon transpired that the tweet had been meant for a personal Twitter account but was ineptly posted to KitchenAid's corporate Twitter feed instead. Accidental it may have been, but an offensive throwaway line for the amusement of friends was now out there as part of the brand's communication with the public. Warranted criticism and unwanted retweets erupted across social media. KitchenAid was looking pretty bad.

To its credit, KitchenAid cleaned up the mess very efficiently. The message was swiftly deleted and replaced by an apology. Whereas some apologies for social media mistakes can seem superficial or half-hearted, Cynthia Soledad, a senior director at KitchenAid with responsibility for the brand, took it upon herself to personally apologise to the president and his family as well as to everyone else on Twitter for the offensive tweet. In addition, she issued a fuller apology to the media outlets queuing up to cover the grandma *faux pas*. It read:

> 'During the debate tonight, a member of our Twitter team mistakenly posted an offensive tweet from the KitchenAid handle instead of a personal handle. The tasteless joke in no way represents our values at KitchenAid, and that person won't be tweeting for us anymore. That said, I lead the KitchenAid brand, and I take responsibility for the whole team. I am

deeply sorry to President Obama, his family, and the Twitter community for this careless error. Thanks for hearing me out.'

The full apology was circulated within a couple of hours and Soledad's readiness to be accountable for a junior's slip-up proved disarming. Media outlets from the *Los Angeles Times* to the *Huffington Post* ran embarrassing stories, but the potential for brand damage from these was lessened by their inclusion of Soledad's words of contrition. For anyone who administers both business and personal social media accounts from the same computer or smartphone, this should be a salutary wake-up call. Pay attention and don't get confused! And if you are easily confused … stick to being nice. It's safer.

For another social media humour cock-up, who better to turn to than condom and sex accessories brand Durex? In November 2011, Durex South Africa posted a series of jokes on its @DurexSA Twitter feed that were sexual in nature and adorned them with the #DurexJoke hashtag. Did anybody honestly think this was going to end well? Maybe in more skilful hands. But as the Reckitt Benckiser-owned brand lurched from one smutty gag to another, it seemed only a matter of time before they would overstep the mark. So it proved when the brand tweeted: 'Why did God give men penises? So they'd have at least one way to shut a woman up.'

The coercion implied by this sleazy joke wouldn't have played well anywhere. In South Africa, where sexual assault is rife, it touched a nerve. A truly horrifying 25% of South African men have raped someone, and almost half of these men admit carrying out more than one attack, according to research released by the country's Medical Research Council in 2009. (This disturbing research was reported around the world at the time, and contemporary reports are still available at the time of writing on the BBC and *Guardian* websites, among others.)

In a society in which rape is so prevalent and such a cause for concern among women, the tweet caused immediate offence. Appalled Durex tweeps expressed their disgust on Twitter and, as is the way with such things, news of the brand's insensitivity hurtled across the internet. Before long, the tweet was forwarded to Jen Thorpe of women's rights group Feminists SA. Stunned, Thorpe used the @FeministsSA Twitter account to point out to Durex that its tweet endorsed violence against women. Durex's semi-literate reply, on Twitter once again, was dismissive rather than apologetic: '@FeministsSA We have posted many jokes, see our timeline . . . And they not violent against woman! Re-read it!!!!!'

Stung into further action, Thorpe penned an eloquent, intelligent piece on the Feminists SA website in which she argued that South Africa's 'incredibly powerful rape culture' is sustained by many things: low conviction rates for perpetrators; an unpleasant criminal justice system that alienates survivors and reduces reporting; a history of violence in South Africa; and inequality amongst the sexes. It is also perpetuated, she concluded, 'by our laughter at jokes that condone violence against women. Rape is not funny.'

Criticism of Durex's behaviour mounted with growing momentum until eventually the brand began to take it seriously. Finally, it tweeted an apology: 'We're really sorry for causing offence today, not intentional. We believe in the rights of woman and safe sex. Thanks for putting us right.'

The joke was not only offensive, its timing was dreadful. Durex unleashed its tweet the day before the start of South Africa's annual 16 Days of Activism for No Violence Against Women and Children campaign. Set against this backdrop, the heavy-handed attempt at humour looked even worse. The way the joke was worded left it open to interpretation and in posting it to Twitter there may well have been no intent to condone sexual violence against women. Yet just as it's a good idea to practise safe sex, brands should practise safe humour – taking precautions against unnecessary risks. A thoughtless quick quip has the potential to inflict lasting damage on a brand.

Durex exacerbated the outrage by not taking the first wave of complaints about its joke seriously. Instead of nipping the crisis in the bud, it fanned the flames. When at last it got round to apologising, Durex apportioned the blame to its creative agency in South Africa Euro RSCG rather than accepting full responsibility itself, even naming and shaming the agency on Twitter. Sure, the agency was culpable for the misjudged tweet, but as far as the public were concerned the joke was made in Durex's name. Pointing the finger at its agency appeared petty and added another layer of sourness to an unpleasant episode.

With the passage of time, Durex seems to have got a better grip on its social media presence. It's interesting to note that the profile information on the official Twitter page of Durex South Africa in 2013 presents the brand as: 'Lovers of safe and consensual sex. Supports non-violence against women.' A lesson has been learned. Perhaps fittingly for a condom brand, it's a lesson learned the hard way.

Like some of its products, Durex is now more sensitive. Yet sensitivity alone is no protection from mishaps. In 2013, a Durex promotion for its SOS Condoms service was hijacked by pranksters. Durex asked people to vote for which city should receive the service, which features a downloadable app that can be used to request an emergency delivery of condoms – handy for those last-minute hot dates. In a careless oversight (from a company that should know all about taking precautions) Durex left the choice of cities open-ended. Leaping on an opportunity for some fun at the brand's expense, a Facebook campaign was launched calling on people to vote for Batman, a city in Turkey – although needless to say, the intention was actually to undermine the whole process by planting the idea that it was the superhero rather than a city that needed condoms in a hurry. The votes for Batman began stacking up amid quips about the caped crusader's sexual activity: I knew it, even with his mask on I could tell by the way he gazed at Robin that something more than the bat logo was in the air. Batman duly won the vote, trouncing far higher-profile cities such as Kuala Lumpur, Singapore, Paris, New York, London and Moscow. Given that Batman is a deeply conservative place in Muslim south-eastern Turkey, there was no chance that SOS Condoms would be launched there. Pow! Just like that the campaign was knocked down – by a joker who knew how to manipulate Batman.

A hash of it - party falls flat as SuBo invitation is misconstrued

On social media, as elsewhere in life, some of the funniest things aren't meant to be funny at all. A truly glorious instance of unintended hilarity is supplied by the record company PR team tasked with promoting Susan Boyle's *Standing Ovation* album. To drum up interest in this compilation of songs from the stage, it was decided that the Scottish singer unearthed by Simon Cowell on *Britain's Got Talent* should host an exclusive 'album listening party' at which she would answer questions from fans. Word of this was spread in November 2012 via a tweet, to which the hashtag #susanalbumparty was appended.

If ever proof were needed that Twitter users will revel in juvenile humour given half a chance, this tweet delivered it. Eagle-eyed, mischievous Twitterati saw that the hashtag could be broken down to read something rather odder than what the record label meant to convey. Gleefully reinterpreted as an invitation to 'Su's anal bum party' – 'Thanks for asking, but please accept my apologies, I have a prior engagement' – the hashtag was soon a trending topic globally. Once this became evident, the original tweet was deleted, although this did little to stop the online merriment at the unplanned double entendre. In more than one sense, this was a backfiring tweet. That said, any embarrassment it caused the performer and record company should be weighed up against the increased exposure gained by it going viral. Maybe being seen as silly is only to be expected when promoting an album which includes a version of the Stephen Sondheim classic *Send in the Clowns*.

Sniggering aside, the way this tweet was mocked should serve as a warning. Don't publish hashtags that can be misinterpreted or wilfully misconstrued! Another example of Twitter confusion was seen following the death of Margaret Thatcher, when the hashtag #nowthatchersdead appeared, and was misread by some as 'Now That Cher's Dead'. By the same token, citing a trending term on social media without any idea what it actually relates to is a snafu waiting to happen. That's what UK-based online fashion retailer CelebBoutique did in July 2012 when ignorantly tweeting: '#Aurora is trending, clearly about our Kim K inspired #Aurora dress.' No, clearly not! While news of Kardashian-inspired fashion is assuredly of great significance, Twitterati were rightly more concerned about the horrific mass shooting at the late-night screening of Batman movie *The Dark Knight Rises* at a cinema in Aurora, Colorado.

Moreover, if referencing other Twitter users in a tweet, take care not to be sloppy. When Prime Minister David Cameron tweeted about welfare reform in 2013, he meant to cite the Twitter handle of government colleague Iain Duncan Smith, Secretary of State for Work

& Pensions. Carelessly, the tweet pointed Twitterati in the direction of a distinctly unflattering IDS parody account instead. Although the incident made the PM appear a bit bumbling in social media terms, it can't be argued that Cameron was clueless about the potential pitfalls of Twitter. In 2009, before joining Twitter, he was put on the spot during a live radio interview as to why he was not yet on the social networking site. Amid chuckling in the studio, Cameron responded: 'The trouble with Twitter, the instantness of it – too many twits might make a twat.' Shortly afterwards, Cameron apologised for his coarse choice of language on air – which only goes to show, it can be just as easy to make a gaffe talking about Twitter as it is when posting on Twitter.

Nestlé and the heavy hand of censorship

While the SuBo blunder can be assessed light-heartedly, the same cannot be said of Nestlé's social media difficulties of 2010. As the world's biggest food company, a hugely profitable global business with many billion-dollar brands in its portfolio, the Swiss giant is a prominent target for criticism. Since the mid-1970s it has faced a series of boycotts relating to claims that it has been 'aggressive' in promoting infant formula as an alternative to breastfeeding in developing countries. In response, Nestlé insists that these days it complies with both the letter and the spirit of the World Health Organization's International Code of Marketing of Breast-Milk Substitutes. Unsurprisingly in the circumstances, this is a company very mindful of reputational issues. Strange, therefore, that it should turn a molehill into a Swiss mountain of trouble when environmental charity Greenpeace went gunning for it.

In this case the issue wasn't baby milk but the use by Nestlé of Indonesian conglomerate Sinar Mas as a supplier of palm oil as an ingredient for products such as the chocolate bar Kit Kat. Greenpeace accused Sinar Mas of unsustainable behaviour relating to the deforestation of Indonesia and the impact of this on endangered species. In March 2010, Greenpeace published a report titled *Caught Red Handed – How Nestlé's Use of Palm Oil is Having a Devastating Impact on Rainforest, the Climate and Orang-utans*. The report alleged that clearing forests to make way for palm oil plantations was one of the main causes for the steep decline in orang-utan numbers in recent years. It pointed the finger at Nestlé as a major contributor to this deforestation by having, over a three-year period, almost doubled its annual use of palm oil to 320,000 tonnes to meet the needs of manufacturing food products such as Kit Kat on a global scale. 'Every five minutes, enough Kit Kats are manufactured to outstack the Eiffel Tower,' the report revealed.

To galvanise support for its campaign to persuade Nestlé to change its ways, Greenpeace produced a video for social media distribution. The 60-second *Have a Break* video was a gruesome play on Nestlé's Kit Kat advertising. It shows a bored office worker taking a break from the mundane task of shredding documents by unpeeling a Kit Kat wrapper, snapping off a finger from the chocolate bar and biting into it. Only there's a twist. It isn't an ordinary chocolate wafer finger; it's the hairy finger of an orang-utan. As the office worker crunches into it, blood runs down his chin and colleagues look on aghast. Graphics using Kit Kat's red and white brand colours urge people to give the orang-utan a break before the video cuts to ugly scenes of deforestation and a concluding exhortation to 'Stop Nestlé buying palm oil from companies that destroy the rain forests.'

It's the kind of emotive campaigning that NGOs (non-governmental organisations) such as Greenpeace do extraordinarily well, but for which they frequently struggle to find an audience much beyond committed activists and diehard supporters. Reaching only a small number of people may well have been the fate of the *Have a Break* video, which Greenpeace posted to YouTube and which had been seen by under 1,000 viewers ... until Nestlé adopted the heavy-handed approach of forcing YouTube to take down the video on grounds of copyright infringement. Presented with this golden opportunity, Greenpeace lost no time in reposting *Have a Break* to another video-sharing site, Vimeo, and alerting its followers on social media to Nestlé's suppression of the video on YouTube. Trying to muzzle its detractors in this way wasn't a smart move by Nestlé. Charges of censorship were now added to allegations of disregard for the environment, hardening the determination of Greenpeace supporters and piquing the interest of a larger audience. Quite a few Greenpeace supporters took matters into their own hands by reposting *Have a Break* to YouTube themselves, while the video Greenpeace posted on Vimeo got 80,000 views in a single day.

Greenpeace did a fantastic job of orchestrating protest, urging people to target Nestlé with critical emails, phone calls and comments on its social media sites, putting the company under sustained pressure. Nestlé was bombarded with over 200,000 emails and the *Have a Break* video was watched by 1.5 million people; that's 1,500 times as many views than before the food group started interfering. Thousands of negative comments appeared on the Facebook page Nestlé had set up aimed at fans of its brands. The 90,000 or so Facebook fans that had been quite happily following Nestlé before the crisis blew up were suddenly being exposed to massive amounts of negative comment about the company's activities. Some of these critical comments featured doctored images of Nestlé logos, for example Kit Kat reworked to read 'Killer', that Greenpeace shrewdly made available on its website and encouraged its supporters to use. Rather than turning a blind eye, Nestlé deleted these images, further compounding the perception that the company did not tolerate criticism and would take steps to snuff out views contrary to its own.

'We welcome your comments, but please don't post using an altered version of any of our logos as your profile pic – they will be deleted,' wrote Nestlé on its Facebook page.

That response went down like a lead balloon. As far as many social media users are concerned, brands and businesses only have permission to participate in online conversations if they respect the rights of individuals to air their views – even if those views are anathema to a brand and are posted to its own fan page. *Do Not Delete* has become established as a social media tenet, a licence for brands to operate in the space, to be observed unless posts are offensive in the extreme. Yet Nestlé's team in Switzerland set about deleting images, links and comments that did not suit it and further inflamed the situation by responding with unforgiveable rudeness to some of those seeking to engage with the company on Facebook about the matter. Combining cluelessness and arrogance with a dearth of interpersonal skills, a Nestlé representative dismissed concerns about freedom of speech and expression in the following exchange:

> Nestlé: *'Here, there are some rules we set. As in almost any other forum. It's to keep things clear.'*

Paul Griffin: 'Your page, your rules, true, and you just lost a customer. Won the battle and lost the war! Happy?'

Nestlé: 'Oh please ... it's like we're censoring everything to allow only positive comments.'

In another Facebook exchange a little later, the tone was just as rude and patronising.

Helen Constable: 'I'd like to know if the person writing the comments for Nestlé actually has the backing from Nestlé? I doubt it. Even a dumb ass company like them would get such an idiot to be their public voice.'

Nestlé: 'I think you missed out the "not" there, Helen.'

Helen Constable: 'Yes well I'm lacking in the first morning NOT NESTLE coffee. I think you missed your manners in your comments.'

This lack of emollience spurred on the detractors, who continued to swarm over Nestlé on Facebook, Twitter and other social channels. The writing was on the wall. Nestlé's response had been a mixture of the shambolic and inflammatory, a how *not* to do it guide to interaction on social media. A climbdown was necessary. It began with an attempt at bridge building on Facebook.

Nestlé: 'This (deleting logos) was one in a series of mistakes for which I would like to apologise. And for being rude. We've stopped deleting posts, and I have stopped being rude.'

Beyond the embarrassment of Nestlé's chastisement via social media, there was a significant, tangible outcome for Greenpeace's campaign. 'By trying to censor us Nestlé in effect mobilised a large community on the web interested in internet freedom who otherwise we likely wouldn't have reached,' Greenpeace Deputy Head of Mobilisation Jamie Woolley tells me:

'The reaction of this community led to a significant amount of online coverage which in turn drove hard news coverage the

day after we launched. It was the first time in the campaign where we really witnessed online news driving hard news in a significant way. And this in turn put pressure on the company to alter its behaviour. We asked people to use this public forum to communicate with the company, but we had no idea what would happen next. It took on a life of its own. Telling members of the public, as Nestlé did, "we welcome your comments, but please don't post using an altered version of any of our logos as your profile pic – they will be deleted" is only going to get more people posting altered logos.'

In the face of all this criticism, Nestlé suspended purchasing palm oil from Sinar Mas and held meetings with Greenpeace to discuss its palm oil supply chain. In May 2010, it joined the Roundtable on Sustainable Palm Oil, a grouping of organisations working towards eliminating unsustainable palm oil production. On 16th September 2011, Indonesian media revealed that Nestlé had resumed sourcing palm oil from Sinar Mas, on the understanding that the supplier was now able to comply with tightened environmental standards. For its part, Sinar Mas had been working with environmental group the Forest Trust on the introduction of a Forest Conservation Policy designed to prevent any deforestation footprint. Greenpeace continues to monitor the situation in Indonesia to ensure that these environmental pledges are not broken. All of which goes to show the enormous power of social media; a power to bring about change which on this occasion Nestlé was unable to resist. When brands try to suppress criticism in the manner of totalitarian states, it's a near certainty that the situation will only get worse.

Stung by the events of 2010, the Nestlé hierarchy realised that some changes were necessary if the company was to avoid a repeat of the social media fiasco. American digital marketing expert Pete Blackshaw was headhunted for the new role of global head of digital and social media, beginning work at Nestlé global headquarters in Vevey, Switzerland in March 2011. Today, Blackshaw describes the events of 2010 as a 'teachable moment' for the company, and evidence for this can be found in the seniority of his own role. He reports directly to the company's global heads of marketing and corporate communications, the twin reporting lines indicating that Nestlé now recognises the impact social media can have on product brand image, sales and business reputation. The company has begun making organisational changes to better address this; what Blackshaw calls 'softening the silos'.

One of the first things Blackshaw did on joining Nestlé was to put out social media guidelines that clarified dos and don'ts for employees and gave advice on speaking with an empathetic voice. A decision was also taken to adopt a less confrontational approach to the misappropriation of logos on social media. Latterly, he has focused on wider issues of resourcing, exploring how the organisation will have to evolve to meet growing consumer expectations of 24/7 responsiveness, so that Nestlé is not caught flat-footed again. Among the key issues he is wrestling with is who should take on the community manager role, how to fund that and how to make sure community management is available around the clock. In the past, that sort of role has been filled by marketing agencies or an in-house brand manager with a passion for social media. Blackshaw sees this as a 'temporary solution', believing that deeper organisational change is called for. He says he has been thinking about digital as 'an operating principle' as much as he thinks about digital as a communications channel:

> 'We're taking a critical look at core service operations and what are the new expectations in a world where your Facebook page seems to suggest to every consumer that you're always on, always accessible. But you've got call centres that close at six and aren't open on the weekend. A lot of that is very complicated operational issues. How do you rethink store hours, so to speak? We may need to think differently about the time we allocate to consumers. Call centres – well beyond Nestlé – have always been a non-strategic cost centre. So, all the incentives have been aligned around fewer consumers through the pipe, less time per consumer. In a social world there are actually really big dividends to be reaped by keeping the conversation open and continuing – that earned media effect.'

With a global entity such as Nestlé, the challenge is to find a solution that will work at scale. On Facebook alone, Nestlé has roughly

130 million fans spread across 630 Facebook pages around the world: that's before taking into account its other extensive social media activities on platforms such as Twitter and LinkedIn. On an average day, Nestlé drops around 1,500 pieces of content across all of its social media sites. And with every piece of content, the company is looking for answers to the following questions: Did consumers like it? Did they engage? Did they share? Or did they vote with their feet and ignore it? Immense amounts of data mining are taking place, as Nestlé strives to better understand not only how its marketing activity is perceived but also to build up a clearer picture of other issues at the heart of its business, such as product performance and customer service. Nestlé is evidently far more social media savvy today than it was a few years ago. It may be painful for the company to admit as much, but the run-in with Greenpeace may have done it a huge favour.

Washing-up liquid that tastes of chicken – Henkel laments low-key T&Cs

In spring 2011 the German company Henkel, owner of brands such as Persil, Pritt and Schwarzkopf, decided that a spot of crowdsourcing was the way to go about reinvigorating its Pril washing-up liquid. It initiated a design competition called '*Mein Pril – Mein Stil*' ('My Pril – My Style'), the aim of which, quite simply, was to encourage consumers to create designs for Pril bottle labels and post them on Facebook where people could vote for them. The winning designs were to be turned into special edition Pril bottles that would be produced in large numbers and sold through normal retail channels. On the face of it, this promised to be a pleasant and mutually beneficial exercise in engaging with consumers – the brand stood to be refreshed by input from the public, while successful participants in the competition would have the pleasure of seeing the fruits of their creative endeavours on supermarket shelves and in marketing campaigns.

What Henkel failed to anticipate, though, was Peter Breuer and his wicked sense of humour. Shunning the carefully pre-vetted choice of graphics on offer, Breuer used a digital drawing tool to put a rough-and-ready looking illustration of a roast chicken on his label and added a slogan to savour: '*Schmeckt lecker nach Hähnchen*' ('Tastes delicious, like chicken'). When Breuer uploaded his creation, this amusing subversion of the crowdsourcing exercise received a warm welcome. Appreciative German consumers began voting for it in their thousands and, taking their cue from Breuer's irreverence, others were soon poking fun at Pril by putting absurdist designs of their own online.

> '*Unfortunately, the number of objectionable, tasteless and in some cases also legally suspect or prohibited designs being submitted increased in the course of the competition. Consequently, Henkel announced that the designs would only be allowed to participate in the competition once they had been moderated and approved by the Pril editorial team.*'
>
> Bettina Klinken, brand PR team, Henkel's Laundry and Home Care division.

From the very start, Henkel had covered itself with conditions of entry that contained the express advisory that it reserved the right to erase, at any time and without warning, design entries that infringed the rights of third parties, featured illegal content or which in its view violated a natural sense of decency, for example on religious or ethical grounds. The problem was that these terms and conditions were not displayed very prominently and went unnoticed by many of the participants. When Henkel began to interfere, criticism of its actions appeared on Facebook. Consumers felt that what had been presented as a democratic exercise was actually a sham; that Henkel was ignoring the voice of the people.

Henkel also included in the conditions of entry the warning that impermissible manipulation of the voting process would not be tolerated and that participants gaining an unfair competitive advantage in this way would be excluded from the competition. When Henkel discovered that voting for some designs was, as Klinken puts it, 'indeed being massively and unfairly manipulated', it deducted the 'impermissible votes' so as not to disadvantage the honest participants. But to many casual observers it was Henkel that appeared manipulative. Protests about the company's behaviour intensified online and this dissatisfaction was quickly seized upon by mainstream media, who started referring to events as a PR debacle for Henkel.

Amid the controversy, the 'tasty chicken' design, which had led the rankings for some time, was withdrawn from the competition by Breuer, who had had enough of the nonsense. Henkel announced in advance on Facebook that it was discounting the votes that did not meet its guidelines, a move which had an impact on the rankings of some of the designs, particularly within the top 30. The most significant change triggered by this revision of the voting figures was the fall from first to third place in the rankings for another subversive design, 'Priiiiil', which featured the roughly drawn head of a furious man with heavily bloodshot eyes, his mouth gaping in a livid scream. For obvious reasons, this design came to be snappily known as Rage Guy.

A good proportion of people who took part in the competition felt that the moral winner of the competition had been sabotaged. Henkel saw things rather differently. All along, its competition rules had made it clear that two winning designs would be selected by jury from among the 10 designs garnering the most votes. As far as it was concerned, the Rage Guy label was still one of 10 winners that would receive a prize. But it had never stood a chance of being one of the two designs to be mass produced to appear in supermarkets. From Henkel's standpoint, the whole purpose of having a jury element to the process was to ensure the two eventual winners − which in the end were nice enough, but about as entertaining as a massive pile of dirty dishes − would be a good fit for the brand. What we have here is a huge disparity between corporate and individual viewpoints. Henkel felt it had played things straight, but some people nevertheless felt cheated and made scathing comments on Facebook accusing the company of election fraud! Klinken says:

'Even though every participant in the competition had to agree to the conditions of entry in advance, these conditions were apparently not or only scantily read and poorly understood. Otherwise, all the participants would have been aware from the start that a jury would be choosing the winning designs from the top 10. The jury was also introduced in a separate,

readily visible and accessible sub-page. The most important lesson learned in this regard is therefore that, in future competitions, we will need to make the conditions of entry more prominent and possibly also place them repeatedly on different pages.'

Henkel also concluded that establishing an online forum for creative design leaves scope for people to abuse the process with tasteless or offensive material. If it were to run a similar competition in future, its feeling is that design entries should only be uploaded and visualised on the internet once they have been appropriately vetted by a moderator (can you hear the groans of the anarchically minded?). Additionally, while offering prizes such as iPads – as Henkel did with Pril – increases the popularity of a competition, it also attracts the attention of 'third parties who may be professionally involved in the manipulation of competition outcomes'. Marketers at Henkel are now of the opinion that a prize draw, offering all participants the chance to win something, appears to be a better solution.

The Pril competition certainly made waves. More than 50,000 creative designs were posted, attracting a total of over 1.6 million votes – far more than Henkel expected. In autumn 2011 the two winning designs were made available in retail outlets as Pril's Design Edition. In a placatory move, Henkel also offered an exclusive special edition of 888 copies of the Rage Guy design, which had proved to be so popular with the online community. All 777 Rage Guy bottles available on eBay were sold within just 56 minutes. There was also strong demand for the 111 bottles in this design offered in a prize draw on the Pril Facebook page. Clearly, Henkel can take some positives from the affair – even if some of the biggest fans of the Rage Guy bottle were making a point that the company would not find flattering. On top of the online criticism from a loud minority, there was even some comical direct action in support of the 'moral winner'. In a fascinating, out-of-control slant on guerrilla marketing – where the consumer rather than the brand manager calls the shots – some Germans printed out Rage Guy labels and went into a supermarket, where they stuck them on the Pril bottles on shelf (special ops, dish cleanliness division), posting a photo of the resulting makeover online. The Rage Guy label had made it into one store at least.

'We were surprised at the negative tone adopted in media reports as discussions on the Pril Facebook page unfolded, particularly in view of the fact that the general response of Facebook users had essentially been encouraging,' Klinken concedes. 'In fact, the criticism that appeared on Facebook was driven primarily by a very small group of users.' Small, maybe, but given the fuss, far from insignificant. There's always the potential when turning to the crowd that anything positive can be drowned out by those in the mob who bay loudest.

What's the worst that could happen? Dr Pepper finally finds out

If you've seen TV commercials for soft drink brand Dr Pepper, you can probably sing this line: 'Dr Pepper, what's the worst that could happen?' Sorry if that song is now insistently buzzing around inside your head. It's a jaunty, catchy jingle. A little annoying, perhaps, but very effective at implanting the brand name into one's memory. Particularly as the storylines of Dr Pepper ads are built around this slogan, pitching characters into awkward and embarrassing situations for comic purposes. Given the coherent way the brand is presented, it's understandable that marketers would want to expand on this theme through digital channels. That was the intention in April 2010 when Coca-Cola, which owns Dr Pepper in the UK, appointed digital marketing agency Lean Mean Fighting Machine to implement a teen-focused brand-building campaign.

The campaign went live the following month. An app available from the Dr Pepper Facebook page offered consumers the chance to win £1,000 in exchange for allowing the brand to take control of their status update. In keeping with the 'What's the worst that could happen?' creative, this meant that young consumers would have their Facebook pages taken over by Dr Pepper with embarrassing status updates such as 'What's wrong with peeing in the shower?' and 'Lost my special blankie. How will I go sleepies?' Oscar Wilde it's not, but the tone was well judged for an image-conscious teenage target audience obsessed by what is and isn't cool and how they appear to others. There were, the agency trumpeted when promoting the campaign, 'hundreds of ways to stitch yourself up'. Teenagers were being encouraged to present themselves as foolish, without knowing in advance exactly how; this was an edgy campaign for sure.

All went well at first. But in July disaster struck. A mother checking up on her 14-year-old daughter's internet activities was appalled by what she found on her kid's Facebook page. She aired her concerns on leading parenting forum, Mumsnet:

> '*I was HORRIFIED to log into FB and see that her status read – "I watched 2 girls one cup and felt hungry afterwards". For anyone who doesn't know what this means, please stay ignorant, for those who do, you can imagine how I felt. This was compounded later on when a quick search through dds [darling daughter's] internet history revealed she had tried to find out what it was for herself. Thankfully, our ISP has a wonderful child filter!!*'

Like the horrified parent, I won't elaborate in explicit detail on the '2 girls one cup' reference as it relates to pornographic material. However, just to clarify what inappropriate territory this is for a brand to stray into, I should point out that it refers to a notorious trailer for a hardcore fetish movie. Despite the extreme nature of the sequence, the reference to it would have been understood by many in the campaign's teenage target audience, due primarily to the 'Reaction videos' phenomenon. A spate of these videos, in which the often ostentatious revulsion of people watching '2 girls one cup' is recorded for comedy purposes (with the hardcore material they are viewing usually out of shot), has swept the internet. Needless to say, these Reaction videos can be easily found on video-sharing sites such as YouTube and Vimeo and have encouraged plenty of curious teens to hunt down the X-rated source material.

While the creative team at Lean Mean Fighting Machine was obviously wise to all this, marketers at Coke had approved the campaign without any idea what was meant by the reference: never a good move. Enlightenment was to come through public outrage. Before long, the thread on the Mumsnet post had generated more than a thousand comments as parents disgusted by the campaign vented their feelings. Inevitably, the story spilled over into the wider media. Introduced as 'Coca-Cola's Facebook fail', the botched campaign was discussed for six and half minutes on the Sky News prime time evening bulletin – with Mumsnet founder Justine Roberts interviewed live on air not pulling any punches in slamming the campaign for both its content and for encouraging kids to set their privacy settings low.

Coca-Cola apologised unreservedly, removed the unwise status update immediately and brought the promotion to a premature halt. A spokesperson sheepishly admitted that Coca-Cola had been unaware what the line meant when green-lighting the campaign but took full responsibility for it, adding that an investigation had been launched into how it had come to be included and that steps would be taken to ensure that nothing like this would ever happen again. Lean Mean Fighting Machine paid the price. The agency, which had been due to work on another Coca-Cola digital marketing campaign, was sacked.

Given the bald fact that Lean Mean Fighting Machine associated a 14-year-old girl with a reference to stomach-churning porn, it's understandable that Coca-Cola would sever its ties with the agency. The brand-damaging wrongness of this juxtaposition made it an open and shut case. But no one is suggesting that the agency deliberately set out to corrupt minors. It picked a well-known internet meme because it knew it would resonate with a good proportion of the Dr Pepper target audience, but in doing so lost sight of how inappropriate this would be for a major brand. Sure, lots of smartphone-wielding, internet-savvy teens already know about '2 girls one cup': in fact, when I was discussing the sensitivities of writing about this brand disaster with my wife, my 15-year-old daughter interjected with, 'Two girls one cup – yeah, that's all over the internet.' And there was me thinking she spent all her time online doing her history homework!

Today's teenagers are anything but naive and are often far more clued up about what is trending online – the good, the bad and the ugly – than their parents. However, that doesn't mean that brands should throw common sense and care out of the window when targeting this demographic. Indeed, the opposite is true. As this chapter shows, many things can go wrong for brands in the febrile environment of social media. So when planning any campaign, it's a good idea to make sure you have an informed answer to this critical question: 'What's the worst that could happen?'

More Facebook fails

- A Wal-Mart/Sheets Energy Strips promotion in the USA asked consumers to Like their local Wal-Mart on Facebook. The store with the most votes would receive a visit from rapper Pitbull. The promotion was hijacked by a prankster who organised a successful campaign to send the music star into 'exile' at a far-flung store. Pitbull took it in good spirits, duly making an appearance at the winning Wal-Mart – on Kodiak Island, Alaska!
- Australian jewellery brand Paspaley's safety procedures were scrutinised by ABC's investigative current affairs programme *Four Corners* following the death of 22-year-old pearl diver Jarrod Hampton. Comments on the subject of the tragedy were deleted from Paspaley's Facebook page in the hours after the programme was broadcast, triggering a social media furore.
- Newly opened retail destination Paradigm Mall in Malaysia 'reassigned' its Facebook page administrator to other duties in summer 2012 after he posted sarcastic comments in reply to complaints about faulty lifts. Here's a taster: 'Paradigm Mall does not know magic. Cannot snap fingers and make changes. You can? Then we want to hire you!' Just like the lifts, the comments didn't go down well.
- Nestlé Australia proudly announced the inaugural Instagram photo on its Kit Kat Facebook page: a picture of a person in a bear suit playing a drumkit with chocolate bars as sticks. The picture was hastily taken down again once people began remarking on its resemblance to Pedobear – a controversial cartoon bear drawing used as an online warning of child pornography. Bemused Aussie Nestlé execs confessed to never having heard of the Pedobear meme.
- In June 2012, feminine hygiene brand FemFresh took down its Facebook page after coming under fire there for using childish euphemisms for the word 'vagina' – nooni, va jay jay, twinkle, froo froo – plus there were even some that didn't sound like cutesy characters from a Disney animation.
- Mad Mex, an Australian chain of more than 30 Mexican restaurants, felt the force of negative comments on its

Facebook page after posting a Photoshopped version of the cover artwork of Justin Bieber's single *One Time*, labelling it the 'Mexican Edition'. The young Canadian pop singer's head was replaced by an image presumably meant to represent a person of Mexican origin. Inexplicably, the replacement head selected belonged to famous Filipino boxer Manny Pacquiao, leading to complaints of racial insensitivity. A knock-out idea.

More troublesome tweets

- The Swedish tourist authorities hit trouble with a campaign to promote the destination by showing the eclectic nature of its citizens. To flag up the 'progressive' attitudes of the country, control of the @Sweden Twitter handle was every week devolved to different members of the public, who were told to be themselves. All went well until June 2012 when Sonja Abrahamsson took her turn and contributed a series of unsettlingly strange tweets, some of which were condemned as anti-Semitic.
- An employee at Singapore's national daily, the *Straits Times*, was left red-faced in 2011 after accidentally posting a vulgar message meant for a personal Twitter account on the newspaper's official @stcom handle: 'omg, fuck you all. seriously' was widely retweeted – not the kind of commentary for which a prominent newspaper would like to be noted. A US employee of ticket marketplace StubHub made a carbon copy error in 2012, compounding their use of the f-word in delight at it being Friday with some untoward workplace image-trashing: 'Can't wait to get out of this stubsucking hell hole.' Is it really that hard to distinguish between personal and corporate Twitter accounts?
- Vodafone's '12 days of smiles' promotion in the run-up to Christmas 2010 certainly got noticed: its #makemesmile hashtag became the most discussed topic globally in the Twitterverse. Unfortunately for the mobile phone operator, the hashtag's prominence hinged on the fact that it had been

swarmed on by protestors making a point about allegations of tax avoidance levelled at the company. To heighten Vodafone's discomfort, it had chosen to live stream these promotional tweets on its corporate website.

- The Australian arm of book publisher Random House was accused of 'sleazy' marketing in November 2012 when appropriating the hashtag #lestweforget and timing a tweet promoting its war books to coincide with the minute's silence held as a mark of respect for the war dead at 11a.m. on Armistice Day.

- 'I find it ironic that Detroit is known as #motorcity and yet no one here knows how to fucking drive,' read the 2011 tweet on the official @ChryslerAutos handle. Not only did the tweet drop the f-bomb, it denigrated the city of Detroit – which Chrysler was lauding at the time in its big-budget TV advertising for the new 200 model, featuring Eminem and the strapline 'Imported from Detroit'. Chrysler was distinctly unimpressed with its social media agency New Media Strategies, even though it sacked the employee responsible for the tweet straight away. The peeved auto maker announced it would not be renewing its contract.

- When British Gas announced a 10% rise in fuel bills in October 2013, the outraged reaction from hard-pressed consumers was entirely predictable. But the energy supplier turned up the heat on itself by scheduling a Q&A about the price hike with its customer services director Bert Pijls on Twitter for the same day. Over 16,000 Twitter users vented their fury using the #AskBG hashtag as their digital rallying point while Pijls sought to apportion blame for BG's bigger bills on rising wholesale energy costs. Although BG was right to engage with its customers, timing the Q&A to take place so soon after people had been stung by the news fanned the flames of discontent and increased the temperature of the vitriol. 'Will you be sacrificing your social media team for fuel this winter?' sniped one consumer, his sentiment echoed by many.

- Kellogg's UK drew consumer wrath in November 2013 by tweeting '1 RT = 1 breakfast for a vulnerable child'. Botanist and BBC TV presenter James Wong was among the many to take umbrage at the flaky wording, observing 'Anyone else find this kinda creepy? Like sayin, "help us advertise or kids go hungry"'. Others were far more forthright in their condemnation of the cereal company, which apologised for its 'wrong use of words' to promote its funding of school breakfast clubs in deprived areas.

Tips and lessons

- Smartphones can be the cause of stupid mix-ups. Make sure no one able to administer a corporate social media account ever confuses it with their private account.
- Do not delete! Take criticism on the chin, responding where appropriate if correction or clarification is required. Material should only be removed if it is extremely offensive or inflammatory.
- There is no need to respond to every bit of criticism. Not everyone on social media is credible or reasonable. Internet trolls are generally best ignored.
- Be clear on who can and cannot create social media content for your brand, who needs to give approval and what type of content can be shared.
- Open-ended posts, such as those asking people what they think of your brand or to complete a phrase, invite trouble.
- Rudeness is unacceptable.
- Be very careful if you are looking to exploit the news agenda/ trending topics.
- Make sure you are clear. Be unambiguous in what you say and don't use any hashtags that could be misinterpreted.
- Crowdsourcing insight from social media has potential but is not an alternative to robust market research.
- Tools such as Google Trends and Boardreader can provide useful insights into what people are saying online about your brand.
- Put in place social media crisis management procedures that define what constitutes an issue and set out the escalation process if a crisis occurs. Who should respond – and how?

Chapter 4

When NPD stands for New Product Disaster

Dismal launches, from the overhyped to the underwhelming

Whether it's the Rubik's Cube or Apple iPad, certain products have that elusive wow factor. They take off because their desirable qualities resonate and they have the attributes to get customers hooked. ('Watch out, or that infernally addictive puzzle cube will get you!'; 'Stop fiddling with that sleek and versatile tablet!') Great products do more than just meet a market need – they are aspirational; and when the marketing behind the launch is pitched right, people will identify with them. While some products are more or less overnight sensations, others are slow burners whose appeal is built gradually. Take the Toyota Corolla. Who could have imagined when the first model appeared in 1966 that this relatively modest vehicle would go on to be the most popular car of all time, shifting over 40 million units? Although, of course, the Corollas rolling off the assembly line today bear scant resemblance to the original model. It's a story of continual improvement.

Great brands cannot remain great brands by standing still. Innovation is necessary in order to sustain consumer interest, exploit new business opportunities and harness technological advances. Microsoft would be long gone if it had not pushed on from DOS software to Windows;

Opel wouldn't have lasted as a manufacturer for 150 years if it had stuck to making sewing machines. But of course, bringing something new to market is risky. Bad timing, inadequate market research and poor product quality are all factors that can contribute to failure, with potentially severe consequences. Even those companies revered as cool, in tune with customers and for seldom putting a foot wrong are not immune to product launch catastrophes. It's no coincidence that many of the worst launches of all time have come from well-established companies that already have popular, often market-leading products. The quest to repeat such success is far from easy, even for those with impressive credentials.

Big bugs and the wilderness - courtesy of Apple Maps

Several tourists stranded in Australia's searing heat were fortunate to escape with their lives after being misdirected by Apple Maps, launched as part of the iOS 6 mobile operating system. Instead of sending them to the town of Mildura, the glitch-ridden new software pointed them 70km in the wrong direction into the middle of the isolated, semi-arid vastness of Murray-Sunset national park, where water is scarce. Police in the Australian state of Victoria expressed extreme concern at the life-threatening nature of the incidents after rescuing people who had been forced to trek through rough terrain in high temperatures without food and water when their cars ran out of fuel.

The many flaws of Maps that emerged after its launch in late 2012 — including parks reclassified as airports, cities relocated out to sea and bridges that seemed to be melting — forced Apple CEO Tim Cook to issue an apology to customers for falling short of delivering a world-class product, together with a pledge that the company was doing everything it could to make improvements.

Normally so sure-footed, Apple was left looking a little lost after this episode. It made sense to attempt to become less dependent on Google after the relationship between the two tech giants became less amicable, but the company somewhat foolishly set itself up for a fall by describing its new product as the 'most beautiful, powerful mapping service ever'. Quite a claim for a newcomer going into battle against Google Maps, which had carefully ironed out the bugs in its own product over time, helped by feedback from the public. And one that appeared ludicrous as screen grabs showing Apple Maps errors circulated online. The mainstream media, meanwhile, reported on Apple's discomfort with gusto and soon found a name for the disaster: Mapplegate.

No one would be daft enough to suggest that Mapplegate inflicted irreparable damage on a brand as mighty and widely loved as Apple. However, there is evidence to suggest that it put consumers on their guard and undermined some confidence in the tech company. A piece published by *Forbes* under the headline 'Yes, Analysis Shows, Mapplegate Did Hit Apple Sales' needs little further explanation, save to say that this analysis was conducted by online reputation specialist Media Measurement. Negative sentiment is uncomfortable for a brand at any time, but coming as this did just a year after the death of charismatic and visionary founder Steve Jobs – who famously returned to Apple in the 1990s to oversee one of the greatest turnarounds in corporate history – it brought with it speculation about the judgement of the leadership team and the future prospects for the business. *This would never have happened if Steve Jobs was still around* was a common refrain. For a business used to basking in rave reviews for its product quality, this was rocky, virtually uncharted territory.

The car that went wrong - the sorry saga of the Ford Edsel

Poor Edsel Ford; he deserved better. The only son of motor industry pioneer Henry Ford, Edsel was groomed to take over the family empire from an early age. Appointed president of the Ford Motor Company in 1919, when only in his mid-twenties, young Edsel showed true flair for automotive styling and a talent for expanding the company internationally, but despite his grand corporate title he was frequently undermined and marginalised from making important business decisions by his mercurial and domineering father. In 1943, at the age of only 49, Edsel died from complications following surgery for stomach cancer.

His elderly and increasingly erratic father briefly resumed the company presidency but was soon succeeded by Edsel's eldest son, Henry Ford II (sometimes nicknamed 'Hank the Deuce' or 'HF2'), who was to play a pivotal leadership role at Ford for over 30 years. In the mid-1950s, a decade after HF2's assumption of power, the motor company board bestowed his father's name, Edsel, on a major new vehicle line. The posthumous tribute was to backfire terribly. As students of marketing history are well aware, the Ford Edsel didn't win the hearts of the American public. It didn't even come close. In fact, it is commonly held up as one of the greatest marketing disasters of all time.

Concerned by the wider choice of vehicles being offered to US consumers looking to trade up from entry-level models by its rivals Chrysler and in particular General Motors, in 1948 HF2 instructed his product planning team to begin exploring options for a new medium-priced car. The advent of the Korean War put these plans temporarily on hold, but by the mid-1950s, in the wake of the successful launch of the sporty Thunderbird and with Ford preparing to go public, the Special Projects Division was hard at work developing what at the time was referred to as the Experimental or E-car. 'The Edsel was really the answer to a question nobody had asked,' says Dr Paul Nieuwenhuis, director of the Centre for Automotive Research at Cardiff Business School. 'Ford felt that as GM was able to operate a far greater range of brands at the time – six: Chevrolet, Pontiac, Buick, Oldsmobile, Cadillac, GMC – it should be able to do the same. Ford had three: Ford, Mercury and Lincoln.' Edsel was its ill-fated bid to create an impressive fourth marque.

Astonishingly, given the closeness to home of the name it ended up with, Ford went to great lengths to find a memorable moniker for the E-car. This even entailed an informal approach to Pulitzer Prize-winning poet Marianne Moore, who offered up some flighty gems such as Mongoose Civique, Resilient Bullet, Varsity Stroke, Andante con Moto, Utopian Turtletop, Intelligent Whale and Pastelogram. It's difficult to imagine why none of that surreal selection ever made the cut. Ford's ad agency Foote, Cone & Belding made myriad name proposals of its own and the car maker and its agency asked employees to chip in with suggestions too, with the result that the pool of potential names swelled to well over 10,000, which were then pruned down to a still intimidating 6,000. The leading candidates were researched among consumers, but no option stood out. Eventually FCB distilled the list down to 10 names, which were presented to the top brass at Ford, who found none of them suitable. In frustration tempered with some canny brown-nosing of the family dynasty, Ford chairman Ernest Breech blurted out, 'Why don't we just call it the Edsel?' No one senior at Ford, least of all Edsel's son HF2, was minded to oppose the idea, even though the name had performed badly in consumer research, evoking prosaic words such as 'pretzel' and 'weasel', in marked contrast to its derivation from Germanic roots pertaining to 'nobility' and 'wealth'. Ford PR Director C. Gayle Warnock, who later in life wrote two books on the Edsel debacle – the snappily titled *The Edsel Affair* and its unimaginative-sounding follow-up *The Rest of the Edsel Affair* (more than a hint of warmed-up leftovers with that one) – was flabbergasted when informed of the choice of name, firing off a memo to a colleague in which he asserted that it would lose the company 200,000 sales. The blundering had begun.

Next up was the styling. When lead designer Roy Brown presented his first clay model of the car to his bosses he got an appreciative round of applause. Yet when the car came on the market, its styling drew plenty of criticism. The Edsel's most distinctive design feature when looked at head-on was a vertical grille with a large chrome oval at its centre. This was disparagingly mocked as a 'horse collar' or worse – some jokers observed the car looked like it was sucking on a lemon while others suggested the grille reminded them of an intimate part of the female anatomy. Brown subsequently moved to Ford's UK operation, where he achieved design success with the Cortina model, yet inevitably when he died in February 2013 at the ripe old age of 96, the magnitude of the Edsel's failure was what figured large in his obituaries. For example, the *Wall Street Journal* headline on his passing read 'Edsel's Designer Took Flop in Stride'.

Ford's big push to claw back share from GM was therefore centred on a car that had both a name and a design that people did not instinctively warm to. 'The Edsel's failure is blamed on several factors,' says Matt Anderson, Curator of Transportation at the Henry Ford Museum and educational institution in Dearborn, Michigan – the home of Ford:

'Some point to the styling. While I agree that the "horse collar" grille is unusual, I certainly don't think that it alone is responsible for the failure. Unusual styling was the order of the day among 1950s American automobiles. The Edsel certainly had features, but I don't know that I'd call them ahead of their time. The spinning speedometer is more gimmick than innovation. The speed warning light, which you could set at a given speed so that it would turn on whenever you exceeded that speed, seems only marginally useful. The Teletouch transmission, in and of itself, was not that radical – Chrysler and Packard both offered the same thing. I will concede, however, that the Edsel was on to something by placing the transmission buttons in the steering wheel. Today steering wheels have buttons controlling the radios, the cruise control and – yes – the transmission.'

So, despite its dubious styling and pretzel-like name, the car wasn't all bad. In fact, as Anderson has described, it was fairly average. However, that didn't prevent Ford from going completely over the top in its marketing, using undue amounts of hyperbole to create unrealistic expectations for a vehicle that was really nothing special. Ford predicted it would sell more than 200,000 Edsels a year, in one fell swoop claiming a 5% share of the US car market. In pre-launch marketing brochures, Ford boasted: 'You've Never Seen a Car Like the Edsel.' In July 1957 Ford launched a teaser advertising campaign in glossy magazines such as *Life* in which the Edsel was simultaneously trumpeted while being shrouded in secrecy: in the ads, the car was either blurred or kept under wraps as a way to encourage excitement and speculation about what it would look like in the countdown to what was grandiosely dubbed E-Day. HF2 himself sent a message to dealers in which he pledged that the Edsel was here to stay. After more hype, the car finally hit showrooms in September 1957. The US public flocked to check it out in their millions, beginning with almost three million on E-Day itself, many having to wait in long queues for their chance to glimpse what was billed as an amazing car; most found themselves decidedly underwhelmed. 'I think Ford "oversold" the Edsel,' says Anderson. 'It promised customers an advanced automobile unlike anything made by the company before. What it delivered was a series of cars based on conventional Fords and

Mercurys. The marketing really was massive. Consider that *The Edsel Show*, Ford's hour-long prime-time promotional special [broadcast by CBS, with a format based on the massively popular variety programme *The Ed Sullivan Show*] featured Bing Crosby *and* Frank Sinatra. Anything launched with that much fanfare really had to exceed expectations to be considered a success.'

The Edsel fell far short, however, selling fewer than 65,000 vehicles in its first year – less than a third of Ford's ambitious target. Sales the following year were even more dismal. The advertising blitz continued with Ford trying to persuade consumers about the personal statement Edsel ownership would make by bombarding them with lines such as 'They'll Know You've Arrived When you Drive up in an Edsel' and 'The Most Beautiful Thing That Ever Happened to Horsepower'. It didn't help matters that some owners of the new vehicle were reporting mechanical problems and complaining about reliability due to some assembly line hitches. A popular joke of the day had it that Edsel stood for Every Day Something Else Leaks. With the Edsel, it seemed that everything that could go wrong did go wrong.

As part of its efforts to create awareness for the Edsel brand, Ford sponsored NBC's Western series *Wagon Train*. Desperate to find a way of boosting interest in the Edsel as the likelihood of it becoming a hideously costly automotive turkey increased by the week, a member of the sales team suggested exploiting the TV sponsorship by offering a free pony. Yes, a free living, breathing pony! Incredibly, Ford went for this idea, buying 1,000 ponies and sending them to Edsel dealerships across the country. In radio ads for the promotion, complete with galloping hooves sound effects, *Wagon Train* actor Ward Bond appealed directly to children – 'Howdy, boys and girls' – urging them to persuade their parents to take them on an outing to an Edsel dealership. Once at the dealership, children could enter the Wagon Train Pony Contest by completing a form in which they had to give the animal a name . . . only if one of their parents took a demonstration drive in an Edsel. When it came time for dealers to draw the winners, many parents opted to take the alternative $200 cash prize instead of a pony that they had neither the space nor the desire to home. Now, to add to the trouble Ford was having selling assets with four wheels, it had assets with four legs it couldn't shift either.

With no sign at all that the alarming downward path of the sales graph could be rectified, even with Ford's substantial investment in advertising and incompetent attempt to harness pester power by bribing children with ponies, in November 1959 Ford announced that it was discontinuing the Edsel, citing disappointing retail sales. It's estimated that Ford lost around $250m on the car – a massive amount for the era. To put that into context, Ford's 1956 initial public offering (IPO), which was at the time the largest sale of stock to the public by a private company in Wall Street history, raised $643m. A lot of the capital generated by investors had been squandered. Those who had forked out for Ford stock could be forgiven for scowling at the mere mention of the word Edsel.

In fairness, some of Ford's misfortune can be attributed to events beyond its control. The launch coincided with the arrival of a recession, which depressed demand for mid-priced cars across the entire sector. Suddenly, as the economic downturn took effect, more people wanted cheaper, more fuel-efficient vehicles. Yet Ford didn't do itself any favours by launching the more expensive models in the Edsel range first and by not making it clear where Edsel sat in the market in relation to the other brands in the Ford family. Consumers struggled to work out whether Edsel was pitched to occupy the market between Ford and Mercury, or between Mercury and Lincoln. The timing of the launch saw Edsel's new top-end 1958 models appear before other manufacturers released their 1958 vehicles into showrooms. At this point, dealers were heavily discounting the remaining 1957 models in their inventory, making the Edsels appear overpriced in comparison. Moreover, Ford did a lacklustre job of explaining a confusing array of different series and models that it launched under the Edsel marque. A total of 18 different models, from station wagons to convertibles, were spread across four different series: Ranger, Pacer, Corsair and Citation. If that all sounds like a bit of a farrago to you reading this now, you can well surmise how challenging it must have been for consumers at the time. Ford shunned simplicity and paid the price for trying to do too much too soon.

'It's important to remember that the Edsel line was a part of a larger strategy in which Ford would expand its product lines to match General Motors almost car-for-car with its models for every purse and purpose. Ford did learn from the Edsel's failure in that they scaled back their competitive

ambitions. Rather than building new divisions to match GM, Ford concentrated on its core brands. I think you can hear some echo of the Edsel lesson in the company's response to our recent Great Recession, during which the Mercury brand was eliminated [in 2010] so that Ford could further focus its efforts and product line.'

Matt Anderson, Curator of Transportation, Henry Ford
Museum and educational institution, Dearborn, Michigan

To its credit, Ford was able to put the Edsel debacle behind it and take some important lessons to heart. When it launched the Mustang in 1964 it had a car blessed not only with a sleek and powerful name, but one that looked the part because it had been designed with a clearly defined market in mind. This time Ford was less inclined towards empty hype and set itself a more modest Year One sales target of 100,000 vehicles. In the event, it sold a remarkable 417,000 Mustangs in the car's first 12 months on the market. In terms of looks and performance, it was everything the Edsel was not, appearing within months of its introduction in the Bond movie *Goldfinger* and as pace car for the Indianapolis 500. Its aspirational nature even caught the attention of kids – according to Ford, 93,000 pedal-powered children's versions of the car were bought for their offspring by indulgent parents in the 1964 Christmas season. What, no ponies?

While the Edsel was incontestably a flop, entering *Webster's* dictionary as a synonym for over-hyped marketing disaster, in later years the car developed something of a cult following. The first Edsel club was founded just 10 years after the car's debut, and today Edsel cars sit proudly alongside other classics at car shows up and down the USA, with vehicles in top condition commanding healthy prices. Perversely, the Edsel's inextricable association with abject failure seems to have added to its desirability and charm among collectors. Rather like a cursed jewel, its position at the heart of abysmal events adds interest to its story.

'I think most automobile historians would agree that, with hindsight, the most unfortunate thing about the Edsel affair is the way in which it tarnished Edsel Ford's name,' says Anderson. 'Edsel Ford had an innate gift for automobile styling and is responsible for some of the most striking cars of his era, including the Lincoln-Zephyr and the original Lincoln

Continental. It is a true irony that his name is now most associated by the public with a car ridiculed for its poor styling.'

Washed to destruction – Persil Power's laundry overkill

The respected business journalist Andrew Davidson wrote a terrific profile piece on Unilever's then chairman Sir Michael Perry, published in *Management Today* in 1995. At first the interview appears to be progressing amiably but then the atmosphere deteriorates to the point where the tension of the encounter is almost palpable. 'You know, you are only going to get monosyllables out of me on this subject,' Perry informs his interlocutor testily after having been pressed for comment. What's the subject? Why the icy reluctance to speak? The answer to both questions is the disaster that was Persil Power.

Appearing as the first commercially available laundry detergent in the UK in 1909, Persil enjoyed a dominant market position for decades under the careful stewardship of Anglo-Dutch giant Unilever (although it should be pointed out that the Persil brand is owned by Henkel in Germany and a number of other markets). But by the early 1990s, in countries such as the UK and the Netherlands, Persil was coming under immense pressure from Ariel, a competing detergent brand owned by Unilever's arch rival P&G. This was a period of cut-throat competition between Persil and Ariel, often called the 'soap wars' and with the launch of its Ariel Ultra product, which was positioned as being scientifically proven to clean better than ever with less powder, P&G seemed now to have an edge over Unilever that would allow it to – please forgive the pun – clean up in the market.

To the sound of rolling drums (from inside washing machines), Unilever set its chemists to work on the fight-back. They came up with a new manganese catalyst that sped up bleaching during the washing process. When it delivered very impressive cleaning results in tests, the go-ahead was given to launch a new version of the famous detergent, Persil Power, containing this potent cleaning agent. So that consumers would be left in no doubt about the capabilities of this new product, Unilever marketers called the catalyst 'the accelerator'.

As senior executives at Unilever were gearing up for the launch, which they were convinced would see Persil cement its ascendancy in the detergent category, they were approached out of the blue by their counterparts at P&G. Having conducted its own tests, P&G was of the opinion that the product Unilever intended bringing to market was too powerful for consumer use. In a highly unusual move, P&G informed Unilever of its concerns and warned that if it went ahead with introducing such a powerfully formulated detergent, the gloves would be coming off in the fight between them. Senior management at Unilever opted to press on regardless, perceiving P&G's ultimatum as a sign that it was rattled, and Persil Power hit the shops in April 1994, marketed as a breakthrough in stain removal. Samples of the new product were sent to 10 million UK households. This was a massive launch. Before long, it would also be a massive failure.

Unilever had conducted most of the testing for Persil Power on new clothes. But its effects on more delicate older clothes were a different proposition. While all detergents damage clothes to some extent, Persil Power was so strong that it could fade and degrade garments drastically even when consumers scrupulously used the recommended amount. As people started complaining that their favourite clothes were excessively bleached or left in tatters after being washed in Persil Power, Unilever executives were faced with the uncomfortable realisation that testing and analysis during the research and development (R&D) phase had been botched. As Unilever pondered what to do, P&G struck. It sent pictures of clothes that had been damaged by Persil Power to national newspapers across Europe. In a press release accompanying the images, P&G twisted the knife by describing the apparel as 'shredded to the point of indecency'. Journalists were understandably delighted that such a colourful story – make that *colourless* story – had fallen into their laps. The coverage was excruciating for Unilever, which soon had to deal with a warehouse full of damaged clothes sent in by consumers seeking recompense, in addition to a reputational nightmare for its new product that was undermining its long-established Persil brand, together with the prospect of lawsuits from some supermarkets.

The *coup de grâce* for this terminally wounded product was delivered by the Consumers' Association in February 2005. After conducting what it described as the biggest test it or any consumer association in the world had ever carried out on washing powder, it concluded that Persil Power did indeed speed up the destruction of clothes, and that clothes washed in Persil Power were only 40% as strong as those washed in Ariel Ultra.

Unilever had little choice but to withdraw the product from market, writing off £57m in its accounts for unsold stock. But the actual cost of the debacle was probably nearer £250m once other factors such as out-of-court settlements, product development and marketing costs are taken into consideration. Small wonder, then, that Sir Michael Perry was evasive to the point of threatening to cut short his interview with Andrew Davidson when the subject of Persil Power came up. This wasn't a debacle that could be patched up by spin: the greater the spin, the more the clothes fell apart.

Sinclair C5 - worst of all gadgets

In a poll carried out for the Gadget Show Live event in 2013, technology fans were asked to name the worst gizmos of all time. At the top of the scrap heap they put the Sinclair C5, the three-wheeled, battery- and pedal-powered vehicle with a maximum speed of 15 miles per hour that was denounced as unsafe for road use on its 1985 launch in the UK. An obsession with developing his plastic-bodied trike, in which drivers felt particularly vulnerable as cars and trucks loomed large around them while they steered using handlebars tucked beneath their knees, was to lead to humiliation for one of the UK's brightest innovators, who only two years earlier had received a knighthood for his achievements on the recommendation of then Prime Minister Margaret Thatcher.

After making his mark with a miniature TV in the late 1960s and the launch of one of the first slimline pocket calculators in 1972, Sir Clive Sinclair became a trailblazer in home computers during the early 1980s, launching the ZX80 – the first personal computer available for under £100 – followed by the ZX81 and the ZX Spectrum, a hugely influential machine that was the most successful computer of its time in the UK, at its height selling 200,000 units a month. With his firm Sinclair Research valued at £134m, Sir Clive was a wealthy man who now had the means to pursue his dream of developing an electric car; a dream he had harboured since his teenage years.

A new company, Sinclair Vehicles, was set up. Lotus cars was contracted to carry out chassis and transmission design and development work, while production was to take place at the Hoover plant at Merthyr Tydfil. The involvement of Hoover was to spawn a persistent urban myth that the C5 was in fact powered by a washing machine engine. It was marginally better than that, although the puny engine could be defeated by steep hills, requiring drivers to break into a sweat and pedal if they wanted to make it to the top. Nevertheless, this lack of oomph was seen as a marketing advantage by Sir Clive. A top speed of 15mph meant that under newly introduced UK legislation, no driving licence was necessary when taking a C5 out on the road. The entrepreneur was convinced he was creating a commercially viable eco-friendly vehicle that would enjoy mass appeal, embracing serious commuters and teenage fun-seekers alike. In Sir Clive's business plan he forecast an ambitious 250,000 sales a year; but just in case the C5 really caught on, the twin production lines at Hoover had the capacity to produce double that amount.

'As a young car design student at the Royal College of Art, I won a Sinclair-sponsored electric vehicle design competition. This led to Clive hiring me on my graduation to set up his own in-house car design studio. Clive was at his peak, I was undecided about a future in technology or car design. At the time this was an amazing, very high-profile opportunity. I became the first employee of the Sinclair Research Metalab in Cambridge. Clive was an extremely intelligent and very generous man, but he failed to understand the difference between a new market, computing, where new behaviours could be expected, and a mature one, transport, where there were more benchmarks to compare against. He totally failed to get the safety and convenience issues. I blew a big hole in the product costings by asking what we were doing about visibility, rear view mirrors, range indications . . . as a designer I was thinking about the customer experience to a degree of detail Clive simply didn't anticipate the need for.'

Gus Desbarats, Chairman, British Design Innovation

The massively over-optimistic sales projections set high expectations for the launch and contributed to some flawed investment decisions that burned through the money Sir Clive had earmarked for the project far faster than planned. A case in point was the expensive injection-moulded vehicle body – the polypropylene shell was reputedly the largest mass-produced assembly of this kind ever made. Despite some tweaking, serious flaws in the product design remained. But with money beginning to run low, Sir Clive took the decision to bring forward the launch date. So it was that the C5 was launched on a bitterly cold day in January 1985 at a marketing and media event at the top of the hill at Alexandra Palace in London. The chilly conditions were far from ideal for showing off an open-topped vehicle fitted with a battery that didn't perform well at low temperatures.

Although priced at just £399, the C5 failed to win over the British public. People were uneasy with the idea of sitting semi-recumbent in a low-slung vehicle. In an exposed cockpit, with their eye-line fairly close to the tarmac, they felt nervous in heavy traffic. Both the British Safety Council and motoring bodies expressed concerns about driver visibility and vulnerability. The AA even labelled the C5 a death trap, fearing that HGV drivers could easily fail to notice the trike and crush it to smithereens because it was so low to the ground. On top of these safety concerns and its lack of power, other drawbacks included the vehicle's weight, fixed gear drive chain and the inability to adjust the seat to give a more comfortable pedal position. Instead of becoming the first electric vehicle to be commercially successful on a grand scale, the C5 was the butt of countless jokes. Its sales figures were dire. Before the year was out, production had ceased and Sinclair Vehicles had fallen into receivership. The following year, beset by financial problems, Sir Clive sold the marketing and merchandising rights for his computer business to Alan (now Lord) Sugar's Amstrad group for £5m. Sugar, today of course the uncompromising face of *The Apprentice*, ruthlessly neutralised a competitor and picked up the pieces with far greater efficiency than a C5 on a freezing day. Although continuing to innovate, Sir Clive has not again come close to the dizzying heights of his earlier career, undone by the whiff of failure surrounding his much-mocked trike.

Desbarats, meanwhile, has emerged from the baptism of fire to build his own successful industrial design business, TheAlloy, and is national chairman of British Design Innovation, the voice of professional industrial designers. One of the great lessons he has taken from his time at Sinclair is that the outcome of the design process is actually a buying specification for everything that comes next – it's an insight, he says, that permeates his work to this day:

> 'The experience of watching the bubble Clive lived in made me very aware of the need to actively seek out, encourage and reward dissenting opinions later on when I was leading my own businesses. I learned early on how to detect and discourage "yes people" of all flavours. My main contribution on C5 was to convert an ugly pointless device into a prettier, safer and more usable pointless device. Ever since I've made sure I get myself involved early in the innovation process, shaping basic configurations, never again satisfied to simply decorate a fundamentally bad idea. It was an incredibly sad experience to watch an unsung team of really excellent professionals, from the Lotus mechanical engineers to the marketing and advertising team at Primary Contact, all doing their work excellently in a doomed, pointless cause. Bad strategy hurt the lives of good people. It was on C5 that I met the best man at my wedding: Chris Fawkes, a really excellent marketing professional, the nearest I've ever had to a mentor and someone to whom Sir Clive owes a great debt. The atmosphere in the Metalab in the 80s was amazing. I went from C5 to design one of the world's first laptops. The experience left me with the very clear emphatic view that we industrial designers aren't the only creative people on the planet and that whatever else went wrong, at least Sir Clive had a go, and put his money where his mouth was. The UK desperately needs a new generation of entrepreneurs with Sir Clive's mojo. But hopefully ones who will get industrial designers like me in earlier when configurations as well as form are being investigated.'

Sycophancy can be ruinous. Indeed, the more successful a business leader or entrepreneur, the greater their need for dissenting voices and regular reality checks.

Bring me the blowtorch - smokeless cigarette Premier fails to set market on fire

Back in the early 1980s, tobacco company RJ Reynolds began secretive development work in Winston-Salem, North Carolina on a new product that was initially given the codename Project Spa. The R&D, which was so covert that in its early years it was conducted without the knowledge of the company's main board, was to lead to the launch in the late 1980s of a revolutionary 'smokeless cigarette'. This product, branded Premier, was intended to lead the fight-back against the anti-tobacco movement amid growing concerns about passive smoking, or secondary smoking as it is called in the USA. With the tobacco industry under fire for its impact on health and facing a shrinking market as a consequence – cigarette sales were falling by just under 2% a year in the USA during the 1980s – Reynolds hoped that Premier would provide smokers with a 'cleaner' smoking experience that was more acceptable to non-smokers in the vicinity.

Superficially, Premier looked quite like a normal cigarette. But when smokers finished smoking it, it was the same length as when they started. And there was no ash. This was because when they lit up, tobacco wasn't burned – it was heated. A charcoal heat source warmed a flavour capsule containing nicotine, glycerol and other ingredients. Once the flavour ran out, smokers knew it was time to discard the cigarette. Although widely referred to as smokeless, this was incorrect. There was smoke, just less of it and of a different nature from that given off by normal cigarettes. Reynolds made a point of calling this smoke 'cleaner', none too subtly implying that it was a healthier option. This did not endear the company to health campaigners.

When the cigarette was introduced, Surgeon General C. Everett Koop opined that it could be used as a sophisticated 'drug delivery system' for smoking crack cocaine and should therefore be tightly regulated by the Food and Drug Administration (FDA) rather than coming under the auspices of the body normally responsible for tobacco products. A coalition of leading health organisations then petitioned the FDA to classify Premier as a drug, expressing the worry that the novel specifications of the product might lure impressionable children into nicotine addiction. Additionally, the American Medical Association called for a halt to the distribution of Premier until there was more evidence that it was safe. This was a product innovation facing concerted opposition.

But it was reaction from the test markets that really finished it off. Consumers complained that they found it hard to light Premier cigarettes. That wasn't the half of it. Once lit, they encountered the twin sensory problems of taste and smell. Revolted smokers compared the taste of Premier to burning plastic and charred sneakers. As for the aroma, the consensus was that the cigarettes reeked of farts, although one smoker blessed with descriptive originality went so far as to say the smell called to mind a burning dog. There seemed to be as much gagging and retching as smoking.

When Premier hit the market in November 1988, Reynolds' parent company, RJR Nabisco, was embroiled in a high-profile takeover bid that was to lead to its acquisition by private equity firm Kohlberg Kravis Roberts. This $25bn deal was at the time the largest leveraged buy-out in Wall Street history and the story of the convoluted behind-the-scenes manoeuvring in the battle for control of this corporate prize and the over-sized personalities of the executives, bankers and lawyers involved is brilliantly recounted in the bestselling book *Barbarians at the Gate* by journalists Bryan Burrough and John Helyar. The tale was so compelling that the book was turned into a movie, with James Garner cast as RJR Nabisco's CEO Ross Johnson. In this context, Premier was a sub-plot within a far larger narrative. Yet as sub-plots go, it was an important one – never more so than when the scale of its failure became apparent. As Burrough and Helyar wrote in *Barbarians*, 'Premier was the first cigarette ever to be returned for refunds. It was the butt of drive-time disc jockey jokes in St Louis and Arizona, where it was being test marketed. The product that was to be the great hope for Reynolds Tobacco was being called one of the great new product fiascos of all time.'

Early in 1989 Reynolds, now under the ownership of Kohlberg Kravis Roberts, snuffed out Premier. The feedback from the test markets was so overwhelmingly scathing that there was no other rational choice to make. All told, Reynolds had invested close to $350m in the project. On being informed of the decision to withdraw Premier from the market, Emanuel Goldman, a tobacco industry analyst with Paine Webber, said he was unsurprised. 'It didn't taste good. It didn't smell good. And you needed a blowtorch to light it.' It has to be said, a flop like that is hard to match.

It seemed like a good idea at the time . . .

- What we need is a cola that looks like sparkling water, or so thought Pepsi in the early 1990s. Caffeine-free Pepsi Crystal aimed to trade on the notion that clarity was akin to purity, but it soon disappeared once everyone realised that as there was no demand for clear tea, coffee or hot chocolate, why would we want a colourless cola?
- Arguably more like a weapon than a toy, 12-inch Lawn Darts were designed to be thrown at targets outdoors. What, you might wonder, could possibly go wrong when exuberantly hurling these pointy-tipped missiles through the air? After the deaths of three children and thousands of injuries, the US Consumer Product Safety Commission banned their sale in 1988. Several manufacturers, including Franklin Sports, made the metal-tipped darts. Safer plastic-tipped versions, unlikely to cut short garden fun by maiming players, are now available.
- There was definitely something in the air in the late 1980s (watch out – it might be a Lawn Dart!) as soup company Campbell's strove to take convenience food to a new level. In 1987 it launched Souper Combo, a range of frozen microwaveable soup and sandwich combinations. Precisely what the world was waiting for: the appetising prospect of sandwiches limply steaming after a quick zap in the microwave. Even for many of America's time-starved or über-lazy, making a sandwich of their own to go with some soup wasn't too daunting an exercise. The TV commercial included a jingle that set the words Souper Combo to the

tune of the Frank Sinatra hit *Love and Marriage*, originally arranged by Nelson Riddle. A bigger riddle was why Campbell's went ahead with this ill-matched frozen duo at all.

- Packaging its Sun Chips in bags that were 100% compostable in 2009 earned Frito-Lay applause for using renewable materials. Sadly, any applause was drowned out by the unusually noisy crackling sounds made by these sustainable bags when consumers delved into them while snacking. A Facebook page, Sorry But I Can't Hear You Over This Sun Chips Bag, was Liked by more than 50,000 people.

- Italian company Fabbrica d'Armi Pietro Beretta has been producing weapons since Renaissance times. The gun maker's reputation is so illustrious and well-established that author Ian Fleming chose to issue James Bond with a Beretta .25 automatic sidearm in his early 007 novels. In the mid-1980s, General Motors introduced a coupé called the Chevrolet Beretta and soon afterwards received a trademark infringement lawsuit from the Italian company – whose work under the Beretta name has been documented since 1526! The matter was settled out of court in 1989, with GM making a $500,000 donation to a Beretta cancer foundation in return for the right to use the Beretta name on its vehicles. To mark the resolution of the dispute, the chairmen of both companies met face to face in Italy and exchanged gifts. GM gave a Chevrolet Beretta GTU coupé (of course) in return for a Beretta hunting rifle and shotgun.

Tips and lessons

- Always ask yourself whether you will be meeting a genuine customer need.
- Make sure you communicate where your new product sits in the market.
- Just because you *can* do it doesn't mean you *should* do it.
- Iron out bugs and glitches before launch.
- Consumer safety should be paramount.

Chapter 5

Stupid stunts

Lethal imbecility and chaos on the streets in the quest to grab attention

---

Brilliant stunts, executed with panache, can make headlines around the world. Consider the amazing coverage Red Bull achieved for its sponsorship of intrepid Austrian skydiver Felix Baumgartner and his record-breaking jump from the edge of space in October 2012. In what has quickly come to be acknowledged as one of the most successful event marketing stunts of all time, Baumgartner generated an estimated £100m worth of exposure for the Red Bull brand as his breathtaking, heavily branded jump was shown on TV in 50 countries around the world, with a staggering eight million people also watching it live on YouTube, while Facebook and Twitter were likewise abuzz with his exploits. But what if Red Bull Stratos had gone terribly wrong? How would the Red Bull brand have been perceived if Baumgartner had lost his life during the perilous, 24-mile descent in which he plummeted faster than the speed of sound?

Fortunately, Baumgartner's triumph makes this an academic question. He and his support team spent five years training and otherwise preparing for the mission, working meticulously to minimise the risks. Their painstaking dedication paid off and they deserve the plaudits they have received. Yet even with the Red Bull team's assiduous attention to detail, there was a point during his freefall when Baumgartner seemed to be spinning out of control. The perils — among them that Baumgartner's blood could actually begin to boil — were very real.

Few stunts are as inherently complex and dangerous as Red Bull Stratos (if many more were, it might bring about the demise of the Hollywood blockbuster). However, the very nature of staging something distinctive and attention grabbing means there is usually an element of risk involved. Marketing stunts that go awry can leave brands looking very bad indeed, particularly if things get so out of control that the police are called. Ignominious outcomes of this kind have happened more than you might suppose. There's a whole sub-genre of failed stunts that can be classed as flops with cops.

Cartoon Network's Boston bomb

Cartoon Network decided that a spot of guerrilla marketing would be a cool way to draw attention to the movie spin-off from the series *Aqua Teen Hunger Force*, a quirky animation about a trio of anthropomorphic items from a fast food menu – I kid you not – called Master Shake, Meatwad and Frylock. New York agency Interference created blinking LED placards intended to resemble minor characters from the show, the Mooninites, and paid a couple of guys to put up around forty of them in and around Boston in the dead of night. During morning rush hour on 31st January 2007, a concerned commuter alerted a Massachusetts Bay Transportation Authority policeman to the presence of one of these devices underneath the elevated section of the Interstate 93 highway near Sullivan Square subway station. The transport police called in the bomb squad and mayhem ensued. Noting that the ad placard shared some characteristics with an improvised explosive device – a power source, circuit board with exposed wiring, and electrical tape – the emergency services took no chances and carried out a controlled explosion to neutralise any danger. Several bridges, a section of the interstate and a stretch of the Charles River were closed as the authorities scrambled to investigate other devices. As a major security operation unfolded, helicopters circled overhead and news crews reported breathlessly on developments.

Once it finally became clear later in the day that this was a marketing stunt, and after panic subsided, city authorities were incandescent with anger. 'It is outrageous, in a post 9/11 world, that a company would use this type of marketing scheme,' Boston Mayor Thomas Menino told *USA Today*. He added that he was prepared to take legal action against Cartoon Network's parent company Turner Broadcasting System to recover all expenses incurred in responding to the security incident. Sean Stevens and Peter Berdovsky, the two men paid to put up the placards, were arrested on the felony charge of placing a hoax device. They were potentially facing up to five years in prison. A week after the campaign, Massachusetts Attorney General Martha Coakley announced that Turner Broadcasting and Interference had agreed to pay $2m in compensation to wipe the slate clean of any civil or criminal claims. The botched stunt was proving expensive.

Jim Samples, the head of Cartoon Network and a 13-year veteran at the company, fell on his sword a few days later. He explained the reason for his resignation in a letter to employees:

> '*I deeply regret the negative publicity and expense caused to our company as a result of this campaign. As general manager of Cartoon Network, I feel compelled to step down, effective immediately, in recognition of the gravity of the situation that occurred under my watch.*'

Criminal charges against Stevens and Berdovsky were eventually dropped after the pair completed community service at a rehabilitation hospital and read out prepared apologies in court. Mayor Menino released a statement saying that he hoped the hearing marked the conclusion of the fallout from the stunt. He added: 'I hope the message goes out to all guerrilla marketers who plan on doing business in Boston that we take the public safety of those who live and work here very seriously.' Indeed. No question, this was a stupid and irresponsible stunt. Yet Cartoon Network was a little unlucky that it panned out the way it did. LED placards were placed in nine other major US cities, without precipitating anything like Boston's huge emergency response.

There's a mysterious footnote to the story. The creators of *Aqua Teen Hunger Force*, Dave Willis and Matt Maiellaro, reportedly wrote an episode for the fifth season of the show called *Boston*, which tackled the marketing debacle and the pandemonium it provoked in New

England. Turner Broadcasting's jittery lawyers were unsurprisingly having none of it and the episode, which was due to appear in early 2008, has never been shown. Willis has joked in an interview that it has been mastered onto VHS and locked in a vault, to be released only after his death. Then again, maybe he wasn't joking. As events in Boston showed, sometimes it can be difficult to make a distinction between the amusing and the serious.

ET, phone home . . . from Latvia - Tele2 and the nonsensical crater of deception

Things are certainly not always as they first appear. On the evening of Sunday 25th October 2009 a meteorite blazed through the sky over Latvia before slamming into the ground in a field near the border with Estonia. A student and his friends who were in the vicinity hurried to the impact site and filmed a jerky video of the still smouldering crater which was uploaded to YouTube and soon found its way on to news websites. With interest escalating, the media assembled, a military unit cordoned off the area and scientists arrived to test for radiation and examine the crash scene. What they found was a 10-metre wide crater that had been excavated using shovels; and the rocks they analysed were definitely not of extra-terrestrial origin. There were also signs of the presence of pyrotechnics. Evidently, this was an organised albeit unsophisticated hoax with a special effects budget far short of *Armageddon* or *Deep Impact*. The student who'd called in the story had gone to ground. Latvian police announced that a criminal investigation was being considered.

Two days after perpetrating the stunt, Swedish telecommunications company Tele2 admitted it was to blame. Its Latvian subsidiary, together with local media agency Inspired, had cooked up the hoax, with the approval of headquarters in Sweden. But why on earth did they do it? Latvia was one of the European countries hardest hit by the economic downturn and was putting in place some biting austerity measures. A spokesperson at Tele2 in Latvia said the stunt had been intended to divert attention from the depressing economic picture and give people something creative and exciting to talk about.

Personally, I'm not convinced that digging a big hole in the countryside and setting fire to some chemicals at the bottom of it is a creative act. There's some extremely muddled thinking at work here. What is the marketing message they were trying to convey? Telecoms brands aren't built on trying to divert people's attention from national economic woes. Trickery isn't a great basis for winning people's trust. If a compelling, rational marketing message was intended, it failed, like the 'meteorite' itself, to materialise.

Tele2 said it was prepared to reimburse the country for the cost of responding to the hoax but the Latvian government was still distinctly unimpressed. Interior Minister Linda Mūrniece vilified Tele2 for 'cynical mockery' at the expense of Latvians and added that she was terminating a government contract with the company in protest. 'The Interior Ministry doesn't want to do business with a firm that promotes itself at our expense,' she said. Instead of ramping up excitement, this bogus act saw Tele2's star fall in Latvia. For brands aiming to pull off a stratospheric stunt, the lesson should be to take a leaf out of Red Bull's book and keep it real.

Smartphone launch triggers BB gun fusillade and ruck - LG foots bill for medical treatment

Brightly coloured balloons arranged into a giant letter G, banners fluttering in the breeze, nice prizes on offer: sounds laid-back, almost idyllic. Yet when LG Electronics launched its G2 handset in August 2013 with a stunt in a Seoul park, what transpired had more in common with a skirmish on the battlefield than a kids' party.

In an exercise to inflate excitement about its desirable new smartphone, LG offered 100 of them as prizes at the launch event in the Korean capital. Vouchers for the free phones were attached to helium balloons, which were then let loose in the park. To improve their odds of bagging a G2, a number of participants treated the event as if it was the urban Korean equivalent of a pheasant shoot, turning up at the park armed with pellet-firing BB guns Others opted for even more dangerous balloon-bursting tools; one woman was spotted brandishing a spear. The omens for everyone emerging from the event unscathed were not good.

When a cluster of balloons drifted back to earth it was pounced on by a determined pack of consumers. In the ensuing melee, around 20 people were hurt as they grappled to get their hands on prize vouchers. Seven required hospital treatment. The botched stunt made headlines internationally and LG was criticised for its inadequate security and public safety procedures. Perhaps LG representatives on the ground should have been handed smartphones with a step-by-step crowd control app pre-installed.

LG released a statement expressing its regret at the injuries. 'We can confirm that seven participants were hospitalised and although none of the injuries were serious, LG takes full responsibility for the unfortunate situation and has offered to cover all related medical expenses,' it said. 'LG is investigating the incident to ensure that such an occurrence can be avoided in the future.'

I'm no health and safety expert, but more rigorous organisation and a ban on objects with a high potential for causing injury would be a good start. Unless, that is, LG's true event marketing purpose was to demonstrate how quickly the emergency services could be summoned on its phones.

Weapons in the marketing armoury – Ubisoft distributor and Dell put the police on edge

Hands up! All those who think scaring people with fake guns as part of a promotion is a good idea, put your hands in the air now! Anyone? Of course there is *someone* who thinks this is a good idea – without the odd weapon-toting buffoon involved in product marketing, the world would be a duller place. Safer perhaps, but definitely duller.

In April 2010 drinkers sitting at tables outside the Degree Gastrobar in the Viaduct Harbour district of Auckland, New Zealand had their Friday night fun interrupted by a man brandishing a firearm. Somebody yelled 'He's got a gun!' and fearful drinkers dashed for cover. 'This guy with bandages on his hands pointed a gun at customers sitting outside. They were pretty terrified,' bar manager Steph Kurtovich told the *New Zealand Herald.* Armed police rushed to the bar. It was only once they had disarmed the suspect that they realised the gun was made of plastic. Two men were cautioned at the scene. The gunman was in fact an actor hired to promote the release on Xbox of Ubisoft's video game *Splinter Cell: Conviction.* He was – incompetently – trying to impersonate Sam Fisher, the black ops agent character who is the protagonist in the *Splinter Cell* novels and violent video game franchise created by Tom Clancy. Monaco Corporation, Ubisoft's distributor in New Zealand, apologised for the 'marketing gone wrong', revealing that it had instructed another company to organise the stunt and claiming that it had no idea a gun would be involved. The police condemned the shenanigans. 'We consider these types of stunts to be very ill-advised and have real concerns a similar one may one day end in tragedy,' said Senior Sergeant Ben Offner.

Less than a year later, in February 2011, police officers in Texas were voicing similar worries. At the Round Rock head office campus of computer company Dell, Bryan Chester and his boss Daniel Rawson decided to stage an internal marketing stunt to impress upon colleagues that the new Dell Streak tablet could interface with Harley Davidson motorcycles. The duo neglected to tell anyone that a stunt would be taking place. With no warning, dressed in biker gear and with his face concealed beneath a black mask, Chester made a menacing appearance at Dell headquarters. Yelling, and carrying a couple of unidentified metal objects that could easily be mistaken for weapons, he demanded that people go to the lobby. Terrified employees presumed the worst. Several called the police to tell them there was a masked gunman in the building. They genuinely thought they were caught up in a terrorist attack or hostage situation. A SWAT team descended on Dell. There they encountered Rawson, who – unbelievably – at first declined to provide information about who the masked man was and what he was doing. Fortunately, he relented and spilled the beans before police confronted Chester elsewhere in the building. Had the SWAT team still been unaware that this was a marketing stunt, there might have been terrible consequences for Chester. Fortunately he avoided having a chalk line drawn around his body, but was arrested on the misdemeanour charge of deadly conduct – an offence under the Texan penal code that relates to putting others in imminent danger of serious bodily injury. Rawson was charged with the lesser misdemeanour of interfering with public duties. 'Someone could have easily been hurt,' admonished Round Rock Police Department spokesman Eric Poteet.

Too hot for Snapple as it gloops the Big Apple

Pondering how to draw attention to its new kiwi and strawberry flavoured ice lolly, drinks brand Snapple hit upon the idea of creating the world's largest popsicle and putting it on proud display in the centre of New York City. This would be an epic undertaking because back in 1997 a group of friends in the Dutch village of Katwijk aan den Rijn had succeeded in making a 21-foot, 20,000-pound monster popsicle ratified by *Guinness World Records*. Unfazed, in June 2005, Snapple introduced its mega-popsicle contender. It was moulded and frozen in Edison, New Jersey, then hauled by freezer truck to Union Square, where it was to be erected by giant crane. At 25 feet long and 35,000 pounds in weight, Snapple's cold colossus was significantly larger than the Dutch title-holder — but to land the record, it had to stand upright. As the summer sun beat down, the frozen treat began melting much faster than anticipated. Sweet-smelling gloop poured off the popsicle as the process of tilting it carefully from the back of the truck began. Cyclists skidded and pedestrians tumbled on the treacherous kiwi and strawberry hazard as it washed into nearby streets. To those affected by the sticky flood, Snapple's brand slogan, 'Made from the best stuff on earth', might have been a matter for debate.

Police and the fire department were called as the pink liquid continued pouring forth. Several streets were closed to allow fire fighters to hose away the oozing pink fluid, bringing traffic to a standstill. On site, ice sculpture specialists advising Snapple expressed concerns that the giant popsicle might no longer be structurally sound. Lifting it any further upright could well have presented a risk to public safety. The record attempt was abandoned with the increasingly slushy popsicle raised to an angle of only 25 degrees and much cleaning up to be done.

'What was unsettling was that the fluid just kept coming,' said Stuart Claxton, the *Guinness World Records* adjudicator at the event. 'It was quite a lot of fluid. On a hot day like this, you have to move fast.'

It seemed that New Yorkers dodging the sugary slick were fleeter of foot than Snapple. The event was a hilarious blunder that made the brand look incompetent. Failing to break the record wasn't in itself a big deal; the bigger problem was that the stunt was a poor advertisement for product quality. Rapid melting is not a characteristic consumers appreciate in popsicles. Except when laughing at the folly of an immense fruity failure sluiced away into the Big Apple's gutters and drains.

Of course, a situation that makes one product look terrible could be perfect for another. Imagine if Dan Aykroyd and Bill Murray had been on hand clad in ectoplasm-proof hazmat suits to face the pink slime coursing through the streets of NYC. Wouldn't that have been a perfect stunt to promote a new *Ghostbusters* movie?

Too cold for comfort - BRMB injures contestants in Birmingham

At least no one was injured by the Snapple stunt. The same cannot be said about a stupendously ill-conceived promotion in August 2001 by UK regional radio station BRMB. The Coolest Seats in Town event was staged outside BRMB's offices in Birmingham. Contestants were offered the chance to win tickets and backstage passes to the Party in the Park music festival featuring pop acts such as Geri Halliwell and Atomic Kitten. To bag the tickets, competitors were challenged to sit for as long as they could on blocks of dry ice – the solid form of carbon dioxide. Dry ice is used in processes such as flash freezing foods and its most notable property is that it is extremely cold. Precautions should always be taken when handling the substance. Oblivious to any danger, BRMB encouraged ticket-seeking young adults to endure discomfort by sitting on dry ice blocks. In doing so, they were coming into contact with a surface temperature of minus 78 degrees Celsius. That's colder than the average mean winter temperature at the North Pole or the even harsher South Pole.

Plucky pop fans toughed it out, sitting on the dry ice until they could bear it no longer, with nasty consequences for their bodies. Four people were taken to hospital with frostbite. Two women and a man had injuries so severe that they necessitated extensive skin grafts and a prolonged stay in hospital of around 10 weeks. Even after treatment, they were left with permanent scarring. 'I was told it was the worst burns the nurses at the unit had ever seen,' one of the injured women later told the BBC. 'The surgeon said that if they had been on my hands or feet, they would have been amputated – that's how serious it was.'

BRMB expressed deep regret over the stunt and paid compensation to the injured contestants. In January 2003, the radio station admitted breaching health and safety laws in a hearing at Birmingham Magistrates' Court and was fined £15,000 following a prosecution by the Health and Safety Executive (HSE). An HSE spokesperson said the stunt should never have happened and that the idea for it was 'quite a stupid one'.

Wee for a Wii and the Crash at Crush – promotional ideas with fatal flaws

The best that can be said of BRMB's idiotic promotion is that no one died. Tragically, that was not the case with a reckless stunt organised by Californian radio station KDND in January 2007. At the time, there was huge hype around and demand for Nintendo's new games console, the Wii. In a laboured play on words it would soon come to rue, the Sacramento-based station devised a now infamous competition called 'Hold Your Wee for a Wii'. Contestants were given huge quantities of water to drink. The person able to consume the most water without urinating would win. Around twenty contestants took part in the stunt at KDND's studios, which was broadcast on the station's *Morning Rave* show.

Two hours into the contest, a female listener named Eva Brooks phoned the radio station to say that drinking too much water can kill. 'Those people that are drinking all that water can get sick and possibly die from water intoxication,' she warned. One DJ replied, 'We are aware of that,' while another added, 'They signed releases, so we're not responsible. It's okay.' Water intoxication occurs when excessive consumption of water lowers salt levels in the body, overloading the kidneys and inducing swelling in areas such as the brain, with potentially fatal consequences.

Just two years before the radio contest, 21-year-old student Matthew Carrington died from water intoxication in a fraternity 'hazing' ritual – also in California – and his death had been widely reported. With no regard for safety, the radio stunt continued. Bloated competitors gave up one by one until just two women remained. They had each downed more than seven litres of water. Jennifer Strange, a 28-year-old mother of three who was hoping to win the Wii for her kids, finally threw in the towel after starting to feel ill. She was heard on air telling DJs that she was in pain. After the contest, Strange called in sick to work, complaining of a headache. Then she went home – where she was found dead a few hours later.

In the wake of the stunt, KDND's parent company Entercom Communications cancelled the *Morning Rave* show and sacked 10 employees, including three DJs. In 2009, Strange's family was awarded $16.5m in compensation after a jury found Entercom liable in a wrongful death lawsuit. Death, job losses and costly litigation: a dumb promotion could hardly go worse.

That said, 'Hold Your Wee for a Wii' isn't the only lethal marketing stunt. As long ago as 1896, out on a Texas prairie, a publicity stunt went so disastrously wrong that its aftermath resembled a battlefield and young ragtime composer Scott Joplin, who may have witnessed the calamity in person, was even inspired to write a song about it called *Great Crush Collision March*.

In the late 19th century, the Missouri–Kansas–Texas Railroad, commonly known as 'the Katy', was expanding rapidly in the Lone Star State. William George Crush, a passenger agent for the railroad, hit upon the idea of staging a head-on crash between two trains as a spectacular marketing extravaganza. The two locomotives – one painted red, the other green – toured the state for months in advance, taking part in scene-setting events to ratchet up excitement. The stunt itself took place near Waco and pre-publicity was so successful that it is estimated that anywhere between forty and fifty thousand people showed up. This temporary city was named Crush in honour of the event organiser, and on the day of the spectacle it was the second most populated city in Texas at the time. Bear in mind, we're talking about an event that took place five years before the beginning of the Texas oil boom and back then the state was a sparsely populated corner of America. It must have been quite a sight, this sprawling encampment in the back of beyond, a late 19th-century Glastonbury festival attracting hawkers, grifters and the plain curious to a celebration of loco madness. Forget oversized popsicles; for the time and the place, this was huge.

After squaring up to each other at close quarters, like boxers before a fight, the locomotives were reversed apart before being sent forward again along the track on a collision course, each hauling seven boxcars. As the trains gathered momentum, their engineers leapt clear, leaving the accelerating trains to smash into one another with enormous force at a combined speed of over a hundred miles per hour. Excited onlookers had been kept back at what was presumed to be a safe distance. Unexpectedly, the impact caused the boiler of one steam engine to explode. Shrapnel was blown into the crowd, with catastrophic results. Two men were killed, a photographer lost an eye and many other spectators were injured in the ill-fated 'Crash at Crush'. While the wounded were tended to and railroad workers dealt with the mangled wreckage, souvenir hunters scoured the debris for mementos. One bystander said the destruction reminded him of his involvement in the American Civil War. As for Crush the man, he was fired that evening – then reinstated by his bosses at the Katy the following day after it emerged he had been assured by engineers that a boiler explosion was almost impossible. Or perhaps because they were early believers in the misguided adage, 'There's no such thing as bad publicity.'

Ambushing sports and abusing animals

- A crucial, close-fought rugby union match between rivals Australia and New Zealand was disrupted during its closing minutes in 2002 when two streakers with Vodafone logos painted on their bodies ran onto the pitch. All Blacks fly-half Andrew Mehrtens was preparing to take an important, possibly game-deciding penalty kick, which he missed. New Zealand lost – had Mehrtens landed the penalty they would have won – and many Kiwis were disgusted by Vodafone's stunt. When it emerged that Vodafone's Australian boss had agreed in advance to pay any fines incurred by the streakers, the telecoms company came under fire for sanctioning an illegal activity.

- Sony was accused of animal cruelty for using a beheaded goat carcass as the centrepiece of a 2007 marketing event in Athens to mark the European launch of computer game *God of War II*. Actually, it was more gruesome than a full decapitation: the creature's near-severed head dangled precariously from a flap of skin with blood dripping onto the floor. Actors in Ancient Greek costume encouraged guests to gorge themselves on offal and topless women fed them grapes. Pictures of the debauched event were published in Sony's *Playstation* magazine under the headline 'Sony's Greek Orgy'. After howls of protest, Sony apologised for the stunt and recalled the 80,000 print run of the magazine.

- Dutch beer brand Bavaria used ambush marketing at two World Cups in a row, seeking to gain coverage at the expense of official FIFA sponsor Budweiser. In Germany in 2006 supporters dressed in Bavaria-branded orange lederhosen were forced to strip to their underwear to gain stadium access. Four years later in South Africa, after a group of 36 young women in matching short orange dresses made it into the Netherlands versus Denmark game and caught the attention of the media and tournament officials, the consequences were more draconian. The group was thrown out of the stadium and two Dutch women involved in organising the stunt were arrested and charged with contravening South Africa's merchandise marks act – if convicted, they faced up to six months in jail. At the same time, FIFA threatened legal action against Bavaria. In dire straits, the beer brand agreed a settlement with FIFA under which the two women were released and allowed to return to the Netherlands and all claims were dropped on the understanding that Bavaria would 'fully respect the integrity of FIFA's commercial programme until the end of the year

2022'. The stunt also triggered the sacking of ITV football commentator Robbie Earle for passing on his allocation of match tickets.

- Anapka the donkey made headlines around the world when she was sent aloft above the Azov Sea in southern Russia in a callous stunt to promote parasailing at a beach resort. The plight of the terrified parasailing beast was captured on video in July 2010. Anapka was subsequently taken to an animal sanctuary near Moscow, where she died of heart failure early in 2011.

Tips and lessons

- Make sure your activity is legal.
- Respect other people – and animals.
- Capturing attention isn't enough. Any event must sit comfortably with your brand and fit your marketing objectives.
- The safety of participants and audience should be paramount.
- Keep it honest and real.
- Avoid train crashes – literal and metaphorical.

Chapter 6

Regrettable rebranding

Marketing makeovers that made it worse

Lip-smacking, thirst-quenching, ace-tasting . . . Brad's Drink. Huh? That's what Caleb Bradham called his soft drink for five years in the 1890s before settling on the more effervescent name Pepsi-Cola. I think we can all agree that the rebranding was a good judgement call.

Wouldn't it be strange to be BackRubbing when hunting for information on the internet? Yes, search giant Google actually started life as BackRub until Larry Page and Sergei Brin reached the conclusion in 1997 that a better name was called for. Google was chosen as a play on the word 'googol' – a mathematical term for the number one followed by a hundred zeros – and intended to express the company's mission to organise the vast amount of information accessible on the internet. Thus one of the world's great brands was born.

Rebranding doesn't have to entail a change of name, however. Sometimes it is about a new look, change of positioning or fresh messaging. For example, P&G has very adeptly rejuvenated its Old Spice brand with a playful series of commercials, 'The Man Your Man Could Smell Like', beginning with the internet smash 'I'm on a horse' spot starring Isaiah Mustafa.

Rebranding is one of the hardest exercises in marketing. Whether a full-blown renaming exercise or a major freshening of identity, such as a revamped logo and new messaging, there are enormous risks when ringing the changes with an established brand. If rebranding is conducted from a position of weakness, rivals and critics smell blood and may close in for the kill. If done from a position of strength, it risks alienating existing customers comfortable with the status quo. And if the outcome is muddled or the reasons for the change are obscure or at odds with the beliefs of important stakeholders, sales can suffer, organisations may be thrown into turmoil and a marketing crisis could be on the cards.

Tailfins and a branding tailspin - research failings lead to BA livery faux pas

When a rebranding goes wrong, problems become apparent pretty quickly. There may be a backlash, some disparaging remarks. A telltale sign that you may have an issue that needs dealing with is when an observer blasts your rebranding work as 'absolutely terrible' and then wraps a handkerchief around it to demonstrate the opinion that it is offensive, unsightly and best concealed. A big clue that you have a truly difficult situation on your hands is when the person wielding the censorious handkerchief is the former leader of your country and her disdain for your fresh brand image is captured on TV cameras and broadcast on the evening news.

That's precisely the scenario experienced by British Airways in 1997 when erstwhile Prime Minister Margaret Thatcher was shown the airline's new livery applied to a model Boeing 747 aircraft displayed on an exhibition stand at the Conservative Party Conference. To the Iron Lady's great displeasure, the Union flag had been removed from the plane's tailfin. With the new Utopia livery, the intention was to introduce a series of artistic ethnic designs from around the world, representative of the many international destinations served by the airline. This cut no ice with the former PM. As she carefully unfolded the handkerchief, her face bore a steely expression of determination combined with a faint hint of devilment. When she berated BA representatives with her views on the matter, emphasising her point with resolute finger-jabbing, it was in that familiar dogmatic tone allowing for no disagreement; a tone that defined her political career and had so often been used to put political adversaries in their place. 'We fly the British flag, not these awful things you're putting on planes,' she said. This was a rare sight, witnessing one national icon receiving a public dressing down from another. It did not augur well.

So what was BA thinking? Market research into BA's old livery had found that some people felt it made the airline appear haughty and detached. UK design agency Newell and Sorrell, which was soon to merge with Interbrand, began working with the carrier in 1995 with the aim of making the airline appear more global and caring – qualities customers told the agency they wanted to see in BA's operations, brand personality and corporate behaviour. At launch, the designers spoke proudly of the new identity as expressing the concept of BA as a citizen of the world. In a nutshell, if you were asked to visualise the airline as a person, what they wanted you to see was a refined, polyglot, multicultural jet-setter; the kind of well-travelled individual who's *au courant* with the world's great museums and galleries. This impression was given further weight by the design approach taken by Newell and Sorrell, which in selecting tailfin artwork for what it called the Collection of World Images was behaving rather like the curator of an international visual art exhibition. Painters, sculptors, ceramicists, weavers, quilters, calligraphers and paper artists from around the world were invited to produce a series of 'uplifting celebrations' of their own community. It was a kind of BA biennale. Pretentious? Just a little.

It's easy to see how BA was seduced by this proposition. But in downplaying its Britishness in favour of a more multinational, somewhat vaguer branding, the airline at a stroke diluted its carefully nurtured brand equity. Even if research might have suggested otherwise, some of the most precious attributes of the BA brand were tightly bound to its close association with, and exemplification of, its home country. Baroness Thatcher was most definitely not alone in harbouring such views. Plus there were a few complaints from air traffic controllers that the new mixed bag approach to tailfin design made it harder for them to identify BA planes.

Sometimes the most telling evidence of a rebranding blunder can be found in competitor reaction. Sir Richard Branson's rival airline Virgin Atlantic could hardly believe its luck and seized on the opportunity it had been gifted. During the 1990s, the relationship between the two British carriers was particularly acrimonious. In 1993 Virgin sued BA for libel and claimed it was waging a 'dirty tricks' campaign against it. BA settled out of court, to the tune of £3.5m in costs and damages. As BA faced growing criticism for the £60m roll-out of its new identity, Virgin took advantage by introducing a Union flag design on the winglets of its aircraft and refashioning the Scarlet Lady emblem found on the fuselage near the nose, placing a union flag in the hand of the 'pin-up' girl. Although there were clearly major factors at work in addition to branding, Virgin's profits rose, while for the year 1998/99 BA posted a painful 61% fall in pre-tax profits. Dropping the flag looked ever more like a misguided move by BA.

In 1999 Virgin Atlantic took things to another level, unveiling a 'new aircraft livery and corporate identity for the millennium' that featured the Union flag on the tailfins of its 25 aircraft, with Branson bullishly claiming that his airline was now Britain's flag carrier. However, with a cunning eye on stealing his thunder, on the eve of the unveiling BA leaked that it was to make branding changes of its own. In an embarrassing reversal, BA revealed that it would be abandoning its ethnic tailfins and returning to flying the flag. BA chief executive Bob Ayling told the BBC: 'It's what our customers want. It is as simple as that. People in Britain want an image which they can respond to as part of their culture.'

How had BA contrived a rebranding fiasco on such a massive scale? Part of the cause doubtless lay in its market research. It had asked the wrong questions of the wrong people, and paid more attention to its overseas markets than to its core British customers. As British passengers were its most loyal customers and accounted for almost half its business, junking brand attributes that they respected and felt comfortable with was bad for business. Sprawling internationalism may have been an accurate reflection of its route network but it wasn't a coherent brand story. In light of its failure, the use of the word 'Utopia' to describe the exercise now appears heavily ironic. When Sir Thomas More coined the name as the title for his 16th-century book about a fictional island society, he deliberately created it from Greek roots in a way that allowed him to make a satirical play on words. While 'Utopia' is usually considered to mean an ideal place, More also intended it to have the added sense of no place at all. And that's where BA's brand drifted to for several years.

Instead of delivering an inspiring take on a post-imperial, multicultural Britain, BA served up what was perceived by many to be a bunch of meaningless squiggles.

Rebirth of JAL's crane - return of the *tsurumaru* brings reassurance

BA is by no means the only airline forced to backpedal on rebranding. Biman Bangladesh Airlines probably holds the record for the fastest reversal of an airline brand makeover. The state-owned carrier unveiled a new look in February 2010. The Bangladeshi government didn't like what it saw and within two months had instructed the airline to revert to the previous branding.

By contrast, Japanese Airlines was more glacial and considered. In 2002, JAL announced that it was scrapping its famous red-crowned crane logo, the *tsurumaru*, which had been introduced in the late 1950s. There was an outcry in Japan, where the crane is revered as a symbol of peace, longevity and good fortune. But the airline pushed ahead in phasing out the *tsurumaru* over a six-year period. Japanese broadcasters even covered the crane's last flight on news bulletins in 2008.

The livery that replaced it saw tailfins painted red, and JAL written in black on a white fuselage. A vertical red and grey swoosh rather clinically bisected the A and the L. Like several other recent brand logos that have tried to replicate the energy Nike has expressed with its swoosh, it was insipid, faceless and unloved. The airline itself was beset with financial challenges, and in 2010 filed for bankruptcy protection. After a period of restructuring, JAL emerged from bankruptcy protection and brought the *tsurumaru* back. Nearly a decade after the announcement of its demise, in 2011 the crane was reborn, with only some minor tweaking to its feathers. It was a potent symbol of better times.

'We adopted the logo with the determination of going back to the basics, when we had the spirit of challenge,' JAL President Masaru Onishi told reporters in Tokyo. 'We want to create a regenerated JAL.' Nondescript branding could never help with a challenge like that. The bland was ditched for the reassuring familiarity of *tsurumaru*.

I don't like Monday - PwC has had better days

Tell me why . . . would anyone rebrand a professional services consulting firm as 'Monday'? That's exactly what accountancy giant PwC chose as the new name for its consulting business in 2002 after turning to branding agency Wolff Olins. Implementation of the rebranding would cost around £75m. This was a serious undertaking with a budget to match. The trouble was, as PwC employees learned of the new name – on a Monday, when else? – many struggled to keep a straight face. Jokes about how switchboard operators would answer the phone – 'This is Monday, hello' – on a Tuesday to Friday were soon doing the rounds. Along with the absurd new name came some ghastly brand positioning collateral: 'Sharpen your pencil, iron your crisp white shirt, set the alarm clock, relish the challenge, listen, be fulfilled, make an impact, take a risk.' Oh my! I'll sharpen my pencil all right, and use it as a weapon to defend myself against this sort of horror.

Greg Brenneman, president and chief executive of PwC's consulting arm, described the brand as 'a real word, concise, recognisable, global and the right fit for a company that works hard to deliver results'. At more or less the same time, PwC staff were telling journalists about how the rebranding was being received with hysterical disbelief in the office.

It's bad enough when outsiders consider a rebranding to be naff or ridiculous. But when a great many people within the organisation consider a new identity inappropriate and absurd, the rebranding exercise has missed its mark entirely. Great brands, it is often said, are built from the inside out. They reflect organisational values and have traction because they are engaging for employees as well as customers. But for all businesses, and particularly so for professional services firms, the most important touchpoint and expression of the brand is to be found through its most convincing advocates – employees. Normally, that's a very good thing. Less so when employees are perplexed to suddenly find themselves working for a company named after the worst day of the week.

Details of the whys and wherefores of the rebranding were displayed on a website with the introducingmonday.com URL. Whether through oversight or parsimony, PwC neglected to buy the .co.uk version of the introducingmonday domain name, which it could have had for a paltry £10. A friend of Rob Manuel, co-founder of online comedy collective B3ta, bought it instead, and Manuel added to the absurdity by creating an animation for the website that literally stuck two fingers (his own!) up at the new identity and included a donkey cavorting to a song with the infantile but undeniably catchy lyrics: 'We've got your name, la, la, la.' He even had the wit to cash in with some satirical merchandise, selling around 100 subversive donkey mugs – mostly to PwC staff. Manuel recalls:

> '*I was careful to not brand them* Introducing Monday *for fear of any lawsuits. They just had pictures of donkeys with the words "We've got your name, la la, la." PwC isn't a brand like Coke: it might have that kind of turnover but it's not a brand in people's faces all the time. There was a sense of* Who are you? We don't care. Go away. *I just joined in, but somehow my mockery hit a note that became the defining note. Fun times, although people told me my fingers were ugly and sinister, which I didn't enjoy much.*'

The ludicrous rebranding was mercifully short-lived. Less than two months after the brand launch, the business was snapped up by IBM, which immediately killed off the Monday moniker. It wasn't missed. The Monday brand was infused with the dispiriting whiff of living to work instead of working to live. PwC may as well have opted for a name like Goodbye Weekend, or the even punchier Stress.

One aspect of the rebranding due diligence process saw PwC pay £3.5m to a company called OneMonday to acquire elements of its name. Under the agreement, OneMonday – a listed holding company for a number of PR and marketing businesses – was given six months to rebrand itself. When this agreement was announced to the markets in June 2002, OneMonday finance director David Dewhurst said his company wasn't yet sure how it would spend this windfall, but added: 'We won't be spending it on rebranding because we can do that ourselves.' By the time OneMonday became Next Fifteen in November 2002, PwC's Monday had been and gone. Perhaps Next Fifteen could have negotiated a way out of its contractual obligation and remained OneMonday. Although it has to be said that in its nod to the familiar Andy Warhol quote about fame, it now had a better, more fitting corporate brand than before. If only Mondays could always disappear so fast.

The significance of Syfy – mockery soon turns to admiration

There was also a fair bit of sniggering when Sci-Fi Channel rebranded as Syfy in July 2009. Shouldn't it be pronounced as 'siffy' some wags wondered, and if so, was it alluding to a venereal disease? Mockery aside, there was actually some sensible strategic thinking at work. 'Sci-fi' is by its very definition a generic term, which made it extremely difficult for the cable channel to secure trademark protection on any branded merchandise it produced. The galactic amounts of sci-fi material on the internet also meant the old brand wasn't easily picked out by search engines. Additionally, the channel was broadening its output into 'imagination-based entertainment', broadcasting more shows that were not pure sci-fi. By settling on Syfy – pronounced as a homophone of its earlier name, i.e. it still sounded the same – the NBC Universal-owned channel had enough continuity to appease hardcore fans, while the new spelling simultaneously offered more leeway for diversifying output.

The second half of 2009 saw the rebranded channel pull in more viewers than at any time in its 17-year history, including a growing number of women. The US rebrand was so successful that the two senior marketers behind it were promoted and it was rolled out internationally. Most rebrandings attract at least some negative feedback. What this goes to show is that some initial sniggering is not enough of a reason to kill off a change of this kind.

From Blackwater to Xe to Academi

Conjuring up a new name in order to lay bad memories to rest is a difficult trick to pull off, as Blackwater discovered when in 2009 it rebranded to Xe Services.

The work of the private security company in Iraq drew worldwide attention in 2004 when four of its contractors were ambushed and killed by insurgents in Fallujah. In what became one of the defining images of the conflict, the mutilated bodies of two of the security guards were strung up on a bridge spanning the Euphrates. The shocking incident raised issues about the accountability and widespread involvement of private security firms working in the region, while Blackwater itself came to symbolise the US policy of hiring mercenaries to undertake assignments that would previously have been handled by the military. In 2005, the families of the deceased launched a wrongful death lawsuit against Blackwater that rumbled on for years before being settled out of court in 2012.

Things went from bad to worse in September 2007. In what is now called the Nisour Square Massacre, Blackwater security guards opened fire on Iraqi civilians, leaving 17 dead, sparking outrage and straining the relationship between Baghdad and Washington. The Iraqi government stripped the company of its licence to operate in the country. A restructuring of the business followed, leading to the 2009 rebranding as Xe and the departure the following year of the company's controversial founder, former Navy SEAL Erik Prince, who sold his stake in the firm to investor consortium USTC Holdings and subsequently set up a new security business in the Middle East.

Xe was chosen as the new brand name for Blackwater precisely because it had no specific meaning. But despite the neutral branding and changes in the ownership of the business, its controversial past meant that Xe was perpetually referred to as 'the company formerly known as Blackwater'. In December 2011, the company's brand name was changed again. New President and CEO Ted Wright said the Academi name represented a strategy refocused on training and security services, adding that it was inspired by Plato's third-century BC Akademia, which produced both the best thinkers and the best warriors.

Maybe in the tough, unforgiving private security business, the regular death of a brand name comes with the territory. Despite its best efforts to distance itself from the past, the 'formerly known as Blackwater' line will continue to stick to Academi just as tenaciously as it clung to Xe.

A company that has conducted over 60,000 private security missions across the globe will be readier than most to operate in the shadows. But it cannot hide from view entirely. Media coverage and campaigning by anti-violence groups repeatedly link the company with its former name. Rebranding can deliver against many objectives, but it can never create corporate camouflage.

Tropicana's chilling sales slump

Brands do need to move with the times. Consumer preferences evolve; packaging or logo design can begin to appear stale; what was once solid and dependable can gradually be perceived as dull and out of touch. Occasionally, therefore, brand managers need to weigh up whether, when and how to refresh. This is a matter of perennial concern in the fast-moving consumer goods (FMCG) sector, where products need to grab attention in split seconds in the busy environment of the supermarket aisle. According to research by POPAI, the global association for marketing at retail, shoppers are planning less, increasingly deciding what to buy when they are at the shelf. POPAI's *2012 Shopper Engagement Study* put the in-store decision rate at 76%, an all-time high. The conundrum for FMCG brands is how best to appeal to the shopper's roving eye. Familiarity has a lot in its favour, but a refreshed brand image may help with standout, alter perceptions of a product and generate interest.

Tropicana, the fruit juice brand owned by PepsiCo, decided it needed to shake things up by pursuing the latter course. It asked agency Arnell Group to overhaul the packaging for its Tropicana Pure Premium line and supported the launch of the new look with an integrated marketing campaign, with high hopes of rejuvenating the fresh juice category. Arnell Group chief executive Peter Arnell – one of the most flamboyant and controversial figures in an industry that arguably has more than its fair share – said a five-month journey had led to dramatic changes in the packaging so that it now implied the notion of squeezing. Out went the brilliantly simple yet instantly recognisable Tropicana image of an orange pierced by a straw. In came characterless packaging that resembled a generic supermarket own label product. It was as if all the life and distinctiveness had been squeezed out of the brand.

When the repackaged product appeared in January 2009 it received a critical mauling from the design community and a thumbs-down from shoppers who found it hard to identify in store, so faceless was the new look. Had the packaging been thoroughly researched with consumers in advance it would surely never have seen the light of day. A facelift is one thing, but this was like when plastic surgery goes terribly, comically wrong and the result is an expressionless mess only slightly reminiscent of the beautiful features that used to exist. Usually a rebranding that receives marketing support will deliver a spike in sales, but in Tropicana's case the opposite happened. No longer recognising the brand easily when peering into store chiller cabinets, many consumers turned instead to its competitors. When the sales figures came in they were frightful. According to Information Resources Inc., between 1st January and 22nd February, unit sales dropped 20%, while dollar sales decreased by 19%, equivalent to $33m in lost revenue, a lot of which had been sucked up by competitor brands Minute Maid, Florida's Natural and Tree Ripe. The rebranding was unequivocally a disaster. Tropicana did the sensible thing and reintroduced the traditional packaging.

Brand owners need to appreciate and protect what is special about their brands and to respect and understand consumers. In Tropicana, PepsiCo has the world's leading producer of branded fruit juices with a pedigree dating back well over half a century. By peeling away the strong visual cues that made Tropicana packaging immediately recognisable in favour of a generic appearance that cheapened and commoditised, PepsiCo took enormous liberties with brand equity nurtured over decades. It really should have had a clearer understanding of the true worth of the Tropicana brand. After all, it did splash out $3.3bn when buying the Tropicana business from Seagram in 1998.

It may be the case that the Tropicana team fell for the *chutzpah* and forcefulness of eccentric design guru Peter Arnell, who owns 1,600 pairs of eyeglasses and just as bizarrely chooses to eat up to 20 oranges a day. In terms of this rebranding fiasco, it's tempting – if facetious – to conclude that Arnell's ravenous appetite for citrus fruit played a part in convincing PepsiCo he was the right man for the job. Unfortunately for the larger-than-life Arnell, less than two years afterwards he was no longer seen as the right man to run the agency he had started. Marketing services group Omnicom, which bought Arnell Group in

2001, sacked its idiosyncratic founder in February 2011, and promptly appointed his wife Sara as the new CEO – there are plenty of twists and turns in the Arnell story! As well as showing some questionable rebranding judgement, Peter Arnell had earned a reputation for himself as a difficult boss. A few days after he was fired, Arnell brought a $1m lawsuit against Omnicom seeking the return of a library of rare books he had assembled, in part with company money. The suit was settled quietly in 2012. Arnell is one of those brilliant, egotistical characters whose name generates a buzz in Adland. He has been behind some wonderful work. But in rebranding Tropicana with so little regard for its identity he proved a key point: a great brand is a potent yet fragile thing that is sustained through consistency. A new look can make consumers take notice, yet if poorly executed it will turn them off.

Gap turns back, JC Penney keeps on changing

It was definitely a case of the latter in 2010 when clothing retailer Gap unveiled a new logo online. Over 2,000 comments about the rebranding were posted on the company's Facebook page alone, many demanding the retailer stick with the traditional logo it had used for more than two decades: a blue square containing the word 'Gap' in white capital letters. The almost universally negative clamour about the new logo persuaded Gap to change its mind in less than a week rather than risk alienating its customers by rolling out the new design. 'All roads were leading us back to the blue box,' said President of Gap Brand North America, Marka Hansen.

That kind of feedback can be enormously frustrating for marketers keen to find exciting new avenues down which to take their brand. Gap wasn't looking to foolishly abandon its brand heritage. The new logo paid homage to the old, with a small blue square featuring in the background to the right, partly behind the letter 'p'. This evolution irked fans of the brand, however, because it failed to offer something stronger or more interesting than what Gap already had. Consumers are naturally resistant to change, so when you do make a change you need to give people a reason to love it.

While Gap at least responded decisively once the dislike of its new logo was clear, department store JC Penney sent out very confused messages when it changed its logo in 2011 and then again in 2012. Three very different logos over the course of just three years suggests a business that is struggling to make sense of its own identity, never mind conveying it convincingly to customers. Indeed, the repeated rebranding is symptomatic of the fact that JC Penney has been wrestling with a number of major marketing issues that I consider at greater length elsewhere (see page 212). Businesses that rebrand more than once in a short space of time are usually not in great shape. If you'd like a snapshot in support of that theory: JC Penney posted a net loss of $985m in the 2012 financial year.

Netflix and its Qwikster debacle

At the end of 2010 Reed Hastings was named *Fortune* magazine's businessperson of the year. A few months later he was among the powerful Silicon Valley elite, including Steve Jobs and Mark Zuckerberg, attending a dinner party with President Barack Obama. But not long after that, having instigated a customer service and rebranding nightmare, his business decisions were being mocked on *Saturday Night Live*.

Hastings co-founded internet movie rental company Netflix in 1997 and oversaw its stunning growth into a multi-billion-dollar business at the expense of more traditional players such as Blockbuster. Netflix was built around the backbone of a DVD-by-post service, but the advent of faster broadband connections convinced Hastings that future growth in the business would be driven by streaming movies and other content to subscribers over the internet.

In summer 2011, Netflix sprung an unpleasant surprise on its US customers, announcing a 60% price increase for its combined by-post and streaming service, from $9.99 to $15.98 per month. Alternatively, customers could have one or the other for $7.99 per month. Investors as well as customers responded very negatively to such a large increase coming out of the blue. Then Hastings sprung his second surprise on those still smarting from the price hike. The DVD business was spun out of Netflix and given a separate brand name, Qwikster. This restructuring was intended to go deeper than a mere name change – and would be of great inconvenience to the well over 10 million customers who had hitherto been using both services. Suddenly they would need to use separate, unconnected websites and have two separate billing accounts. This needless over-complication was a massive backward step in customer service and it triggered another huge wave of complaints. No one much seemed to like the Qwikster name either.

As if all of this were not bad enough, the impression that the move had been ill thought through was reinforced when it became clear that Netflix had not taken steps in advance to acquire the @Qwikster Twitter handle. That account was already in the hands of a young man called Jason Castillo, who media covering the story took great delight in referring to as a 'foul-mouthed pothead'. Castillo was partial to rude language and druggy references in his tweets and had adorned his Twitter account with an avatar picture of Elmo the Muppet smoking dope. His account had been dormant for around a month until Netflix announced Qwikster, at which point a massive rise in followers led Castillo to the realisation that he might suddenly have a valuable Twitter handle in his possession. There followed a series of semi-literate teen-speak Twitter musings from Castillo on how this good fortune might lead to him striking a deal and 'making bank'. Hardly the kind of image Netflix would have wanted for its new brand. Having antagonised customers with a price rise and the high-handed introduction of Qwikster, it was now appearing inept. This was not only embarrassing but financially damaging; customers were turning their backs on the business.

Just three weeks after it had been announced, in early October 2011 Netflix nixed Qwikster. 'Consumers value the simplicity Netflix has always offered and we respect that,' said a contrite Hastings. 'There is a difference between moving quickly – which Netflix has done very well for years – and moving too fast, which is what we did in this case.' If anything, Hastings was even more penitent when Netflix reported its financial results later that same month. The company had lost 800,000 subscribers in the previous quarter, nearly 3.5% of its customers, and it was the first time in years that its US customer base had declined rather than grown. 'We've hurt our hard-earned reputation, and stalled our domestic growth,' Hastings told Wall Street. Investors were unhappy.

Netflix stock dropped 37% on the news, to just over $75 per share. Four months earlier, before Netflix had cooked up this massive mess for itself, its shares were worth almost four times as much. There's nothing to be said in defence of Qwikster. Other than it was kicked into touch. Qwik-ly.

A first-class disaster – how Consignia was consigned to history

Unlike the impetuous birth of Qwikster, the rebranding of the UK's Post Office Group to Consignia in 2001 came about as the result of an intelligent and thorough process that seemed to leave no stone unturned. Yet it is often cited as one of the biggest corporate branding disasters in history. The evolution of the Consignia brand is a fascinating story; its demise even more so. For this was brand as scapegoat, slaughtered in public for expediency at a time of bitter organisational upheaval.

In the run-up to the new millennium, Post Office Group took a long hard look at the increasingly diverse and complicated nature of its business and the challenges it faced, from cost-effective service delivery in the UK to the growing threat of international competition. Brand consultancy Dragon was brought in to conduct a comprehensive review of corporate strategy, market research and marketing strategies and to explore what impact changes to these might have over the next five to 10 years. Dozens of individual management interviews were conducted at group level and with senior figures at the key businesses: Royal Mail, Post Office Counters, ParcelForce and SSL, which handled TV licensing. Dozens more focus groups followed with employees at all levels in key locations across the UK.

'We then expanded that research into their customer base, in a number of different markets, in Europe, USA and Asia,' says Keith Wells, who led the Dragon team. 'I even interviewed a number of MPs to get the government's view.' This work took months to complete, and was progressing as planned, when Wells was told of a new initiative called Shaping for Competitive Success (SCS).

Deregulation in Europe presented Post Office Group with threats and opportunities. Dragon's work shifted to fit into the context of planned major organisational changes being developed under SCS. For years, privatisation of the Post Office had been a political hot potato. No government had wanted to press ahead with it for fear of the controversy and strike action it might provoke. However, increased competition was pushing aside these barriers to change. Plans were formulated to switch commercial status from a government agency to a PLC – in which the government would initially own all the shares. The SCS project took the existing operating structure of the four businesses under the Group, and turned it into one of multiple business units further split into market-facing business units and service delivery units. 'These would use a mix of the existing brand names, in whatever could be the best way,' recalls Wells. 'Add to this the freedom the Group was now given to invest in or acquire businesses abroad, of which I think they made 15 in the time we were working with them, and you can see how a complicated matrix might evolve.'

Under the new structure, in which major client relationships would be managed and developed at a senior level and across international boundaries, it made sense to position the Group as an 'integrated distribution company'. Logically, the next step was that this should be expressed through a single brand name (like DHL, TNT, FedEx), otherwise customers would be faced with a panoply of names and contact points.

Dragon started with the names already being used, but found serious drawbacks with each. The Post Office was seen as out of date and incapable of offering the full range of modern services; Royal Mail had a terrible reputation for industrial action and was not perceived to be the kind of organisation that clients would look to for consultancy-type relationships; ParcelForce received cross-subsidisation from the other businesses, which could not be extended into other markets. There were also some more practical problems: for instance, names already registered and in use by other postal administrations in markets the Group was targeting. Royal Mail was also at this stage ruled a non-starter for a further reason. 'There were some genuine concerns about trying to act as a "Royal" anything in those countries in which royal families were already living and cherished,' says Wells. 'Think of how the UK press and population would react if Dutch or Thai or Danish companies tried to set up here as "royal" entities.'

Pressing forward in the quest for an appropriate name, Dragon whittled potential names down to a long list of 12, from which three final contenders were taken out to international quantitative research among a sample of 8,000 people. The survey was conducted twice – to be doubly sure of the findings. This is the exercise from which Consignia emerged as the winner. Wells liked it for several reasons, one of which was a dictionary definition of 'consign': to entrust to the care of.

The name was registered three years before the rebranding came into effect as the wheels of change were otherwise moving slowly. The massive restructuring of the SCS programme couldn't be accomplished overnight and Tony Blair's Labour Government, sensitive to public opinion, took its time. Given that the rebranding affected the organisation responsible for the 'Royal' Mail, Buckingham Palace was also consulted. In January 2000, Trade and Industry Secretary Stephen Byers unveiled the Postal Services Bill that would allow the organisation to become a public company and spoke of the necessity for Post Office modernisation. 'It has served the country well for more than 350 years, but now it needs to change so that it can compete effectively,' said Byers at the time. A little under a year later, on 9th January 2001, the Post Office Group revealed that it would be changing its corporate brand name to Consignia when it switched to becoming a state-owned limited company. It also revealed that it had spent £500m on international acquisitions.

At the launch, Post Office chief executive John Roberts said the Consignia name would be seen 'principally by our corporate customers in the financial services, telecommunications, home shopping, utilities and advertising and marketing sectors, who together account for nearly a third of our annual £7.5bn turnover'. This was reported by BBC News among others. Yet later that day, on the BBC evening news bulletin a vox-popping reporter stood outside a Post Office branch asking old ladies how they felt about 'going down the Consignia'. Other media outlets also ran stories in which the nature of the rebranding was misreported, implying that the new overarching corporate brand would be seen on the High Street.

Looking back, Wells regrets that more wasn't done to set the record straight about the fledgling brand. 'Never assume that people have "got it" even when the research tells you they have,' he advises. 'What I would do differently now is to make sure every single instance of inaccurate reporting be jumped on and corrected.'

Behind the scenes, tracking among the key clients and other target audiences showed over 90% understanding of the new name and strong acceptance of it – a marked contrast to some of the sniping at the name reported by the media. The Consignia brand was seemingly connecting with its main target audience and would almost certainly have survived had its introduction not coincided with the worst financial performance in the organisation's history. In a bid to stem rising losses of over £1bn a year, in December 2001 Consignia announced it would have to make up to 30,000 redundancies. Unions were furious and threatened strike action. Businessman Allan Leighton, who had been involved in turning around ailing supermarket group ASDA and then selling it to US giant Wal-Mart for £6.7bn, was brought in by the government as chairman early in 2002 with a brief to stem the losses. One of his first acts was to reveal in a TV interview with David Frost that he wanted to axe the Consignia brand, for reasons of credibility rather than for a commercial rationale. Public criticism of the name flared up again following Leighton's comments. Shortly afterwards it was officially announced that the Consignia brand was to be scrapped in favour of Royal Mail as the organisation slimmed down and re-focused on core activities.

Never one to mince his words, Leighton today remains adamant that the rebranding to Consignia was a 'stupid call' given the centuries of heritage the organisation could exploit from its well-known existing brands. Tellingly, as a populist and pragmatist to his bones, Leighton was fully aware that by killing off a ridiculed brand that had come to be associated with a dire time in its history, he could stamp his authority and decisiveness on the organisation. As a dynamic new broom sweeping away the Consignia brand, he could disassociate himself from the management regime that had contributed to the ugly financial picture he had been hired to rectify, which meant overseeing painful mass lay-offs, branch closures and selling off non-core parts of the business.

'Changing to the Royal Mail made brand sense but also helped me show "things were changing" and unlike in the past, poor decisions got reversed. Also I wanted to signal a change: new leadership who did not hide from tough decisions. When

things needed changing speed kicked in. We did not take months to do things as in the past.'
Allan Leighton, former non-executive Chairman, Royal Mail

So the Consignia brand came and went at a cost of £1.9m – and has been roundly pilloried ever since as a prime example of wastefulness and ineptitude. Yet is should be pointed out that even if the organisation had stuck with the Post Office name it would probably have incurred in the region of £1.5m in costs by adding PLC to its name across a vast array of stationery and documents to comply with the Companies Act. Ironically, if Wells and the rest of the team had been less mindful of potential wastefulness, the new brand would have appeared earlier and may have stood a far better chance of survival. But it was agreed that it would have been madness to commit to one set of changes, then to another as soon as the new commercial status was confirmed.

'In retrospect, we might have suggested launching the new name with no reference to the change in commercial status. That way, the business would have had three years to establish itself, and the organisation would have been seen to be performing okay, at least to begin with. In the light of its decreasing performance, people might have been asking "What's gone wrong at Consignia?" rather than saying, "It's all gone wrong because of/since they changed the name." But that's hindsight, and I still believe it was right to tie the physical and commercial changes to the brand change.'
Keith Wells, Director, Dragon Brands

Understandably, Wells is aggrieved at the way the rebranding to Consignia has been lazily dismissed as a dumb exercise. The work was caught up in a maelstrom of ill-informed opinions, and sucked down into oblivion by the weight of disappointment in the organisation's performance. No brand can paper over cracks as large as those that affected the organisation that for a short while bore the Consignia name. A brand can't hold together what bigger forces will pull apart. I don't think Consignia was a wonderful brand name. However, it was fit for purpose and undeserving of all the opprobrium that was heaped upon it. Honestly, is it any worse than Accenture or Novartis or Diageo or Mondelēz, or a host of other corporate brands in this vein?

In Need of Rebranding?

- The Dolphin tinned tuna brand, heavily advertised in Egypt, features a smiling dolphin on its label. Some consumers in the Middle East have wondered at the choice of brand name, given the number of dolphins killed by tuna fishing over the years.
- UK sandwich chain Pret a Manger launched its own brand Virgin Mary crisps early in 2013, a spiced tomato flavour with a name that alluded to the non-alcoholic version of the Bloody Mary cocktail. After complaints from consumers and religious groups, the chain took the product off shelves after just a few days, donating unsold stock to the homeless.
- Japanese health drink Pocari Sweat is very popular in its domestic market, but would probably benefit from a name change if it tried to crack English-speaking markets. Another Japanese drink, Calpis, has the somewhat less off-putting name Calpico outside Japan.

Tips and lessons

- Think twice before dispensing with a name, logo or brand image that has served you well in the past.
- Conduct focus groups to help winkle out any problems that may not have been pinpointed at the early planning stage.
- Make sure a new brand identity is relevant, meaningful and able to harness useful brand equity that has already been built up, as well as being fresh.
- Don't proceed with a rebranding until you have secured all the necessary web domain names and social media handles.
- Always bear employees, customers and other stakeholders in mind. How will the rebranding benefit them?
- Timing can be crucial. Rebranding at a time of bad news for your product, service or corporate brand may be perceived as a smokescreen.
- Remember there is far more to a brand than a name that will appear on your product, in ads or on your website. Will the rebranding be sufficiently flexible in nature and tone to work across all touchpoints?

Chapter 7

Can you believe it?

When fakery, falsification and scams come to light

Not everything is as it might at first appear. During the 1930s and 1940s, notorious Dutch art forger Han van Meegeren used Bakelite to harden the oils in paintings he passed off as the work of Old Masters such as Frans Hals and Johannes Vermeer, thus giving them the semblance of age. Today's masters of manipulation use digital techniques, often to soften the lines on the faces of models or to rework their physical proportions, thereby making them appear younger or slimmer. For marketers, faking it can be a temptation that's hard to resist. Photoshop and other digital tools allow images to be retouched, enhanced and distorted with relative ease, as never before. Where boundaries lie in terms of what may be deemed a fair and true advertising image can be contentious. Sometimes, even when it's clear where a line should be drawn, marketers overstep the mark. The possibility of being found out isn't always a deterrent.

Occasionally boundaries are crossed without the knowledge or explicit consent of brand owners. From time to time, scam ads or unapproved virals ostensibly promoting a brand are produced by creative teams to further their own interests – for example to heighten their profile, pick up awards or help secure new business. If these creative teams behave unethically or incompetently, allowing content that may be detrimental to a brand to reach a wider audience, brand owners may find themselves caught up in an unpleasant mess. But before we get on to the finger-pointing and who-did-what, let's talk about the beauty industry and its tricks.

Beauty and trickery - L'Oréal, Dior and P&G retouch too much

Here's a piece of advertising trivia for you. What do Julia Roberts, Twiggy, Rachel Weisz, Christy Turlington, Penelope Cruz and Natalie Portman have in common? All six female celebrities have featured in print ads for cosmetics brands in recent years that have been banned by the UK's advertising watchdog, the Advertising Standards Authority (ASA), for being falsified in one way or another. *Star Wars* actress Portman appeared in an ad for Christian Dior mascara which was censured by the ASA in October 2012, because the Hollywood A-lister's eyelashes had been retouched. Dior conceded that a 'minimal' amount of retouching had taken place to stylistically lengthen and curve Portman's lashes, but argued that the look did not go beyond what consumers could achieve by using the product themselves. The ASA dismissed Dior's stance and ruled against the ad on the basis that it was misleading. The watchdog concluded it had 'not seen sufficient evidence to show that the post-production retouching on Natalie Portman's lashes in the ad did not exaggerate the likely effects of the product'.

As is frequently the case with complaints to advertising regulators, the complaint against Dior was brought by a competitor; in this instance, L'Oréal. Interestingly, the French beauty group has itself been a repeat offender when it comes to retouching. Four of the other five ads mentioned above were for L'Oréal products – the fifth, featuring the model Twiggy, was in 2009 for P&G's Olay Definity eye illuminator. The four upheld complaints against L'Oréal were:

- Rachel Weisz – L'Oréal Revitalift, 2012. The ASA considered that the image had been altered in a way that substantially changed Weisz's complexion to make it appear smoother and more even.
- Julia Roberts – Lancôme Teint Miracle foundation, 2011.

- Christy Turlington – Maybelline Eraser product designed to conceal crows' feet and dark circles around the eyes, 2011.
- Penelope Cruz – L'Oréal Telescopic Mascara, 2007.

The campaign for L'Oréal Telescopic Explosion, which included press and TV advertising, claimed the mascara could deliver eyelashes up to 60% longer. Whatever the truth of that boast, L'Oréal was made to look ridiculous when it emerged that the Spanish star of blockbusters such as *Pirates of the Caribbean 4* was actually wearing false eyelashes during the shoot. Critics had a field day at the company's expense. There's even an amusing parody of the commercial by comedienne Ronni Ancona, in which L'Oréal is restyled as L'Unreal and is well worth a look on YouTube.

Beiersdorf has also been censured for retouching images, in a print ad for Nivea Vital Anti-Age cream that claimed the moisturiser visibly reduces wrinkles, improves firmness and helps prevent age spots. Unconvinced, the ASA banned the ad in August 2013 citing a lack of scientific evidence that the product could deliver such results, after concluding that lines and wrinkles on a model's face had been dramatically reduced in order to misleadingly exaggerate the performance of the moisturiser.

Of course this isn't a phenomenon unique to the UK. P&G has also been pulled up for digital manipulation in the USA. A print ad for its CoverGirl NatureLuxe Mousse Mascara featuring the visage of singer-songwriter Taylor Swift, her eyelashes lushly resplendent, claimed to double the volume of lashes but bore the small print disclaimer that: 'lashes were enhanced in post production'. The National Advertising Division (NAD), one of the bodies involved in the self-regulation of the US advertising industry and responsible for checking the veracity of ads, was, to paraphrase a Taylor Swift hit, 'never, ever, ever' going to stand for that. Part of NAD's remit is to ensure that product demonstrations in national advertising are accurate and truthful – which means that images cannot be made more flattering to the advantage of a product by using digital trickery. 'You can't use a photograph to demonstrate how a cosmetic will look after it is applied to a woman's face and then – in the mice type – have a disclosure that says "okay, not really",' NAD Director Andrea Levine witheringly told *Business Insider*. P&G discontinued the campaign and agreed not to reproduce the doctored image of Swift or to repeat any of the unsubstantiated product claims made in the ad.

Policing the use of Photoshop and other digital tools with regard to the dishonest distortion of images is far from easy for bodies such as NAD and the ASA. Would P&G have been caught if it had omitted any mention at all of post-production enhancement? Maybe. Then again, maybe not. Other advertisers unethically using digital techniques to smooth, soften or exaggerate have undoubtedly slipped through the net. Being found out for the abuse of Photoshop often comes down to being shopped by competitors. There's a hard and ugly side to beauty advertising. As far as cosmetics and fashion ads are concerned, what you see isn't always what you get.

Although some pressure for tightening up the rules has been applied, the political will for change internationally has to date been patchy. In 2009, French MP Valérie Boyer called for a law requiring ads that had been digitally altered to carry a bold printed notice, while in the UK the Liberal Democrats have come out in favour of similar legislation, including a complete ban on retouching in any ads aimed at children under 16. In 2011, Norway's Equality Minister Audun Lysbakken said he would like to see 'warning labels' on Photoshopped ads, particularly those in which models had been made to look thinner. Lysbakken was taking the view that ads 'cleaned up' to make women appear skinnier could have a damaging effect on teenage girls' self-image, leading them to starve themselves in pursuit of 'unobtainable ideal bodies'. Backing up his stance was a paper signed by 45 international experts on body image, *The Impact of Media Images on Body Image and Behaviours*, which concluded: 'Media images that depict ultra-thin, digitally altered women models are linked to body dissatisfaction and unhealthy eating in girls and women.' It's a damning assessment. But like many catwalk models, significant change has so far been thin.

Among the most egregious examples of Photoshop revisionism is a 2009 Ralph Lauren ad in which model Filippa Hamilton, dressed in designer check blouse and blue jeans, stands with hands resting on hips, just below her slight waist. However, on this occasion the word 'slight' fails to do the image justice. The airbrushing is so extreme that the model's waist appears narrower than her head! Amid barbs that the image was 'grotesque', Ralph Lauren promptly apologised. Despite welcoming the apology, eating disorders charity Beat slammed distorted fashion advertising of this kind as 'highly toxic to young and vulnerable people'.

The psychological impact of beauty advertising is an emotive issue. Advertisers should always be mindful that the influence of their images runs far deeper than the product they are promoting. Although under pressure to sell clothes and make-up, advertisers also have an obligation to behave honestly and responsibly. The boundaries of what is permissible may appear to lie on shifting sands, but consumers have an increasingly acute sense of what they believe to be acceptable and are more than ready to hold to account those brands that have transgressed. Websites such as Photoshop Disasters have brought examples of digital deception to a wider audience, and many ordinary people today have access to design software and with it an understanding of what is possible in the way of image manipulation, which means they often view advertising images with a healthy dose of scepticism. Yet even when it is intelligently targeted, advertising is not seen only by the well-rounded majority. It is the job of advertising to present products in a favourable, enticing light; but it is irrefutably a step too far to offer up an unachievable, warped ideal of womanhood that is skeletal, unblemished and distorted by unnaturally accentuated eyelashes.

Out of the blue - unapproved advertising is explosive for Kia and VW

Most great advertising is created by agencies. That's not to say that wonderful work can't come from in-house teams, because there are some outstanding exceptions, but in the main it's creative teams at agencies that deliver the best advertising. Why? Most obviously because that's what they're set up to do. A carefully nurtured creative environment, coupled with the opportunity to work with like-minded people on a variety of assignments, usually for several different clients, is an enticing proposition for the cream of copywriting and design talent. Promises of glamour and creative satisfaction prove irresistible to a stream of hot young talent with a voracious appetite for success and a yearning for recognition. Adland is adept at selling itself; you'd expect nothing less.

When agencies do good work for clients, this tried and tested model is hard to beat. Sometimes, although the faces on the teams change, client/agency relationships can endure for decades. For example, in 2013 Unilever celebrated its 110th anniversary of working with agency JWT. In what is often seen as a fickle business, there are many relationships that have stood the test of time. Agencies can live and breathe their clients' brands and are often able to express and re-energise them more powerfully than clients could themselves. If on occasion they get it hopelessly wrong by coming up with an idea that is offensive and entirely at odds with what a brand stands for, no harm is done because the client simply rejects it and the idea never sees the light of day.

And that should be that. Only of course it isn't. Not always.

While normally a virtue, an agency's capacity to generate plenty of ideas can sometimes cause havoc. Creative exercises and pitch preparations can throw up all sorts of concepts and 'solutions' that marketers would not wish to see associated with their brand. From time to time, shockingly ill-suited material leaks out and goes viral. In the worst cases, damage limitation activity is necessary – which is galling for those clients who didn't like or even know about an idea in the first place.

A frequent contributor to the emergence of such rogue material is the marketing world's obsession with awards. Just as actors relish the kudos of winning Oscars, Emmys, Tonys and BAFTAs, and athletes strain every sinew for medals, trophies and *palmarès*, creative agencies crave the prestige bestowed by awards such as the Cannes Lions, CLIOs, D&AD Pencils, One Show and on and on through a host of other celebrations of excellence in marketing communications. Picking up a major award can cement an agency's reputation and be the making of a creative team. Agencies often flag up the awards they have won prominently on their websites and highlight creative prizes in their new business credentials, in the knowledge that approval from their peers bestows a certain cachet and enhances their credibility with clients. However, the pursuit of recognition can sometimes cause a rush of blood to the head.

Every June, over ten thousand members of the global advertising industry converge on the sunny South of France for the Cannes Lions

International Festival of Creativity at which awards are dished out amid much back-slapping bonhomie, avid networking, worthy seminars and the consumption of prodigious amounts of canapés and alcohol. At the 2011 festival, one trend precipitating discussion among the top creatives enjoying themselves on the French Riviera was the burgeoning success of advertising from Brazil – in the Lions that year, Brazil was the fourth most awarded country, with São Paolo ranked as the third most creative city in the world. Yet among all the genuinely good entries from Brazil, there was a campaign that made some people distinctly uneasy. This campaign came from an agency called Moma Propaganda, based in, you've guessed it, São Paolo, which landed two awards: a Silver Lion in the Press category and a Bronze Lion for Outdoor work.

Although advertising awards are sometimes decided on effectiveness and hard metrics, there is a large dose of subjectivity in the process – just as in judging the best author in a book prize or the best actor in a movie – and the announcement of the winners usually provokes plenty of disagreement with the decisions reached by the jury. That's perfectly normal. However, the two awards bestowed on Moma in 2011 caused some genuine shock.

Both ads were for the car maker Kia and were designed to promote the Kia Sportage SUV, placing specific emphasis on its dual-zone air conditioning. If I tell you that the ads are now known as the 'Kia paedophile ads' you will understand why their success in the awards would lead to disquiet. Playing with the strapline 'A different temperature on each side', the ads were split in half, with a different style of illustration on either side: to the left, the pictures were wholesome and in the style of cartoons aimed at children; to the right, the drawings were much more lifelike and erotically charged. In the execution called 'Teacher', the panel on the left shows a teacher and a little girl aged around seven, both with cute oversized heads, standing in a classroom separated by a desk on which a red apple perches. The teacher is rendered with a kindly smile and in a speech bubble asks the little girl, 'So where should we start?' In the accompanying illustration, although they are wearing the same clothes as before, the teacher and the student are portrayed very differently, standing flirtatiously side by side, he with chiselled jaw and broad shoulders, she now with the curvaceous body of a teenager, her legs and midriff provocatively on display because she is wearing a micro mini skirt and has her school blouse hitched up with a knot. Responding to the teacher's question about where to start, she says: 'How about anatomy?' There's no mistaking the sexually suggestive nature of the work. The ad appears to be promoting a car by using the abuse of trust implicit in an unethical sexual relationship between a teacher and pupil, with the even more disturbing message that pre-pubescent girls are to be confused with curvy young women thrown for good measure into this unsavoury mix. Disgusting, in every sense. Although seemingly not so to the members of the Cannes Lions jury who saw fit to garland the Kia ads with awards.

There has long been something of a disparity between the kind of controversial, off-the-wall work that gets many advertising creative directors excited and the sometimes more mundane advertising that actually helps brands sell products and services. Awards juries have a tendency to pick the edgy; often to the detriment of advertising that truly delivers what clients need. Maybe I'm too trusting of humanity, but I believe I'm on safe ground saying that paedo-fantasy is not the key to attracting the overwhelming majority of people to a car. There are literally hundreds of better ways to highlight the virtues of dual-zone air conditioning. Quite what they were thinking in Cannes when awarding Lions to these Kia ads is beyond me. There's no suggestion of any corruption or unethical behaviour on the jury, but plenty of evidence of a colossal lapse in taste combined with a blatant disregard for what might be seemly and appropriate content for a mainstream car company. However, the machinations of awards juries is a subject best left to another kind of book entirely. What is of concern here is the impact of such advertising on the Kia brand.

Aghast and perplexed by the decision, some of the more sensible creative talent (they do exist!) at Cannes made sure the ads would be judged by a bigger jury by spreading them virally online – where of course they were met with revulsion and derision. Why hadn't they leaked out onto the internet before, when they initially appeared in Brazil? For the simple reason that they had never been used in an advertising campaign. These were scam ads, created by the agency for the purpose of winning awards and boosting its profile with a bit of cheap scandal. Kia was in the dark about their existence, until it suddenly found itself embroiled in a controversy in which it was accused of using paedophilic images to advertise its Sportage model.

'Neither us at headquarters nor our distributor of Kia vehicles in Brazil, Kia Motors do Brasil, had any knowledge of this creative work done by Moma nor of its submission to Cannes. Furthermore, the ads were never run in public other than Cannes posting them on their website, and were then taken from there by various media outlets.'

Michael Choo, General Manager of Global Public
Relations, Kia Motors, South Korea

On the record, Kia sounds calmly diplomatic. Off the record, its marketers and PR staff were absolutely livid; first and foremost with the chancers at the Brazilian agency, but also with the organisers of the Cannes Festival. Why on earth, Kia quite reasonably wanted to know, did the judges give awards to scam ads with a dubious theme, landing Kia with a reputational crisis relating to something it had known nothing about? The festival organisers launched an investigation and a month later announced that Moma was to be stripped of its two awards. In an official statement, chagrined Festival CEO Philip Thomas said: 'The Cannes Lions rules state clearly that if requested, proof must be provided that campaigns ran, and were legitimately created for a fee-paying client. Despite many conversations, Moma Propaganda has not provided the proof we require and therefore the Lions have been withdrawn.'

It's probably fair to say that most people will struggle to understand why they were awarded in the first place.

Paedophilia, thankfully, isn't a natural angle for car marketing. Neither is suicide bombing. That's why in early 2005 Volkswagen had to go into crisis mode when a spoof video with a terrorist theme began circulating on the internet and was widely mistaken as a legitimate commercial for its Polo model. The action in the ad is as follows. A suicide bomber gets into a VW and drives it to his target, a restaurant where diners are eating al fresco, comes to a halt and presses a detonator button. This triggers a massive explosion, complete with fireball, inside the car. Yet despite the force of the blast the car doesn't disintegrate. Then comes the tagline payoff: 'Polo. Small But Tough'. VW was concerned that consumers would believe it was responsible for this distasteful ad and set about trying to track down who was behind it, at the same time threatening legal action on the grounds that the video was both libellous and infringed the German auto maker's intellectual property.

It soon emerged that the video was the brainchild of London-based creative duo Lee Ford and Dan Brooks, commonly known as Lee and Dan (like Ant and Dec, but with terrorism jokes). Lee and Dan had made the video for their showreel, with the help of film-maker Stuart Fryer, and presented it to VW's ad agency DDB London in the hope of picking up some work – they were unsuccessful.

It's unclear how the video made its way on to the internet, but once there it spread fast. VW was determined to distance itself from the fake ad and indicated it was prepared to be as tough as its cars if necessary. Now in a sticky situation, Lee and Dan turned for advice to David Price Solicitors, a specialist media law firm. Eventually a settlement was reached. Lee and Dan apologised for the spoof commercial, made it clear that there had been no input into the video from VW and admitted the work infringed the car company's trademark and was libellous. In return, VW agreed not to pursue the pair for damages.

It got out there somehow – Ford and Hyundai court controversy

One reason VW was so determined to set the record straight was that some other tasteless viral ads doing the rounds were rightly perceived by consumers as having been sanctioned by brand owners in some way. For example, in 2004 a video for Ford's SportKa provoked controversy and sparked condemnation from animal charities. In this video, a curious cat climbs onto the car to investigate its open sun roof, which snaps shut, decapitating the unlucky feline whose headless body then slides down the windscreen. Unlike Lee and Dan's 'Terrorist' video, the SportKa ad was made by an officially retained agency, in this instance Ogilvy & Mather. The video was presented by O&M to Ford with a view to it being used for viral marketing purposes, but was apparently rejected by the client on taste grounds. And yet it found its way on to the internet. Protests from the agency that the video had slipped out accidentally rang a little hollow. Plausible deniability may work for advertisers and agencies some of the time, but consumers are increasingly on their guard against cynical marketing ruses. Anyone who thinks a strategy based on leaks is risk free should take a long hard look at the career of Julian Assange.

Although the appearance on the internet of car ads that are 'not meant to be there' is a relatively new phenomenon, it is also part of a pattern in which we can see history repeating itself. Shift into top gear and take the road from 2004 to April 2013. This time it is Korean car manufacturer Hyundai issuing a public apology for 'any offence or distress caused' by a European video for its ix35 model it claimed it never approved, or even instructed to have made. The marketing agency that did make it, Innocean Worldwide, also apologised and said the film had been posted on YouTube for just one day to get consumer feedback on a 'creative idea employing hyperbole to dramatise a product advantage without any other commercial purpose'. Just one day on YouTube? More than enough time to ensure that the video would be spread virally. Just as much to the point, Innocean isn't an independent agency – it is owned by Hyundai.

So, what was this hyperbolic idea that caused distress through the dramatisation of what the ix35 has to offer? The video, called *Pipe Job*, depicts a despondent middle-aged man trying to kill himself. After shutting himself in his garage and making it airtight with masking tape, the man runs a tube from his exhaust pipe into his car, gets into the vehicle, turns on the engine and waits to be overcome by the fumes. In no way to be confused with a shameless attempt to stir up publicity through controversy – who would ever do that? – the creatives behind the ad gloss over all those tediously conventional issues associated with attempted suicide, such as depression and desperation, in order to make an eco-friendly marketing point about engine emissions. You see, the ix35 is powered by hydrogen fuel cells, which means, as the video tagline has it, '100 per cent water emissions'. As you'll have worked out by now, this brings us to the video's hilarious conclusion: the hapless suicidal man survives his attempt to gas himself. Oh, how we laughed!

What next? More would-be suicides throwing themselves piteously into the road only to have their anguished lives spared by Hyundai's superior braking technology?

The backlash against the video was predictable and widespread, with print, broadcast and online media all covering the story. One of the most poignant of dissenting voices came from within the advertising industry itself. Young advertising copywriter Holly Brockwell wrote an open letter to Hyundai and Innocean on her blog in which she explained how the video made her sob because it brought back horrible childhood memories of her own father committing suicide in his car:

> 'I understand better than most people the need to do something newsworthy, something talkable, even something outrageous to get those all-important viewing figures. What I don't understand is why a group of strangers have just brought me to tears in order to sell me a car. Why I had to be reminded of the awful moment I knew I'd never see my dad again, and the moments since that he hasn't been there. That birthday party. Results day. Graduation.'

All too often, in the desperate search for memorability, the ad industry is drawn towards edginess – but creative teams need to stop short of poking fun at those who really are close to the edge.

Unapproved . . . approved – WTF WWF?

International conservation charity World Wildlife Fund (WWF) has also found itself at the centre of heated debate about shock tactics. In 2009 a WWF print ad (and later a video version) emerged that drew condemnation around the world for its gross insensitivity. The ad, *Tsunami*, featured dozens of passenger aircraft Photoshopped into attack formation in the skies above Manhattan, apparently converging on the Twin Towers of the World Trade Centre in a deliberate re-imagining of the 9/11 atrocity.

The point the ad made so brutally was that the Boxing Day tsunami of 2004 killed 100 times as many people as the horrendous terrorist attack on New York City in 2001. When confronted by this tasteless shocker, the US office of WWF rushed out a statement claiming it was being 'inaccurately' linked to the ad, implying that it was an idea that had been rejected. But to the wildlife charity's mortification it soon came to light that the crass ad had been sanctioned after all – in Brazil! There it had been created *pro bono* by agency DDB and approved by a junior member of the WWF team to run in a Brazilian magazine. DDB and WWF then issued a joint statement conceding that the ad had indeed been created and approved for use but that it had been a mistake to do so. The error, it explained, was due to 'a lack of experience on the part of a few professionals from both parties involved' who were trying to get across the message that nature is a powerful force ... as is the contempt of people who feel they are being manipulated by cynical or gratuitously offensive advertising ploys.

Denying the truth - Hi-Tec, Witchery and VisitDenmark string us along

In trying to sustain an illusion that makes a viral video compelling viewing in the first place, for instance that it is a genuine story independently told rather than a piece of concealed advertising, several brand owners have been prepared to feed lies to the public. Running shoe brand Hi-Tec released a fun video called *Liquid Mountaineering*, which used special effects to make it look as though people were running on water – but brought a sour note to the campaign by denying any involvement in the viral for a month to foster speculation about its origin, before eventually coming clean and shamelessly releasing a short 'making of' film.

Worse still was the behaviour of Australian clothing retailer Witchery and its agency Naked Communications, which in 2009 created a video called *Man in the Jacket* as a sneaky way to promote a new menswear line. In this video, a pretty young lady named Heidi spoke direct to camera while apparently sitting in her bedroom, giving it the home-made feel of so many videos to be found on YouTube. She described a brief encounter with an unidentified man who had captured her heart when they spoke for a few minutes at a café, but on departing had left his jacket behind, which Heidi retrieved and brought home. Now, like Cinderella in reverse, Heidi hoped to track down her Prince Charming by using this item of apparel. Feigning infatuation, she sniffed and stroked the 'beautiful' jacket, clutched it to her body and then held it up to the camera so that viewers could appreciate its striped silk lining. A stalker with a fetish for men's clothes, she was on the hunt for her jacketless quarry.

With the viral spreading, the media began to take an interest in Heidi's story. Scepticism about its authenticity grew. But when quizzed by journalists, Heidi asserted hers was a genuine quest for love and even gave a national TV interview to that effect. Unconvinced, the media dug deeper and unearthed the reality. As a headline in the *Sydney Morning Herald* succinctly put it, 'You've been had: Sydney Cinderella's jacket man exposed as viral ad.' The woman in the ad was an actress and Heidi wasn't her real name. Naked and Witchery were caught on the back foot by the speed with which the media got to the truth. Instead of being able to control a 'reveal' and give the viral a positive spin, their deception became the focus of the story. It didn't reflect well on them. Naked claimed the campaign helped change perceptions of Witchery for the better, but by its own admission research also showed that a quarter of people had lost respect for the Witchery brand. To my mind, that's an awful outcome for a campaign. Offering up a big chunk of brand integrity in return for sustaining a trifling amount of mystery in a video for a few days doesn't strike me as a worthwhile trade-off. Consumers may be comfortable with brands being playful but they detest feeling conned. Transparency matters.

Thousands of miles away, VisitDenmark tried a similar ruse, but with a raunchier dimension – this time a young woman spoke to camera cradling her baby, ostensibly the result of a drunken one night stand with a tourist whose name she had forgotten and whom she was now trying to track down via the internet to let him know he was a daddy. The aim was to present Denmark as a broad-minded and exciting place. But when the Danish media found out the paternity appeal was a hoax, awkward questions were put to the tourist board about why it would want to present Denmark as a destination in which drunken women had spur-of-the-moment unprotected sex with visitors to the country whose names they could not even recall.

Laying 'astroturf' online - Edelman flogs for Wal-Mart

The importance of transparency and honesty in business is underlined by the Edelman *Trust Barometer*. Edelman is the world's largest PR firm, employing more than 4,500 people across 66 offices worldwide. Every year for over a decade it has carried out its Barometer research, exploring people's faith in business, government, NGOs and the media.

In 2013, this ran to interviews with 31,000 respondents in 26 different countries. It will come as little surprise that, globally, government (48%) has a lower trust score than business (58%). Yet that is not at all to say that people believe the majority of businesses will be straight with them all the time. Only 18% of people trust business leaders to tell the truth regardless of how complex or unpopular it may be. Damningly, it is in the more developed markets that trust in business is at its lowest. There is, it seems reasonable to conclude, something of an international crisis in confidence in the integrity of business.

For the most part, Edelman counsels its clients to be open and straightforward. But there have been occasions when its own business ethics have been called into question. In a hugely embarrassing episode for the PR firm and one of its major clients, in 2006 Edelman became embroiled in an 'astroturfing' fiasco. Astroturfing is the marketing industry's witty term for creating fake grassroots; engineering support for a brand so that it appears to be spontaneous and unconnected directly to its communication activities when in fact the opposite is the case. When this kind of activity involves the creation of fake blogs, in communications parlance these are often referred to as flogs. As the terminology, with its emphasis on fakery attests, this is a dishonourable and misleading way to set about achieving communications goals. And to be fair, most reputable marketers would not condone this sort of approach.

Unwisely, Edelman chose to create two flogs for its supermarket client Wal-Mart. The most high-profile of these was called 'Wal-Marting Across America'. It was purportedly the work of a man and woman called Jim and Laura who were chronicling in words and pictures their travels across the USA in an RV (mobile home). The couple made a point of stopping at Wal-Mart stores because of the friendliness of the staff, who were often gushing about their wonderful working conditions, the quality and good value of its products and the ease of finding space for a large RV in its parking lots. It wasn't just the seafood at Wal-Mart's fish counter that smelled fishy. Some of the people who happened upon these Wal-Mart-praising tales of life on the road sensed that they weren't as independent as they were made out to be. Due to its size – in 2011 it made \$419bn in net sales – Wal-Mart is a closely watched corporation. Before long, people began to look into what was actually happening. It soon became clear that the authors of 'Wal-Marting Across America' were not exactly intrepid, independently minded adventurers but were in fact being funded by Working Families for Wal-Mart, a group set up to counter criticism that the retailer was not a family-friendly employer. Working Families for Wal-Mart was the surreptitious concoction of Edelman and had a flog of its own. *Businessweek* broke the story under the headline 'Wal-Mart's Jim and Laura: The Real Story'. Under mounting pressure, Edelman revealed an involvement in the creation of the astroturfing content it had previously chosen to hide.

The PR firm had been caught practising the antithesis of what it preached. As one of the leading lights in the PR sector, Edelman was involved in framing best practice guidelines for online communications and members of its leadership team had lectured others on the need for openness and integrity in the blogosphere to enable people to judge for themselves if they were reading material that was being presented through the filter of vested interests or bias. So the revelation that the firm had flouted the ethics it espoused was of immense embarrassment and laid it open to allegations of hypocrisy. Such allegations were personally felt as, despite its global standing, Edelman is a family business, set up in Chicago in 1952 by Dan Edelman, one of the pioneers and all-time greats in the field of PR.

I had the pleasure of meeting Dan Edelman at his company's London offices in 2002 when I interviewed him for a profile piece published in the *Financial Times* to mark the agency's 50th birthday. Then a sprightly 82-year-old, Edelman was still working a demanding five-day week as company chairman, continuing to share his expertise with staff and clients, having stood aside as chief executive a mere six years earlier when he handed over the reins of power to his eldest son, Richard. At the time, Dan, who sadly passed away in January 2013, was characteristically more interested in looking to the future instead of dwelling on his numerous past achievements. He was keen to talk up the growing maturity of PR as a discipline and predicted a bright outlook for the Edelman business on the basis that clients were still discovering its values and potential impact. 'We feel that public relations will increasingly be important because our business is based on establishing relationships with stakeholders, whether they are customers, employees, shareholders, the financial community or regulators,' Dan elaborated to me with an entrepreneurial twinkle in his eye. It's safe to surmise that the model for relationships he alluded to in 2002 was rather more transparent than the astroturfing duplicity that emerged four years later. To make matters worse for itself in 2006, Edelman broke another golden rule of PR by taking its time to respond to the crisis, allowing speculation and criticism of its actions to accrue unanswered for several days. It was a full week after the *Businessweek* story ran that Richard Edelman, himself a noted blogger, wrote in his influential blog: 'I want to acknowledge our error in failing to be transparent about the identity of the two bloggers from the outset. This is 100% our responsibility and our error; not the client's.' It's a jarring chapter in its long history that Edelman would like to see buried, presumably beneath natural turf.

But here I am, digging it up once again. Despite the embarrassing nature of the episode for his business, when I get in touch with him in the USA, Richard Edelman is kind enough to share his thoughts on the matter with me:

> 'You have to be transparent on sponsor and funding: always, whether in mainstream or social or blogs. We had not done a good enough job of educating our global Edelman team on this fundamental principle. This was a collective failure that we have remedied through continuing education and strong quality control.'

Bribes, undisclosed relationships and sock puppetry - Utkonos, *SZ* and more

Among the other cases of astroturfing that have come to light in recent years is a campaign by Russian online retailer Utkonos, which in 2007 paid prominent bloggers on LiveJournal, a very popular social media platform in Russia, to simultaneously publish text praising the company for its high quality, low prices and fast delivery. When other bloggers deduced from the broadly identical nature of the posts that this was essentially hidden advertising, they began to criticise the bloggers paid by Utkonos for being greedy and underhand, and attacked Utkonos for running a rotten, deceitful campaign. Reputable media take care to make a clear distinction between editorial and advertising content – which from the standpoint of brands seeking exposure can also be differentiated as 'earned' versus 'paid-for' coverage. To make distinguishing between the two straightforward, any advertising created in an editorial style should be marked up with the words 'advertorial', 'advertisement feature' or similar.

In Russia, although the media landscape has changed tremendously in the post-Soviet era, some ethical and reporting integrity question marks remain. The NGO Reporters Without Borders ranked Russia a lowly 148th out of 179 nations in its *Press Freedom Index 2013* (in case you're wondering, Somalia, Syria, Turkmenistan, North Korea and Eritrea were the five lowest-ranked nations). There is even a specific Russian word for bribery in exchange for media coverage: *zakazukha*. Indeed, in 2001, when the International Public Relations Association (IPRA) launched its Campaign for Media Transparency, designed to reduce unethical practices in the media such as bribery and astroturfing, IPRA's president at the time, Alasdair Sutherland, continually referred to the initiative as the fight against *zakazukha*. (At this point, given that this is a chapter all about openness and honesty, I think it prudent to declare that I have worked on a freelance basis as IPRA's head of editorial content for over a decade ... and in all that time have never been offered a single bribe. Not even to write about IPRA here!)

The IPRA campaign inspired a Media Transparency Charter which has been adopted by PR practitioners and media outlets across the globe. Yet despite the guidelines and good intentions, there will always be instances of dubious or unethical behaviour, with the blogosphere, review sites and citizen journalists often top of the hit list in those markets where traditional media outlets are hard to corrupt. In 2009, an employee of technology company Belkin was caught offering to pay people to write positive reviews of the company's products, while in the same year Honda was criticised for astroturfing when it published pictures of its new Crosstour vehicle on its Facebook page: the car's design met with a wave of negative comments, which were then countered by some incredibly positive views – the latter, it was soon discovered, had been written by a Honda product manager who had failed to mention his status in the company when posting his praise. Plenty of restaurants, hotels, musicians – and authors! – have benefited from favourable reviews from friends and family on sites such as Amazon and TripAdvisor over the years, and of course many of these reviews have been far from objective and impartial. There have even been occasions when authors themselves have created fake online identities to sing the praises of their own work or trash the literary efforts of rival writers; a grubby, clandestine practice known as 'sock puppetry'. Shame on you, historian Orlando Figes, crime writer Stephen Leather and other abusers of reviewing integrity – beware the zombie Lamb Chop, slippery Pinocchio and other malevolent puppets haunting your dreams! However, consumers are in the main alert to such unsophisticated, small-scale goings-on and are eminently capable of disregarding information that strikes them as insincere.

It is when more powerful marketing machinery is applied to such antics that people feel greater cause for concern. This reminds me of the snide old joke that gives the definition of PR as organised lying. For obvious reasons, consumers do not warm to the notion of a concerted effort to pull the wool over their eyes. In 2010, one of Germany's leading newspapers, *Süddeutsche Zeitung* (*SZ*), gave the impression that it was trying to do just that when using the blogosphere to promote the launch of its new iPhone app. *SZ* brought in Swiss social media marketing agency Trigami to help it create a buzz. Trigami had a network of 15,000 bloggers with which it seeded content. In this instance, Trigami paid selected bloggers to write positively about the app and even gave them modules of pre-prepared text to drop in so that it required minimal effort. When one blogger spilled the beans, the story was quickly picked up by *SZ*'s competitors, who wrote negative articles about *SZ* buying positive reviews. Hardly the kind of behaviour one would expect from a quality newspaper that would be expected to stand firm in defending the honesty and integrity of critics and reviewers writing on its own pages. *SZ* stopped the campaign immediately due to the damaging criticism. Its editorial staff, who pride themselves on scrupulous journalism, were dismayed that their reputation for fairness and impartiality had been undermined in this way. In a timely demonstration of its editorial objectivity, the news outlet reported on its own blunder under the blunt heading *Unsuccessful Marketing*. That must have hurt.

How, then, did a sophisticated media owner manage to cook up such an amateurish mess for itself? Peter Bilz-Wohlgemuth, the senior product manager responsible for online marketing at *SZ* apologised and explained that the problem had been caused by a misunderstanding during the briefing process. When talking to Trigami, Bilz-Wohlgemuth had expressed the hope that the campaign would deliver many positive reviews. This sentiment was misinterpreted by a member of staff at Trigami, who implemented an advertorial campaign designed to ensure that the content would be uniformly (some might say mindlessly) positive instead of arranging for bloggers to write independent, warts-and-all reviews. Participating bloggers were also told to write favourable comments about the product on the Apple App Store. Although Trigami – which in 2011 merged with social media advertising company ebuzzing – had instructed its bloggers to highlight the fact that the *SZ* app 'review' was part of a promotional campaign, this wasn't always very clear. Trigami founder Remo Uherek released a statement apologising for the failure of his agency's internal quality controls that led to it running the advertorial campaign rather than implementing what the client intended. This was an uncomfortable episode for both parties.

SZ did not set out to deliberately deceive. However, the margins between what the public is comfortable with and what it considers dubious can be fine indeed. People had greater expectations of the *SZ* brand than what they detected in its behaviour in the blogosphere: a newspaper that would undoubtedly take the moral high ground if, say, it was publishing a story on a political party buying votes, should not appear to be buying reviews. Brands are built on belief. Any marketing behaviour that undermines that belief is a danger to the future health of a brand.

No right to be there

- In 2009 a tourism promotion campaign for landlocked Canadian province Alberta featured images of a beach in Northumberland, UK. When the faux pas came to light an Alberta government official apologised for having 'screwed up'. Capitalising on an unplanned PR opportunity, Northumberland Tourism declared itself thrilled that Alberta was 'promoting the beauty of the North of England, which is often neglected'.
- French government agency HADOPI, which was set up to police copyright protection on the internet, came into being following a convoluted legislative process. In January 2010, France's Minister of Culture Frédéric Mitterand unveiled HADOPI's logo, remarking that the new agency 'finally had a face'. Within hours it came to light that the logo made use of a custom typeface created by graphic designer Jean François Porchez and belonging to France Télécom. HADOPI hadn't sought the copyright owner's permission to use it. This would have been embarrassing for any organisation, but for an anti-piracy body it was excruciatingly farcical. HADOPI's design agency Plan Créativ had to quickly rework the logo using a different typeface.
- In September 2012, US health insurance company Health Net got some rough treatment in the media for a billboard campaign when it transpired it was using fake customer testimonial tweets in the ads to praise its health plans. Feel a bit sick, anyone?

Tips and lessons

- Photoshop should not be used to deceive.
- Never lie to the public, even if that means losing an element of impact or surprise in a campaign. Long-term brand reputation is more important than short-term gain.

- Be transparent in all your marketing and communications activities.
- Don't infringe anyone else's copyright.
- Ensure your advertising is accurate and truthful.
- Make sure no one publishes advertising/promotional material pertaining to your brand without your explicit permission.

Chapter 8

Wide of the mark

Patronised consumers, mistargeted products and inharmonious partnerships

Targeting is crucial, even for brands with broad appeal. Simply put, if you don't know who a product or service is for, how can you position or promote it properly? And if you have no insights into your audience, how on earth can you motivate them to buy? Big brands do a lot of market segmentation and of course target audiences can be defined by all manner of characteristics such as age, gender, location, shopping history, income, values and many behavioural attributes. Defining and understanding a core target audience provides firm foundations for the development of new products and marketing communications campaigns.

One of the biggest asks in marketing is to take a brand associated with a particular target audience, with all the perceptions and baggage that entails, and make it appealing to another audience. This is what car maker Mercedes has sought to do with its A-Class series. Mercedes has long been associated with the sedate, luxury end of the car market and its buyers consequently tend to be older, more affluent consumers. With the new A-Class, one of its most important launches for decades, Mercedes is aiming for a younger demographic and needs to liven up its brand for a Generation Y audience (those born in the early 1980s or later). Armed with the insight that younger adults expect to drive content and conversations — as much as they like driving good cars — a Twitter-led TV ad was created by agencies Maxus and AMV BBDO. Mercedes' #YouDrive jumped on the dual-screen trend. On Twitter, viewers steered the course of the action in a real-time story told over commercials shown during *X Factor*, for example choosing between options #hide and #evade shown on different screens, with the most popular hashtag tweeted determining how the pursuit sequence would progress. With the Gen Y demographic in mind, the commercial was shot on the streets of Lisbon and told the story of an urban music star and his female companion trying to get to a secret gig that the authorities want to close down. It's a marked counterpoint to the impeccably groomed, smug executive listening to a string quartet on the sophisticated in-car entertainment system while gliding serenely along empty scenic roads that one might otherwise presume to see in a Mercedes spot. A couple of months after launch, the A-Class had taken 6.2% of the UK hatchback market, and 77,000 leads had been generated. Significantly, the average age of people enquiring about the A-Class was ten years younger than the typical Mercedes-Benz average, an indication that the targeting had worked.

However, taking aim is no guarantee you'll hit your target. Some who have tried and failed might wish they'd picked up a scattergun and fired wildly into the air instead.

Hurray for the demise of Animée - Molson Coors misjudges the market

The Animée story starts in 2009 with the formation of the BitterSweet Partnership by the UK arm of Molson Coors Brewing Company. BitterSweet's *raison d'être* was to find ways to make beer more appealing to women. Research showed that women accounted for only 17% of beer sales in the UK and that 79% of women either rarely or never drank beer. Further data led Molson Coors to believe that with the right female-friendly beer product, it could tap into a £400m market. The company initiated a major two-year new product development programme with consumer insight at its heart. Over 30,000 women were questioned about why they don't drink beer, with the brewer seizing on a finding that many women believe that all beers look and taste the same and therefore struggle to tell them apart. This insight underpinned the product formulation and packaging strategy.

In autumn 2011 Molson Coors launched its carefully researched new beer with the support of a £2m advertising campaign bearing the strapline 'Hurray for Animée'. The 'light sparkling, finely filtered' bottled beer had an ABV of 4% and was available in three variants: Clear Filtered, Zesty Lemon and Crisp Rosé. Product design was unashamedly feminine, rather like putting Cath Kidston in charge of reimagining the livery for JCB. Bottle labels and multi-pack design featured muted blues and silvers, teamed in the case of the flavoured variants with lemon or pink graphical elements in keeping with the drink's colour. The main label illustration, presumably intended to put a feminine twist on the beer's ingredients, resembled a floral arrangement by the Women's Institute, possibly destined for the local church hall. Hopefully the creators of such pretty things, already exhausted by the terrible mental effort of trying to distinguish between different beers, were able to rest their dainty hands for a while so as to be refreshed before getting on with further gender-appropriate activities such as cupcake decoration and making themselves presentable in time for the man of the house's return.

The brand plan was for Animée to be positioned as feminine and sophisticated, without being patronising. Unfortunately a large chunk of the target audience felt very patronised indeed. Although there is a rich tradition of fruit-flavoured beers, most famously Belgian lambic-style beers, the Animée variants came across as contrived, appearing to have been formulated to pigeonhole women based on assumptions about the flavours many enjoy in other categories, for example wine, rather than evolving out of a genuine brewing heritage. For many, this made Animée seem phoney, and more like an alcopop than a real beer. In a piece for the *Guardian*'s 'Word of Mouth' food blog, Sophie Atherton wrote that rather than breaking down the barriers between women and beer Animée merely succeeded in producing a bottle that 'looks like it contains sparkling water' and wondered whether the £2m launch advertising budget wouldn't have been better spent on staging events to introduce women to Molson Coors' existing beers.

Meanwhile, on tasting the product, respected beer expert Melissa Cole went as far as to pronounce, 'If anyone can identify anything even approaching a normal beer flavour in any of these drinks I'll eat my hat,' and later offered to happily bury any remaining bottles by digging a hole with her own bare hands. Somehow I doubt she'd need the assistance of smelling salts to get the job done. Faced with sluggish sales, apathy and derision, a year after launch Molson Coors bowed to the inevitable and announced it was withdrawing Animée from the UK market and disbanding BitterSweet. While the product may not have tasted bitter, the experience did – the Animée brand had failed.

Patronising your target audience is never a smart move and Molson Coors was undoubtedly guilty of that. Moreover, in positioning the product so blatantly as a beer for women, the brewer ensured that it alienated male drinkers. Considering that men constitute the overwhelming majority of the beer market this wasn't a very commercially astute direction to take. Yet for brewers with an eye on growth, increasing the size of the female beer market remains a realistic ambition. There is little to suggest that more women can't be persuaded to drink beer, and indeed some beer brands in the UK and elsewhere have proved adept at attracting female consumers. One of the biggest turn-offs female consumers have is the sexist nature of a lot of mainstream beer advertising, which sends out the signal that this is a product that is not for them. The answer to converting more women into consumers of beer is more likely to lie in giving authentic brands cross-gender relevance than in brewing up the alcoholic equivalent of fake lashes.

Bic's belittling biro – a poison pen response from unimpressed women

Molson Coors is by no means alone in developing product targeted at women only to endure a backlash from an audience resenting the perpetuation of stereotypes. The Bic for Her pen was mocked by consumers who strove to outdo each other by posting sarcastic product reviews on the Amazon website. Bic's perception of its target audience appeared to be that they were women who, each time they looked in the mirror, saw a Barbie princess reflected back at them. Available in a range of pretty pastel colours such as pink and purple, and presented as having a slimline barrel 'designed to fit comfortably in a woman's hand', the targeting of Bic for Her pens was undeniably adept at provoking a reaction. The trouble was, that reaction was an overwhelmingly facetious one as women vented their displeasure at being lumped into a feeble damsel in distress or vacuous homemaker demographic. Not wanting to miss out on the Bic-baiting fun, men joined in as well and before long there were hundreds of humorous reviews on Amazon.

'It would be hyperbolic to say that I woke up the next morning to a brand new me,' wrote reviewer Amy Hudson. 'In reality, it took about 3–4 days for the changes to become apparent. I started wearing tighter clothes and impracticable shoes. On the third night, my hair grew six inches, going from a manageable shoulder skimming bob to a length that requires much more work and hair care products. The men at the office see me differently as well! Finally, I am getting compliments on the way I look instead of my abilities!'

While another reviewer chimed in with: 'My husband has never allowed me to write, as he doesn't want me touching men's pens. However when I saw this product, I decided to buy it (using my pocket money) and so far it has been fabulous! Once I had learnt to write, the feminine colour and the grip size, which was more suited to my delicate little hands, has enabled me to vent thoughts about new recipe ideas, sewing and gardening. My husband is less pleased with this product as he believes it will lead to more independence and he hates the feminine tingling sensation (along with the visions of fairies and rainbows) he gets whenever he picks it up.'

Reviews in this vein continue for page after page. To anyone unconnected with the Bic brand, it's a lot of fun. And of course this kind of reaction is not without precedent. The Veet for Men hair removal brand has also found itself the butt, if I can use that word in the context of the product, of a flurry of excoriating humour as reviewers poked fun at its potency. If you are tempted to check these out, be warned: they are hilarious but crude.

The big difference between Veet and Bic is that while reviews of the former centre on male ineptitude regarding product usage – and in fact many praise the product's depilatory effectiveness – Bic was being roundly condemned for its patronising approach to women. As the reviews mounted up, bloggers and media outlets took notice and stories about the criticism began to appear across the internet. Inevitably, this encouraged even more people to write scathing reviews, triggering yet more coverage elsewhere.

Bic neglected to secure the @bicforher Twitter handle, leaving the way clear for a parody account to emerge. By October 2012, traditional media were getting in on the act. Comedian Ellen DeGeneres devoted a monologue to Bic for Her on the *Ellen* TV show, even shooting a spoof commercial ironically lauding the pen for being able 'to stand up to all your wild mood swings'. Bic's reputation was taking a pounding because it was targeting a product in a way that implicitly belittled many of the people it wanted to win over.

As it happens, this is not the only Bic product launch to have left the brand with its knickers in a twist. Back in the 1970s consumers were bemused as Bic, having successfully extended from pens into disposable lighters, stretched its brand too far by launching disposable underwear. Disposability aside, people struggled to see much connection between Bic's existing product line and a move into undergarments. In fact, to many it seemed plain weird and the brand extension swiftly flopped. A cheap fragrance, Parfum Bic, also proved short-lived. Although targeted as a value for money drugstore scent in the USA, and supported by a multi-million dollar marketing budget, Parfum Bic still missed the mark. Even at the value end of the fragrance market, consumers desire a degree of sophistication, allure and mystique – qualities not typically associated with throwaway plastic lighters and inexpensive ballpoint pens.

History has a strange way of repeating itself, as can be seen by the launch of Zippo the Woman perfume, licensed from lighter brand Zippo – and voted the worst brand extension of 2012 in an *Adweek* reader survey in association with Parham Santana.

Given that it has been synonymous with stationery since the launch of its Cristal ballpoint in 1950, Bic is arguably on far safer ground when focusing on pens. Yet as the mistakes made with Bic for Her illustrate, it's foolish to take a target audience for granted.

The Dodge La Femme - by appointment to her majesty . . . the American woman

I'd love to know what racing driver Danica Patrick makes of the Dodge La Femme. Back in the 1950s, Chrysler was trying to figure out how to appeal to the growing number of women taking an interest in cars. World War II heralded enormous changes in American society, with millions of women entering the workforce, and in the post-war years brand owners were keen to exploit an increasingly independent and self-confident female market. With this in mind, Chrysler launched the Dodge La Femme in 1955, a vehicle based on its Custom Royal Lancer model. But, just as Animée and Bic were to do over half a century later, it overdid the daintiness. Marketed as the first fine car exclusively for women, the 1955 model had a two-tone rose pink and white exterior, while the interior featured richly woven Jacquard fabric with a pastel rose tapestry design. A 'stylish' rain cape, 'chic' umbrella and 'stunning' fitted shoulder bag – all in a shade of pink matched to the car – came as part of the package. The four-page dealer brochure, in which pink was prominent once again, had the obsequious coverline, 'By appointment to her majesty … the American woman' on a ribbon-like background over an illustration of a glamorous lady. The content of the brochure wasn't spoilt by any grubby, tedious facts about engine capacity or fuel economy, but fortunately there was room enough to talk about 'dainty rain boots for unexpected showers'. Probably not a phrase Jeremy Clarkson has had occasion to use when reviewing a car.

By way of context, it should be pointed out that the 1950s was the decade that culminated in the launch of the Barbie doll. And it was not until 1963 that Betty Friedan published *The Feminine Mystique*, that landmark work in modern feminist writing. Yet even in this era before the women's liberation movement emerged, Dodge's positioning of La Femme came across as condescending. The cars attracted little interest in showrooms and sales were slow. After just two years, Dodge's female-focused vehicle was axed. Marketing a car on the basis of its pretty accessories really didn't make a lot of sense. What came across was a very patronising, masculine view of what women should like about a car. Even in the pre-women's lib 1950s, women weren't buying it.

Skincare in the dairy aisle - Danone gets its distribution strategy wrong

Functional foods, or nutraceuticals as they are sometimes called, have evolved into a big business. An increasing overlap between the fields of nutrition and healthcare has seen a boom in new food products formulated to offer general wellness or even disease prevention and control benefits. According to a study by Transparency Market Research, the global nutraceutical market was worth $142.1bn in 2011 and is expected to reach $204.8bn by 2017. There is serious money to be made.

In 2007 French food giant Danone went for a piece of the action with the launch of yoghurt brand Essensis in France and several other European countries. Yoghurt is a mainstay of the Danone business and there were high hopes that this latest addition to its dairy brands portfolio would perform well. Essensis, though, was no ordinary yoghurt. Its ingredients included borage oil, vitamin E and green tea extract. Amid claims that regular consumption would beautify the skin, it was positioned as an edible cosmetics product. A high-profile multi-million-euro French TV ad campaign showed young women not only eating the product but flaunting their flawless complexions and delightedly stroking their wrinkle-free faces while admiring their reflections – in a spoon! The commercial talked up the antioxidant and probiotic nature of the product and cited scientific evidence for its efficacy. It even included a short sequence of on-screen graphics to illustrate skin being refreshed by consumption of the yoghurt. This celebration of eating for the sake of beauty finished with the rhyming tagline 'nourrit votre peux de l'intérieur' – 'nourishes your skin from within'. The slogan also made its way on to product packaging.

Although the product was positioned as radically different due to its beauty claims, Danone pursued a conventional yoghurt distribution strategy. Essensis appeared on supermarket shelves alongside established mass-market yoghurts, where its beauty claims were an uneasy fit and its premium pricing, compared to other products in the yoghurt category, made it appear expensive. The advent of the global economic downturn certainly didn't help matters, as European consumers began to weigh up purchases more carefully. But what really doomed the brand was the way Danone mishandled targeting. In our beauty-obsessed world there probably is a place for a product like Essensis; however, that place is somewhere more stylish and exclusive than the supermarket. After an initial burst of interest after launch, sales of Essensis began to decline. Danone tinkered with product taste, but the changes it made had little impact on the downward trend of the sales graph. In 2009, two years after its high-profile debut, Danone withdrew Essensis.

Danone may have blundered in the yoghurt aisle, but it is actually a sophisticated player in the functional foods market. In the same year it launched Essensis, Danone acquired medical nutrition company Nutricia and has steadily grown turnover at that business by around 10% a year, to the point where Nutricia generates well over €1bn in annual revenue and is a healthily (what else?) profitable part of the Danone empire. Where Nutricia excels is in delivering products that have specialist benefits – some of which may only be used under medical supervision. A huge part of its marketing revolves around building relationships with patient and professional groups. That's a very different and much more effective targeting model than was the case with Essensis.

Bring on the singing Spongmonkeys – Quiznos' mascots too creepy for many

Denver-based fast-service restaurant chain Quiznos built its reputation on toasted sandwiches and developed its business using the franchising model so popular in the fast food sector. Today Quiznos restaurants can be found all over the USA and in 25 other countries, although tougher economic times precipitated the closure of around a thousand outlets between 2007 and 2009. It is very much a challenger brand when compared against the market leader, Subway.

In 2004 Quiznos and its ad agency, the Martin Agency, set out to make its brand seem cooler to 18–24-year-olds. The answer to their brief seemed to lie across the Atlantic in London, where web animator and singer-songwriter Joel Veitch was demonstrating his knack for creating entertaining memes popular with young audiences. Veitch was behind the creation of the Spongmonkeys, a bulbous-eyed pair of furry creatures partial to shrieking out humorous songs in videos that were animated in an intentionally jerky style that made the creatures look as if they were levitating. One of these videos was for a Veitch-penned song called *We Like the Moon*, in which the Spongmonkeys sang not only of their affection for the celestial body but also of their random liking for cheese and zeppelins and marmots. The song was reworked for a Quiznos TV commercial as *We Love the Subs*, with the Spongmonkeys this time considerably more focused in singing their approval of tasty, crunchy, warm toasted sandwiches. They also sang about the 'pepper bar' that is a popular feature of Quiznos restaurants. As the Spongmonkeys were already a proven viral internet hit, Quiznos harboured hopes that they would catch on as memorable brand icons, even referring to them as 'spokesthings'.

What Quiznos hadn't bargained for was how negatively the Spongmonkeys would be perceived by many consumers. While the raw quirkiness of the work struck a chord with a young audience, many older consumers didn't much like the idea of a restaurant chain promoting itself using characters that reminded them of rats. Screechy, bulgy-eyed rats at that. Viral internet success story they may have been, but the Spongmonkeys weren't playing well to middle-aged Middle America. Quiznos received around thirty thousand calls and emails about the campaign, and traffic to its website quadrupled, so the Spongmonkeys were certainly effective at capturing attention, although opinion was deeply divided as to whether they were fun brand critters or repulsive tuneless vermin.

Polarising ad campaigns get talked about and can be very good for business. However, this wasn't the case here. Down on the ground, a lot of Quiznos franchisees weren't happy with what was happening. 'In our area we've had nothing but negative comments and sales will prove that it hurt business,' Huey Mack, owner of a Quiznos franchise in Mobile, Alabama railed to the media. Another franchisee in Texas complained to the *Houston Chronicle*: 'They said the ad did well with test groups. But how can that be? It's putting me out of business. I've lost customers.' Elsewhere, other franchisees were getting fed up with fielding complaints about the commercial, and several put up signs in their restaurants directing anyone wishing to complain to corporate head office. In their view, distancing themselves from the brand advertising was a necessary move to protect business. And in any case, they'd had enough of dealing with questions about why rats would be used to advertise a restaurant.

Amid growing franchisee unrest and mounting consumer complaints, Quiznos pulled the Spongmonkeys campaign from mainstream national networks. However, the commercials continued to air on MTV for a while longer. This speaks volumes because the fundamental problem here was one of mistargeting. If the strange creature that is a Spongmonkey has a natural habitat, it is the internet. Beyond that, it is also capable of flourishing in an environment with broadly similar conditions, such as music TV, where the viewer demographic *just gets it*. In relation to generating buzz through its advertising, Quiznos did a good job, and it was a bold move to experiment with an internet viral style on mainstream TV. Lots of twenty-somethings and teens loved it; plenty of more mature consumers didn't like it at all. The commercial is still remembered – though not always fondly – for its originality. In 2011, the Spongmonkeys found a place in a *Time* magazine feature on the 'Top 10 Creepiest Product Mascots' of all time. Personally, I like the ad and the reason for doing it. There's sound logic in a challenger brand with a limited marketing budget taking a novel approach to TV advertising to achieve standout. If they'd stuck to targeting a youthful demographic with the Spongmonkeys, this campaign could have been a real winner.

Defining and understanding a target market is absolutely fundamental to marketing, for both product development strategy and message delivery. Data analytics tools allow for audiences to be segmented as never before and market research is more sophisticated than ever. All the same, it's still easy to get targeting terribly wrong. Businesses usually understand themselves far better than they understand their prospects and customers. We live in an age of personalised one-to-one marketing communication *and* 'big data', in which we risk being swamped by the sheer volume of information being dispersed. The danger here is that marketers end up formulating strategies on the basis of data that is so broad as to be meaningless or so narrow as to define segments too specific to be commercially viable. A target market profile should always ring true. Once it does, there's no excuse for offending or baffling your target audience. Otherwise you end up bewildering Middle America with Spongmonkeys, asking French shoppers to search for beauty products amid the Greek yoghurt or patronising British women with girly beer.

Off-message partnerships – from fallen heroes to unsuitable tie-ups

In the arduous sport of competitive cycling, Lance Armstrong endured his share of crashes that inflicted painful 'road rash' on his body as it skidded along the tarmac. But no fall from a bike will have hurt the Texan as much as his fall from grace after his admission of doping following years of rumours that he was a drugs cheat. Disgraced, stripped of his unequalled seven Tour de France titles, panned for his lack of candour even when giving a confessional interview to Oprah, it was inevitable that sponsors such as Nike, Trek cycles, RadioShack and energy food brand Honey Stinger would turn their backs on him. Where Armstrong was once the yellow jersey-wearing golden boy of cycling, the iron-willed team leader whose astounding deeds on two wheels following recovery from cancer were matched only by his epic fundraising prowess, now he was damaged goods; tainted, imbued with too many negatives for his face to be comfortably associated with prominent brands.

The Armstrong revelations also led to Dutch bank Rabobank pulling out of the sport of which it had been a prominent sponsor for 17 years, following several doping scandals on its own team. Despite ending its title sponsorship with immediate effect, Rabobank honoured its financial contract with the Netherlands-based professional team, allowing riders to compete as part of the unbranded Blanco Pro team in the early part of 2013 before Belkin stepped in as a new title sponsor on the eve of the 100th Tour de France.

I'm a big fan of the sport, so cycling's problems with substance abuse fill me with sadness – particularly for the many clean athletes who sacrifice so much in their punishing training routines only to be unfairly suspected of cheating. Although he understood the reasons for them, it was clearly galling for 2013 Tour de France winner Chris Froome to have to deal with questions about doping from the sports press pack day after day throughout the three-week duration of the race. In the post-Armstrong era, cycling has embraced more rigorous anti-doping measures and it's reasonable to conclude that it is a far cleaner sport than it has been in a generation. Given that the Grand Tours in particular – the Tour de France, Vuelta a España and Giro d'Italia – are among the world's great sporting events, they present wonderful marketing opportunities.

In the wake of Tiger Woods' extramarital affair in 2009, AT&T, Accenture and others bailed out of their sponsorships of the golf superstar rather than risk having their good names undermined by reflected ignominy. Nike stood by Woods, taking the stance that his problems were not relevant to his sporting conduct, but was less forgiving of sprinters Marion Jones and Justin Gatlin, who, like Armstrong, saw their athletic achievements discredited due to their entanglement in doping scandals.

Dealing with controversy has been a recurring theme for Nike. In 2007, Nike terminated its sponsorship contract with National Football League star quarterback Michael Vick of the Atlanta Falcons after he pleaded guilty to participating in an illegal dogfighting ring. Vick served 20 months in jail but on his release made a successful return to the NFL with his new team, the Philadelphia Eagles, and in 2011 was re-signed by Nike, which told CNN, 'We support the positive changes he has made to better himself off the field.' When Oscar Pistorius was arrested for murder in February 2013, the sports gear maker had to get out of the blocks like lightning – the ad it was running on the South African Paralympian's website bore the headline 'I am the bullet in the chamber.' In light of the charges laid against Pistorius, this ad was suddenly wholly inappropriate and was removed forthwith.

Sponsorships and celebrity partnerships can be a hugely effective way for brands to heighten profile, whip up interest and garner kudos. Yet if a scandal occurs or the relationship goes off message, it can lead to serious problems. Here are some more tie-ups that turned out to have a notable downside.

- Car insurance company Churchill has twice dropped comedians from its TV ads after they picked up driving bans. Vic Reeves was penalised for drink driving in 2005, while Martin Clunes was disqualified in 2012 after repeatedly being caught speeding. Not an unreasonable course of action for a company in the business of rewarding safe motorists with favourable premiums. Clunes thought otherwise. 'I was very surprised by their reaction,' he complained in a 2013 interview with the *Radio Times*. 'It was neurotic and very heavy-handed. Quite rude, actually. They never said goodbye. They never said thanks.' Thanks for taking our money and then embarrassing us?

- When Germany's leading poultry brand Wiesenhof announced a two-year shirt sponsorship of Werder Bremen in August 2012 it prompted the resignation of the Bundesliga football club's 'environment ambassador', the prominent Green Party politician and celebrity fan Jürgen Trittin, in protest at the new sponsor's factory farming practices. In his letter of resignation to Werder Bremen's President, Klaus-Dieter Fischer, which attracted abundant media coverage, Trittin outlined his views on the dangers of intensive mass animal farming for the environment and concluded with the words '*Lebenslang Werder – kein Tag Wiesenhof*', which can be translated as 'Werder lifelong – Wiesenhof never'. The sponsorship furore was followed by an undistinguished season for the team on the pitch.

- A 1988 US TV commercial for beer brand Michelob starred rock guitar legend Eric Clapton. Although the soundtrack to the ad is excellent, Clapton was an unlikely choice of brand ambassador given his long-standing battle with alcoholism, including a spell in rehab earlier in the decade. Clapton has since set up the Crossroads treatment centre for drug and alcohol addiction on the Caribbean island of Antigua.

- In September 2012, the world-famous Tivoli Gardens amusement park and pleasure gardens in Denmark announced that Kopenhagen Fur would be its official Christmas partner for three years. As part of the deal, a shop selling fur garments was opened at the leisure attraction. 'It is a perfect showcase where we can demonstrate why Danish mink farmers are the world's elite,' said Kopenhagen Fur CEO Torben Nielsen at the launch of the partnership. Anti-fur campaigners responded with demonstrations of their own, staging a torchlight protest outside the park gates on the opening night of the 2012 Christmas season and launching an online petition calling for the partnership to be dissolved.

- Kerry Katona, singer with pop group Atomic Kitten and reality TV star, has seen many of the turbulent ups and downs of her personal life played out in the spotlight. In 2008, she was declared bankrupt at the High Court in London after failing to pay a tax bill. Given her well-known history of money problems, payday loans company PDB, which trades as Cash Lady, decided that Katona would be the ideal public face of its brand as many of its customers had financial difficulties of their own and would therefore be able to relate to her. Katona duly fronted a TV commercial with the strapline 'Fast Cash for Fast Lives'. In May 2013, after receiving 30 complaints about the campaign, the ASA banned the ad, labelling it irresponsible and concluding that by playing on Katona's celebrity status Cash Lady might lead some vulnerable viewers to believe that high-interest payday loans could be used to fund the kind of lavish lifestyle enjoyed by the rich and famous. Katona was eventually dropped as the face of Cash Lady when she filed for bankruptcy a second time in July 2013.

Infineon takes the wrong track

In 1999 the German engineering and electronics giant Siemens spun off its semiconductor business into an entirely new company called Infineon Technologies. During its subsequent IPO in 2000, Infineon CEO Ulrich Schumacher dressed in motor racing overalls and drove a Porsche race car along Wall Street to mark the company's stock exchange listing. To a small degree, this was a nod to the CEO's namesake, Formula One multiple world champion Michael Schumacher, but for the most part it was an opportunity for the boss to indulge his passion for motor racing by weaving it into the publicity activity surrounding his company's switch to public ownership. A keen amateur racer himself, the CEO even had an old Porsche engine on display in his office and roped racing legend Mario Andretti into his New York Stock Exchange stunt. Determined to deepen his company's involvement with motor sport, in 2002 Schumacher oversaw the signing of a sponsorship deal which entailed renaming Sonoma Raceway in California – a track that stages NASCAR and IndyCar events – the Infineon Raceway. Although Infineon supplies chips to the automotive industry, the sponsorship was a poor choice for a fledgling technology brand looking to build its presence in the business-to-business market. Race fans were in no way its primary audience. In March 2004 Schumacher was peremptorily ousted from the Infineon board, and later that year Rainer Westermann was lured from his job running Burson-Marsteller in Germany to take up the position of Corporate Vice President, Communications with responsibility for marketing communications, branding, PR and sponsorship. What he found on arrival horrified him.

> 'The company continued to invest heavily in racing sponsoring even after several years of only losing money. With the contract [to rename the Sonoma Raceway] came the right to create paraphernalia with the Infineon logo. Soon, the brand became associated with the raceway rather than the company. When our people were asked at the US border who they worked for, inevitably, the reaction [from immigration staff] was "NASCAR". Even the Wall Street Journal ran a story, "Infineon adds new races to portfolio." In a presentation designed to convince me to continue with the investment, the racetrack management argued that they generated $25m worth of advertising equivalent. My response was that that was part of the problem, because Infineon had a marketing communications budget of less than $2m per year in the USA.'
>
> Rainer Westermann, Corporate Vice President,
> Communications, Infineon

Infineon's marketing messages were being drowned out by the sound of souped-up engines and distorted by the passion of race fans.

That the sponsorship was an ineffective waste of money was bad enough. Worse, corruption issues began to emerge too, as Westermann explains:

'When I became head of communications, race car sponsoring was a liability to Infineon because there were allegations of side deals, personal benefits for senior management. Within my first 12 months we lost a member of the executive board who admitted to the police that he had taken bribes in context with using his office to secure sponsoring deals for the promoter. Race car sponsoring became a symbol of everything that was wrong with Infineon and we paid again good money to get out of our contractual obligations.'

It's all too easy for heads to be turned by glamorous sponsorship opportunities. Supreme athletes and the magnificent cathedrals of modern sport have an undeniable attraction. Yet in the hard-nosed world of business, the only time to succumb to temptations of this kind is if they present marketing answers that are perfectly in line with brand image and corporate goals.

Tips and lessons

- Be clear on who your audience is and how your product sits in the marketplace – segmentation, targeting and positioning are cornerstones of marketing best practice.
- A gap in the market may present an opportunity, but it may also exist because it doesn't warrant filling. Always ensure there is a genuine demand for a product.
- Never patronise your audience.
- Take care to get your distribution strategy and media planning right, so that your product appears to its advantage and your advertising messages hit your target audience with minimal wastage.
- There are risks in pinning brand reputation on a star name. If cheating, criminality, infidelity or other indiscretions occur they can hurt a brand.

Chapter 9

Baffling brand extensions

Daft stretches and crazy category hops

To hit the sweet spot with a brand extension, it needs to be seen by the target market as a logical move. Consumer reaction should be 'Ah! That makes sense!' or, better yet, 'What took them so long?' Pet food brand Iams' expansion into the pet insurance market ticks the boxes in this respect. Although food manufacturing and financial services are markedly different types of business, to the general public the step from animal nutrition to animal health issues is but a small one. Crucially, it is a step that does not put the core values of the Iams brand under strain. Imagine, by contrast, if it had been unleashed into the field of mortgage payment protection cover. It's still an insurance product; but one that sits ill with the brand – unless people have started taking out mortgages on palatial kennels for their furry friends, that is.

In truth, Iams launching mortgage cover would be about as logical as a move into lingerie by bottled water brand Evian. But Evian has already done that. And not just with ordinary underwear. The Evian Water Bra was a short-lived bra/bikini top with a pocket designed to hold water – Evian, presumably – to keep breasts cool. Yes, really. (*Eau* dear!) You can see how they talked themselves into it: 'We're a water brand, and this is an innovative garment that makes great use of what we're about ... water.' Yet while H_2O is the common theme, this is the kind of gimmicky approach that can cheapen rather than enhance a brand in the public's eyes. Evian boobed uncoolly with this one. Someone really ought to have poured cold water all over the idea.

Pursued by a cyber lynch mob - Kraft's Vegemite snack attacked

Here's a little test. Spot the odd one out: iMac, iPod, iPhone, iPad, iSnack 2.0. Almost certainly you'll know it's the last one on the list. Even if you don't recognise the name you'll have picked it by a process of elimination because Apple's pre-eminence in consumer-tech means its big product brands are familiar worldwide. But iSnack 2.0, what *is* that? To me it sounds like a USB-powered treat dispenser. A device you could sync with iTunes so that when certain songs on your playlist begin, it pops out tasty sweets. Yet the truth is rather different – and a whole lot stranger. Would it surprise you to learn that iSnack 2.0 was actually a jar of food? More than that, a new variant of a food product so well established in its country of origin that it is a symbol of national identity? The launch of iSnack 2.0 offers a cautionary tale about how *not* to name a brand extension to an edible national treasure.

That national treasure is Vegemite, a spread made from concentrated yeast extract. It has been popular in Australia for 90 years and is considered a quintessentially Australian product – one that even gets a name check in the international pop hit *Down Under* by Men at Work. Yet despite its iconic status, sales of Vegemite were in decline and there was a weakening of brand equity. Vegemite's owner Kraft Foods had taken its famous brand for granted for some years and it was beginning to show signs of a lack of customer focus. Simon Talbot, Kraft's Director of Corporate Affairs for Australia and New Zealand, realised that some marketing innovation was required and set his brand team to work.

Extensive social media analysis of brand image identified a gap in the market for a line extension involving a blend of Vegemite and another of Kraft's iconic brands, Philadelphia cream cheese. There was already a strong precedent for uniting Vegemite and cheese in the shape of Cheesymite scrolls – bread with cheese and Vegemite – a popular snack that had long been available from bakers in Australia and New Zealand. Research found that consumers would be interested in a product that was easy to eat on the go, and that could be dipped into or spread straight from the jar. The increasingly multicultural nature of Australia meant that there were a growing number of consumers born outside the country who had no cultural connection to Vegemite. By extending the Vegemite range to include a product with a new taste, Kraft hoped to appeal to a younger, more multicultural demographic. It also hoped to develop a product that was appealing throughout the day, whereas the original Vegemite had a strong association with breakfast time. Once Kraft had got the product formulation right, it needed to find a name. Cheesymite was not an option as the trademark was already owned by Australian bakery franchise group Bakers Delight. Talbot and his team decided to involve the Australian public in the search for a name to create a buzz around the product.

In July 2009 jars of Vegemite mixed with cream cheese began appearing in store, promising a 'deliciously different Vegemite experience'. Beneath the Vegemite and Kraft logos was a cut-out label urging consumers to 'Name Me'. Around 48,000 Australians and New Zealanders obligingly submitted suggestions, with a cash prize on offer to the winner. As the weeks rolled by, there was plenty of good-natured speculation about the outcome. During this time, the nameless brand extension performed well, selling around a million jars a month – impressive for a newcomer in a market of just 22 million people. To further ratchet up excitement and awareness, Kraft booked an expensive advertising spot in the middle of the showpiece Australian rules football AFL Grand Final match in which to proudly unveil the new name. And before the ad aired, the name was announced to the crowd in the stadium. As we know, the name chosen from the entries by the marketing team – and which secured unanimous boardroom approval – was iSnack 2.0. It was picked because it alluded to innovation, and no doubt also with an eye on accumulating some reflected glory from Apple's i-range of gadgets.

The reaction was terrible. People thought it was a bad joke, many believing that the true name would be revealed the following day. When the realisation dawned that it wasn't a hoax, Vegemite lovers voiced their indignation on social media. Thousands of Twitter posts attacked the name choice and at least a dozen Facebook groups sprang up in opposition to iSnack 2.0, vilifying Kraft for messing with an Australian icon. Someone even started up a website called 'Names that are better than iSnack 2.0'. Dean Robbins, the 27-year-old graphic designer from Perth who dreamed up the winning name, also came in for some personal abuse from internet trolls. As BBC News Asia Pacific reported, one enraged Vegemite fan said Robbins should be forced to run through the streets of Sydney 'wearing nothing but a generous lathering of old-fashioned Vegemite as retribution for his cultural crime'. With threats being made against him, Kraft took no chances and spirited Robbins and his young family out of Australia for a short break in Bali. Media coverage of the affair was intense and the social media vitriol kept on coming. Kraft had to decide whether to ride out the storm, change the name immediately or let the people vote again for a new name. After three days it reached the conclusion that the iSnack 2.0 name wasn't worth defending and took the latter path.

> 'We were in lockdown and the media just kept at the story. So we had to hand it back over to the public to find a new name. We developed a web page in record time and got 50,000 customer votes in five days. They chose the name Cheesybite. The great irony was that we'd sold three million jars, which is the best trial rate for a consumer product in Australian history, beating Coke Zero. And when we announced the name change, people were out there buying iSnack 2.0 because it was to become a memorabilia item. So many people thought it was all a stunt from the beginning, the most masterfully orchestrated PR stunt in all of history. But it wasn't. The fear of leaking to the nation that we had a new Vegemite stopped appropriate consumer testing; this was a mistake. What we did do right was respond quickly and in a manner befitting a national icon: i.e. let the people decide.'
>
> Simon Talbot, Director of Corporate Affairs for
> Australia and New Zealand, Kraft

At the second time of asking, consumers were presented with a choice of just six names – some of which were popular suggestions from the initial vote. Vegemite Cheesybite proved to be a comfortable winner, taking 36% of the poll, ahead of Vegemite Smooth in second place with 23%. Kraft showed some corporate humility when they held the second vote, using inclusive phrases on its website such as 'Have your say' and 'We've listened and taken on your feedback.' There was clear acknowledgement here that the status of Vegemite as a national treasure meant that the public had a genuine sense of brand ownership.

Domestic reputation management of the Vegemite brand wasn't the only issue on Kraft's plate, however. Larger corporate reputation matters at a global level had to be factored in too. On 7th September 2009 Kraft made a £10bn takeover bid for Cadbury. That bid was swiftly rejected by the Cadbury board. But at the time of the iSnack 2.0 blunder, executives at Kraft were working behind the scenes preparing a hostile bid for the British confectionery group. Given that iSnack 2.0 had become a laughing stock, questions were being asked about the credibility and judgement of the Kraft management team. The situation required swift resolution so as not to undermine Kraft's takeover plans.

Thankfully, the new name for the brand extension steadied the ship. Jars of iSnack 2.0 were snapped up as collectors' items and when the product hit the shelves rebranded as Cheesybite it continued to sell well. Vitally, the new product did not cannibalise sales of the original Vegemite. In fact, the opposite was true – the pattern of a decline in Vegemite sales was reversed, with all the publicity helping drive a temporary 5% rise in sales.

Today, Talbot is still at Kraft – although in the post-Cadbury acquisition era, and under the new corporate umbrella brand Mondelez, it is a far bigger business in Australia now than it was in the iSnack 2.0 days. What's fascinating about iSnack 2.0 is that it was a good product innovation burdened with an atrocious name. The insight behind it was right and as sales show, it has an appealing taste. To its credit, Kraft has maintained a strong focus on innovation in Australia and New Zealand – sometimes successfully, sometimes less so. In 2011 it launched My First Vegemite, a lower-salt, milder-flavoured version of the original product that is aimed at kids. Although well received at first, sales of this brand extension proved disappointing and My First Vegemite was discontinued in 2012.

Looking back, Talbot accepts it was a mistake for Kraft to stage a naming competition (the original one) and then pick as the winner a name that wasn't the most popular choice. It's small wonder that such an approach should trigger public venom. 'We fronted one of the branded world's first cyber-lynchings,' Talbot tells me ruefully.

Don't hold your breath for iSnack 3.0.

Are you single, baby? Gerber goes for an immature line

Had social media been around in the 1970s, without a shadow of a doubt Gerber would have been the victim of a cyber-lynching too. In 1974, the baby food manufacturer attempted to stretch its brand into the adult food market. But the products it brought out seemed as though they belonged in the nursery. Gerber's marketing strategy was to target college students and other single adults with easy meals for one. If you consider the subsequent success of products such as Pot Noodle, there's compelling commercial merit in the idea. However, Gerber neglected to think through what adults would find appealing.

Mediterranean vegetables, creamed beef and blueberry delight were among the savoury and sweet products in the Gerber Singles range. These small servings were sold in jars almost identical to those of Gerber baby foods. The contents seemed pretty similar too: let's hear a big hooray for fruit purée! It's no surprise that American adults didn't respond positively to meals infantilised in this way. Solitarily spooning gooey food out of a jar doesn't call to mind a pleasant culinary experience; nor is it likely to do much for a person's self-esteem. The unsettling – and frankly kind of oddball – sense that this was baby food for lonely adults was accentuated by the Singles name. Just as cigarette brand Strand found to its cost in the 1950s (see page 18), associating a product with loneliness can lead to an early demise. So it proved for Gerber Singles, a brand that had no chance whatsoever of reaching maturity. If it left any sort of legacy, I like to think of it being the inspiration for Eric Carmen's 1975 power ballad, *All By Myself*. Although perhaps a better choice of hit, from the same year, might be Bay City Rollers' *Bye Bye Baby*.

Putting pop songs of yesteryear to one side, Gerber failed because it looked to extend its brand on the basis of what it already had and knew (baby food in jars) rather than gaining a proper understanding of what its adult target market would truly warm to. As a result, it found itself with a product aimed at a peculiar niche market that was too small to be viable: singletons with arrested development.

Weird cross-category leaps

Making the leap from one category to another is particularly challenging for brands. A handful of what are often called parent brands, such as Virgin, GE and to a lesser extent Disney, have proved both strong and flexible enough to flourish across multiple categories. However, these are very much in the minority. Taking a well-known brand into an entirely new market has its temptations as there is always the hope that the name recognition factor and comfort of established brand values will prove to be a useful springboard. One of the most notable cross-category success stories is the Caterpillar clothing line, which has made sense to consumers because the rugged workwear image is in line with the tough and durable characteristics of the construction and mining machinery company's equipment. Other cross-category stretches have proved far less sensible. Here are some examples.

- In 1982, toothpaste brand Colgate launched a line of frozen ready meals. Colgate Kitchen Entrees bombed. While obviously consumers could see a connection between food and dental care, the idea of associating minty toothpaste with their evening meal was too hard to swallow. What next? Candy *floss*, anyone? Oh.
- Sweaty denim, engine oil, old leather. That's what I imagine a biker to smell like. Motorcycle maker Harley Davidson thought otherwise when it brought out a perfume in the 1990s. True Harley fans excited by the power, toughness and style of Harley bikes saw it as an off-message move that conflicted with what drew them to the brand. Undermining the essence of a brand is as reckless as taunting a gang of Hell's Angels. The mystique of the Harley brand lies in its machines; the distinctive deep spluttering rumble of their engines. That doesn't translate to the dainty application of scent. The perfume, plus a few other off-brand extensions like wine coolers, disappeared faster than a hog speeding along

an open highway towards a fat California sunset. Rumour has it that Chanel No 5 was a better transmission lubricant in any case. Harley Davidson is a very extendible brand with the kudos to work on a wide range of merchandise, but even its rugged bikes can't go everywhere.

- Kiss me, cheesy lips! Sounds pretty off-putting to me too. Although apparently not to cheesy snack brand Cheetos, which in 2005 teamed up with lip products company Lotta Luv to launch a cheese flavour lip balm. 'Dangerously cheesy' cautioned the packaging. Consumers heeded the warning, sparing their lips and, more important, their tongues. About as logical as Monterey Jack shaving foam or Parmesan shower gel. Which brings us to . . .

- . . . Clairol Touch of Yoghurt Shampoo. This 1979 launch failed to win over suspicious consumers, who didn't warm to the idea of washing their hair in yoghurt. Reportedly, a handful of confused folk even tried to eat the product. Today's consumers are more receptive to yoghurt as a shampoo ingredient for pampering their tresses, but without a public education campaign to set them straight, many 1970s shoppers were bewildered and reluctant to welcome this newcomer into their bathrooms.

- Twenty years after Clairol failed in its efforts to associate yoghurt with glossy hair, glossy magazine *Cosmopolitan* discovered that slapping its brand on a yoghurt range struck people to be just as odd. The short-lived range of low-fat yoghurts introduced in 1999 featured flavours such as peach and cherry. But while the raunchy Hearst-owned women's title may have written about inventively enjoying yoghurt in the bedroom from time to time, that wasn't nearly enough for its brand to muster a convincing presence alongside yoghurt products with genuine heritage and less tenuous reasons for their existence.

- Catering and the hotel business are natural bedfellows: hotel guests need feeding. So it's far from ridiculous for a restaurant company to consider expansion into the hotel sector. However, it becomes a different matter when the business in question is McDonald's, a brand with deeply entrenched perceptions globally as a purveyor of fast food. In 2001

McDonald's opened two Golden Arch hotels in Switzerland, one at Zurich Airport, the other at Lully between the cities of Lausanne and Berne. These four-star establishments were designed with spartan decor in stark colours and boasted McDonald's restaurants open round the clock, which for somnolent Switzerland was a rarity. Aside from its catering expertise, McDonald's was unquestionably able to call upon a lot of operational skills that could be adapted for the hotel business; you can imagine that a company well versed in running a slick drive-through service could turn its hand to providing guests with a speedy check-out. But ask yourself, is a place that evokes Ronald McDonald and Happy Meals somewhere that business travellers would want to unwind at the end of a hectic day? The foray into hotels failed to take off and after two years McDonald's pulled out. Location certainly wasn't a problem – the restyled Zurich Airport and Lully hotels have in recent years been run successfully as part of the Park Inn by Radisson chain. McDonald's had the right competencies but wrong brand image for the hotel business, and if they wanted to appeal to the German-speakers in Switzerland it probably didn't help that Arch sounds a little similar to the German word for bottom!

- Since its beginnings in Colorado in the 1870s, Coors has promoted the fact that its lager is brewed with Rocky Mountain spring water. In 1990, Coors tried to make an even greater virtue out of this pure H_2O by launching bottled sparkling water in original, lemon and lime, and cherry flavours. The familiar Coors logo featured prominently on the label. Americans who'd been conditioned for over a century to think of Coors as a beer brand were nonplussed. After a trickle of sales, Coors washed its hands of the water category.

When more equals less - Crest and Kit Kat go over the top

In his 2004 book *The Paradox of Choice: Why More is Less*, American psychologist Barry Schwartz mounts a persuasive argument that too much choice causes anxiety. Flying in the face of conventional wisdom that choice is always good, Schwartz asserts that decision making becomes a daunting prospect for consumers when there are too many alternatives. Some may buy a product and afterwards question whether they have made the right decision, while others will be so overwhelmed by the number of options they may be deterred from buying at all. Schwartz is by no means alone in subscribing to this view. Other psychologists have conducted research into 'choice overload' and 'consumer hyperchoice'.

The thesis Schwartz advances throws up some fascinating issues for marketers. In the realm of mobile phone handsets and other consumer-tech devices, product is often marketed on having more or better functions than rival or previous models. However, for most consumers, wouldn't a product that sacrificed a few non-essential functions in favour of improved ease of use actually be a better option? Choice overload can be just as much a factor when it comes to brand extensions. According to the Food Marketing Institute, US supermarkets carry anywhere between 15,000 and 60,000 different items (referred to in the grocery trade as SKUs – stock keeping units). With such an abundance of choice before them, it's no wonder that shoppers increasingly struggle to reach a decision. Brand owners may accidentally make things a whole lot more stressful for consumers and damage sales of their own products by over-extending to the point of confusion.

P&G's toothpaste brand Crest is an illuminating case in point. In the 1980s it took toothpaste line extension to extremes, presenting consumers with a bafflingly excessive amount of choice in flavours and attributes, from tartar control to teeth whitening to gum protection via many more. At the height of this folly, an astonishing 52 versions of Crest toothpaste were available and it looked as if one aim of this hyperchoice strategy was to have more varieties on sale than there are bristles on a toothbrush. So much choice made it hard for consumers to work out which was the right product for them. 'When Crest had one product, its share soared above 50 per cent,' writes Matt Haig in his book *Brand Failures*. 'By the time Crest had 38 products it was down to 36 per cent of the market. As soon as there were 50 Crest toothpastes, its market share dipped to 25 per cent and fell behind Colgate.'

Nestlé also discovered the drawbacks of choice overload when swamping the UK market with line extensions of its venerable Kit Kat chocolate-covered wafer. Kit Kat was launched in the 1930s and was for decades the top selling chocolate bar in the UK – its famous slogan 'Have a Break, Have a Kit Kat' was dreamed up by Donald Gillies at JWT in 1958 and has been in use ever since. In 1999, with sales beginning to flag, Nestlé introduced Kit Kat Chunky as a line extension, which initially boosted sales. Emboldened by this positive outcome, the company set about introducing a wide range of new Kit Kat flavours between 2003 and 2005. Sweet-toothed consumers could try the following Kit Kats and more: blood orange, Christmas pudding, dark chocolate, lime crush, red berry, strawberries and cream, Seville orange, mango and passion fruit, white chocolate, and lemon and yoghurt. A lot of these flavours didn't have wide appeal and, as with Crest, consumers were overwhelmed by the amount of product available. Some even complained that they found it difficult to pick out the original bar, which for many remained their favourite, from among the confectionery clutter created by Kit Kat.

The flavour variants weren't expensive to produce – there was no need to retool the manufacturing line; it was merely a case of altering recipes – but the exercise proved costly for the brand. As the *Wall Street Journal* reported in July 2006, under the headline 'Flavor Experiment for Kit Kat Leaves Nestlé with a Bad Taste', UK sales of Kit Kat plunged 18% in two years. In tune with Schwartz's paradox, far greater choice was eroding sales overall. Most of the new flavours were not going down well, even with staunch Kit Kat fans. Nestlé and its distributors found it increasingly difficult to shift stock to retailers without cutting prices to the bone. 'They were flooding the market,' Arshad Chaudhary, head buyer for wholesale group Bestway told the *Wall Street Journal*. 'Initially, we were comfortable with one or two varieties, but when they started coming out with another one every few months, it became a joke.'

Bowing to the inevitable, Nestlé withdrew nearly all the exotic flavours from the market. In the years since, its line extension activity within the category in the UK has been much more tightly focused, concentrating on new product formats ahead of a flavour free-for-all.

Good line extensions work when consumers are well disposed to an established brand and are comfortable with the way it is stretched. From a marketer's standpoint, they offer far lower risk than creating an entirely new brand. On the downside, every extension weakens the equity of the core brand. Extending too often or too far generally invites trouble.

Ironically, outside the UK, in countries where the Kit Kat brand is not as long established and expectations of what it should offer are less rigid, it is a different story. In markets such as Germany, some of the exotic flavours have gone down well. But it is Japan, a country well known for its appetite for innovation – and for what in other parts of the world might be considered unusual or even strange – that offers a remarkably contrasting story. Catering to an appetite among young Japanese consumers for faddy foods and special editions, Nestlé has rolled out over 200 Kit Kat flavours in the land of the rising sun, many available for limited time periods only, others with their distribution restricted to specific geographical regions. Among the weird Kit Kat varieties to have appeared are soy sauce, green tea, ginger ale, miso, blueberry cheesecake, lemon vinegar, grilled corn, Camembert cheese, wasabi and red potato. Believe me, I'm not making this up – and I could go on, but my tastebuds are screaming *stop*! Nestlé has proved adept at tapping into the Japanese passion for collecting. Moreover, in Japan Kit Kats are frequently bought as gifts rather than merely as snacks to keep hunger at bay. A linguistic quirk has helped Nestlé with its efforts in this respect. The name Kit Kat sounds a lot like the Japanese phrase '*Kitto Katsu*', which roughly translated means 'surely win'. This phrase is popularly used to wish students well when sitting exams; as a result, in Japan Kit Kats are appreciated as good luck gifts.

For Kit Kat, success in Japan and the UK requires two substantially different marketing strategies. In Japan, more really *is* more – not only in terms of the vast number of varieties that have helped Japanese consumers get their food novelty fix, but because the brand symbolises far more than a favourite snack product. Conversely, the UK experience showed that, as in most markets, flooding a category with line extensions is usually a recipe for misfortune. '*Kitto Katsu*' is a lovely phrase; however, in the field of brand extension there's no such thing as a sure thing.

Tips and lessons

- Is there a compelling reason to stretch your brand? Could a new brand without any baggage do a better job?
- Too much line extension confuses consumers and is often detrimental to the core brand.
- Market need is a better starting point than ease of production when considering brand/line extension.
- There will be a backlash orchestrated on social media if you are seen to be taking liberties with a cherished brand for which the public feels a degree of ownership.

Chapter 10

Lost in translation

Causing cross-cultural confusion and
international offence

In a famous and typically bizarre Monty Python sketch about an English–
Hungarian phrasebook, John Cleese plays a Hungarian tourist in London
attempting to communicate with a shopkeeper. The comedy stems from
the fact that the lines read aloud from the phrasebook are anything but
faithful translations. From nonsensical phrases like 'My hovercraft is full
of eels' to the downright provocative 'Do you want to come back to
my place, bouncy bouncy?' the tourist unwittingly bemuses and insults
the shopkeeper. It's a piece of cross-cultural incomprehension, given
a darker twist because the book publisher has deliberately set out to
undermine communication.

Even where there's no Pythonesque saboteur to contend with, it's
all too easy for brands to slip up when moving into or launching
marketing campaigns in new territories. Cultural sensitivities, linguistic
nuances and local market customs all present potential banana skins.
Yet globalisation has emboldened brand owners of all kinds to surf
its powerful waves, particularly those facing market saturation or
otherwise struggling for growth in their domestic territories.

Without question, there are huge rewards for brands that establish
themselves among the global elite. According to branding consultancy
Interbrand's *Best Global Brands* Report for 2013, the world's three
biggest brands – Apple, Google and Coca-Cola – are worth more than
$79 billion. That's each, not collectively. Apple alone is worth not far

south of $100bn. Even the 100th ranked brand, clothing retailer Gap, is worth almost $4 billion. Internationally popular brands pull in big bucks. However, even top-tier globally established brands that have transcended their country of origin still make culturally or linguistically embarrassing mistakes from time to time; smaller brands just starting out on an international journey will find themselves at even greater risk of cross-cultural blundering in their marketing efforts. There's plenty that can be lost in translation.

Ikea's missing women – airbrushing for Saudi market causes consternation

Sometimes brands trying to address the cultural sensitivities of a market can end up tying themselves in knots. That's what happened to Swedish furniture retailer Ikea in October 2012 when it came to light that women had been airbrushed out of pictures in the Saudi Arabian edition of its product catalogue. Women rarely feature in advertising campaigns in Saudi Arabia, and when they do their legs, arms and hair are usually covered, in line with the country's Sharia-inspired strict dress code. When Starbucks entered the Saudi Arabian market in 2000, it dropped the iconic long-haired siren from its logo, instead scaling up her star-topped crown to form the central image of its roundel. This of course drew criticism from those opposed to Saudi Arabia's position on women's rights. A dozen years on, therefore, it was no surprise that when the international media got hold of the Ikea story and published side-by-side images of the Saudi catalogue version with the women removed next to the original shot published in other catalogue editions, in which (needless to say) they were present, the retailer was heavily criticised for censorship and for putting commerce ahead of values.

Although Ikea is a private company, it is one of Sweden's foremost brands and as such is a powerful representative of Swedish culture abroad, and its familiar blue and yellow colours reflect those of the Swedish flag. Sweden's Minister for Gender Equality Nyamko Sabuni was distinctly unimpressed and sounded off on the matter to the Associated Press. 'For Ikea to remove an important part of Sweden's image and an important part of its values in a country that more than any other needs to know about Ikea's principles and values, that's completely wrong,' she said.

Ikea issued a statement expressing regret over the issue: 'We should have reacted and realised that excluding women from the Saudi Arabian version of the catalogue is in conflict with the Ikea Group values.' Bear in mind, this is the same company that in the 1990s ran one of the first (albeit little shown) TV commercials in the USA to feature a gay couple – and received bomb threats in response. Obliterating women in an act of censorship certainly didn't look good to many Ikea customers in markets around the world more used to a liberal, inclusive stance from the brand. It was certainly a cross-cultural blunder of far greater magnitude than the sometimes quirky Swedish product names it bestows on furniture lines, to the occasional amusement of shoppers; for example the robustly named Fartfull work bench.

While Ikea merited the criticism it received for the Saudi catalogue incident, for the most part it is right and proper for brands to be mindful of causing offence on cultural or religious grounds. Nike deserves praise for withdrawing some products from its Air range of basketball shoes in the mid-1990s after Muslims claimed that a logo on the footwear resembled the word 'Allah' written in Arabic script. The sportswear brand recalled 38,000 pairs of shoes worldwide, apologised and made a $50,000 donation to an Islamic elementary school in the USA. These prompt actions helped forestall a boycott of its products by Muslims around the world. Conversely – an apt word to use when writing about footwear brands – UK sportswear company Umbro attracted the ire of Jewish groups in 2002 with its Zyklon trainer. Zyklon B was the name of a genocidal gas used in the Holocaust death camps. Umbro changed the name of the shoe, claimed its naming had been coincidental and apologised. The Board of Deputies of British Jews slated Umbro for its 'appalling insensitivity'.

It is by no means the only brand in recent times to have Nazi connotations. In August 2012 a pair of Indian entrepreneurs opened a men's clothing store in Ahmedabad, which they called Hitler. Coincidence would certainly not pass muster as an excuse in this case, given that the logo on the store fascia incorporated a Swastika within the dot of the letter 'i'. Although the Swastika is actually an ancient

Indian symbol that is still widely seen in the country, the store used the tilted version that the Nazi Party adopted as its emblem. After a stream of complaints, predominantly from abroad, municipal authorities in the state of Gujarat tore down the store sign after the owners had reneged on a promise to remove it themselves.

That most of the complaints came from outside India is no surprise given that the majority of Indians have only a sketchy knowledge of European history and 'Hitler' is often used as a synonym for someone bossy. A successful Hindi TV soap opera, *Hitler Didi* – its title referring to a strong female character making it on her own in a man's world – launched in 2011.

But in trying to understand why anyone would brand a clothing store Hitler, there's a fascinating insight to be had that's worthy of note for anyone looking at cross-border marketing. Point of view can be a factor as significant as cultural and language differences. By this I mean that from India's perspective, the struggle against Germany during World War II weakened the British Raj and accelerated the path to cherished independence and partition in 1947. In this context – and, clearly, I mean *in this context alone* – Hitler can be seen as a catalyst for freedom. Consequently, Hitler is a figure less likely to be demonised in India than in most other parts of the world. This is an extreme example, but it illustrates the key point that you need to be alert to the subtle differences in points of view to be found when crossing borders. The familiar adage 'Think Global, Act Local' sums this up well. To succeed internationally, brands must have a consistent global strategy. But that strategy needs to have sufficient flexibility built into it to allow some latitude when implementing marketing activities at a local level. Technology has shrunk the world and given us more in common with others thousands of miles away – yet we are not all the same.

Not British! Irish steaming as Starbucks serves up national muddle

Mistaking one nationality for another is obviously to be avoided in marketing activity, all the more so if it stirs up long-rumbling issues of colonialism. Starbucks managed to do just that with a promotion to mark Queen Elizabeth II's Diamond Jubilee. 'Show us what makes you proud to be British,' the coffee chain tweeted to its followers in June 2012. Not only did the tweet appear on the Starbucks UK Twitter feed, it also inadvertently went out to the two thousand-odd followers of its Irish Twitter handle. 'Right now someone in Starbucks Ireland is wishing there was a Twitter version of the memory wipe thing from *Men In Black*,' shot back one aggrieved Irish follower; while Graham Linehan, writer of cult sitcom *Father Ted*, lambasted Starbucks as 'clueless' – and worse!

There are rare occasions, however, when cross-cultural blunders can actually create opportunities for brands. A good case in point comes from the London 2012 Olympic Games. In the early days of what was widely agreed to be an impeccably run Games, the organisers made an embarrassing mistake. The North Korean women's football team walked off the pitch in protest because the South Korean flag was erroneously displayed at the stadium in place of their own. Spotting a wonderful tactical opportunity, Specsavers opticians rushed out an amusing print and online ad promoting eye tests, which featured the flags of both North and South Korea, as a light-hearted jibe at the organisers' expense.

Of course, there's a world of difference between accidental confusion and deliberate discrimination. Anything that smacks of the latter is almost guaranteed to see a brand come in for justifiable criticism. Italian fashion brand Dolce & Gabbana provoked outrage in Hong Kong in January 2012 when it appeared to be discriminating against the local population. Security guards at the flagship D&G store in Hong Kong were accused of preventing Hong Kong residents from taking photos of the outside of the store, while turning a blind eye when wealthy visitors from the Chinese mainland and elsewhere in the world used their cameras. D&G may well have been trying to protect the anonymity of Chinese government officials who would not have wanted their shopping sprees for exclusive fashion in Hong Kong brought to wide attention on the mainland, where luxury goods are heavily taxed. Whatever its motives, locals resented being treated as second-class citizens. Over a thousand protestors took to the streets outside the store, forcing it to close early one weekend, while on social media and elsewhere online criticism intensified, with one anti-D&G Facebook page accumulating over twenty thousand fans. D&G quickly rushed out a statement saying, 'We wish to underline that our company has not taken part in any action aiming at offending the Hong Kong public.' The neutrality of this did little to placate hostility to the brand. After more than a week of further criticism, D&G released a rather more apologetic statement, which it posted in its Hong Kong store windows:

> *'We understand that the events which unfolded in front of the Dolce & Gabbana boutique on Canton Road have offended the citizens of Hong Kong, and for this we are truly sorry and we apologise. The Dolce & Gabbana policy is to welcome the Hong Kong people and that of the whole world respecting the rights of each individual and of the local laws.'*

High tax levels on luxury goods in mainland China has been a key factor driving the rise of shopping tourism among the Chinese *nouveau riche*. Another reason is precautionary: avoiding the fakes prevalent at home. Research from the World Luxury Forum found that luxury spending in China in January 2013 fell to its lowest level for five years ($830m), but at the same time, China's increasingly moneyed middle classes were spending ten times as much on luxury goods abroad, with the $8.5bn in sales for January 2013 representing a substantial 18% rise on the comparable period in 2012. Paris is among the favoured destinations of China's jet-setting luxury shoppers. Roughly a million Chinese a year now visit the French capital, a number that is set to continue rising, and for the most part they are welcomed with open arms by luxury boutiques and top hotels, some of which have adapted their menus to include more tea and noodles to cater to Chinese tastes. However, while in Hong Kong wealthy Chinese visitors appear to receive positive discrimination, the same is not always the case elsewhere. In a 2012 interview with fashion title *Women's Wear Daily*, Thierry Gillier, founder of the Zadig and Voltaire label, said of a new boutique hotel that he plans to open in Paris in 2014: 'We are going to select guests. It won't be open to Chinese tourists, for example. There is a lot of demand in Paris. Many people are looking for quiet, with a certain privacy.' Gillier's remarks provoked anger in China and he quickly backtracked, claiming in an apology that he was not being anti-Chinese but that his 'clumsy' comments were intended to highlight the fact that his exclusive 40-bedroom boutique hotel would not be open to 'busloads of tourists'.

Brand names that didn't travel well

Travel broadens the mind, but not every person and not every brand is able to do it well.

- Mist is the German word for manure. Small wonder that Irish Mist (liqueur) and Mist Stick (Clairol curling iron) had limited appeal in German-speaking markets. But back in the 1960s Rolls-Royce was sensible enough to drop the proposed Silver Mist name for its new luxury car in favour of Silver Shadow so as not to undermine its chances in Germany.

- While Rolls-Royce's U-turn saved it from embarrassment and Toyota prudently tweaked the name of its MR2 coupé to the MR in France (so it didn't sound similar to the French word for 'poo'), there are other instances of car companies being less aware of the credibility issues raised by the local slang meanings of their model names in certain countries: Ford Pinto (Brazil – little penis), Mitsubishi Pajero (Spain – masturbator) and Toyota Fiera (Puerto Rico – ugly old woman) are names vehicle owners probably would not want to brag about.

- The most famous auto example of the lot is the launch of the Chevy Nova in Latin American, where 'no va' means doesn't go. Not a characteristic most would want in a car! It's a merry story of blundering, but one that's inconveniently diminished by the facts. The Nova actually sold reasonably well in the region, despite the odd strained joke among locals about its name, because although sharing the same letters, Nova and 'no va' are pronounced differently, and the word nova is in wide usage and familiar in phrases such as 'bossa nova'.

- P&G's medications brand Vicks had to be rebranded to Wick in Germany as its original name sounded like the German F-word. Tissues brand Puffs is also unlikely to score a hit for P&G in the German market without a name change – Puff is German slang for brothel.

- The joint venture between giant Russian energy company Gazprom and Nigerian National Petroleum Company was proudly announced on a 2009 visit to Africa of Russian President Dmitry Medvedev. Strangely for a venture of this type, it has a name that sounds like a gangsta rap act: Nigaz.

- Japanese tour operator Kinki Nippon rebranded in several markets after receiving requests about kinky sex tours.
- A marketing campaign for Schweppes Tonic Water in Italy tanked when the product name was mis-translated as 'Schweppes Toilet Water'. However, there is no truth to the widely spread rumour that energy company Powergen had an Italian subsidiary with an easy-to-misread web domain name. The www.powergenitalia.com website does in fact exist, but the business behind it supplies something quite different from electricity – unless, that is, you are using the word 'electricity' as a metaphor for excitement in the bedroom.
- Cooking sauces company Sharwoods launched its Bundh sauces range in the UK with a £6m advertising campaign. Amused Punjabi speakers got in touch to point out that in their language Bundh means 'arse'.
- Italian mineral water company Traficante had some undesirable fans in Spain – where traficante means drug dealer.
- Both Ben & Jerry's (ice cream flavour, 2006) and Nike (black and brown trainers, 2012) have had to backtrack and apologise after bestowing the name Black & Tan on products. While the companies had intended to reference the classic drink combo of stout and pale ale, for many Irish consumers the name evokes the despised group of British military irregulars feared for their indiscriminate brutality during the Irish War of Independence at the beginning of the 1920s.

Slogans that didn't travel well

- In the late 1970s US computer company Wang introduced a new slogan designed to highlight its commitment to customer service. However, the marketing team in the UK was exceedingly reluctant to implement it. 'Wang Cares' sounded a bit too *hands on* to British ears.
- A Swedish vacuum cleaner brand ran a memorable campaign in the 1960s, with the strapline: 'Nothing sucks like an Electrolux'. Hopefully product quality was better than the ad implied.
- Translating global slogans into Mandarin Chinese can be a

challenge. In Taiwan, Pepsi's clarion call to consumers, 'Come alive with the Pepsi generation' was mangled into the more oddly ghoulish 'Pepsi will bring your ancestors back from the dead'. Famously, when Coca-Cola launched in China in the 1920s its brand name was rendered as the frankly surreal 'bite the wax tadpole'. But it's a myth that Coke itself made this blunder – the error appeared in a Mandarin language ad for the brand produced by some over-eager Chinese shopkeepers. But Kentucky Fried Chicken mistranslated its well-known 'Finger Lickin' Good' slogan into 'Eat your fingers off' when entering the mainland China market in the late 1980s. Tasty!

- In a Mexican campaign, Parker Pens managed to mix up the Spanish word for embarrass with 'embarazar' – which means to impregnate, thereby getting itself into an inky mess by promising that its pens 'won't leak in your pocket and impregnate you'. Good to know, as when writing I'm a firm believer in safe text.

- US airline Braniff played up the luxury of its leather business class seats in a 1980s radio and TV campaign in Mexico, using the line 'Vuelo en Cuero', literally 'Fly in Leather'. But the voiceover sounded like 'en cueros', which means 'naked'. Nude executives or mile high club cavorting were probably not the sort of business class images the airline wanted its campaign to deliver – but the work certainly got it noticed.

Fighting the Denglisch tide - Douglas, Schlecker and others confuse Germans

Parlez-vous Franglais? Sprechen sie Denglisch? Or another tongue exasperatingly mangled and diluted by English?

The global supremacy of English as the language of business presents marketers with amazing opportunities. However, slipping English into marketing communications in countries where it is not the national language needs careful consideration. At times, it can work well, conferring a uniformity that may be useful for cross-border campaigns and adding a dash of cool or aspirational internationalism. On the downside, there is always the possibility that it will be poorly received, resented for trampling all over the heritage of the native language in an act of linguistic and cultural vandalism, or simply not fully understood. Why use English, many outraged inhabitants of other countries have wondered, when my own language has adequate if not better words for the job?

In Germany in 2004, the debate about Denglisch in marketing caught fire – Denglisch is a portmanteau word created by combining the German words *Deutsch* (German) and *Englisch* (English), in the same way that Franglais is a conflation of the French words for French and English. Denglisch can also refer to the creeping rise of English phrases or expressions in the German language. In May that year, Germany's leading daily financial newspaper *Handelsblatt*, in association with market research agency Dialego, published consumer research into the most popular advertising slogans in the country, ranking them in a 'hit parade' on the basis of memorability. At the time, quite a few German companies and international companies active in the German market were using English-language slogans. None of them scored well in the *Handelsblatt* chart. This also chimed with research by Cologne-based branding consultancy Endmark, which found that English-language slogans were frequently misunderstood by German consumers.

Further evidence that marketing claims made in German were more effective than those made in English came from the findings of research by Isabel Kick, a statistician from Dortmund, published in July 2004. Kick conducted an experiment in which 10 advertising slogans widely used in Germany were played to 24 volunteers. Five of the slogans were in German, the other five in English. Skin resistance measurements, rather like those used in lie detector tests, were conducted on the volunteers as they listened to the slogans. Kick discovered that the German slogans triggered a much stronger reaction among the volunteers, suggesting more of an emotional connection. The English slogans provoked less of a response, suggesting they were not as well received and probably not as well understood as those delivered in the listeners' mother tongue.

Interestingly, McDonald's had reached the same conclusion just a few months previously. In February 2004, it ditched the English-language slogan it had used prominently in Germany for several years, 'Every time a good time', replacing it with *'Ich liebe es'* – which of course means 'I'm lovin' it'. According to a report in German news magazine *Der Spiegel*, research among McDonald's core target audience of 14- to 59-year-olds had found that only 59% were able to correctly translate 'Every time a good time', a shockingly low number as far as the burger chain was concerned, given that it had used the slogan for years in its TV advertising.

One of the slogans that Endmark looked at and that also featured in Kick's research was 'Come in and Find Out', used by major German retailer Douglas, a specialist in perfume, books, jewellery and confectionery. What Douglas wanted to suggest with the slogan was that its shops are a path to exciting product discovery, but many puzzled Germans interpreted 'Come in and Find Out' as 'enter our store and look for the exit'. Hardly an invitation to linger and test some perfume; it said goodbye rather than speaking of a good buy. With the shortcomings of its slogan under discussion in the media, Douglas could see the writing on the wall – writing that was definitely in German. Before the end of the year, Douglas ditched 'Come in and Find Out', replacing it with *'Douglas macht das Leben schöner'* ('Douglas makes life better'). Several other major brands also dispensed with their English slogans at around the same time, among them Germany's national airline Lufthansa, which got rid of 'There's no better way to fly' in favour of *'Alles für diesen Moment'* ('Everything for this moment').

Although a setback for the rise of Denglisch, this was by no means a rout. English remains commonplace in German advertising campaigns, as any visitor to the country and its German-speaking neighbours Austria and Switzerland will discover. There is plenty of research to back this up. Online advertising portal Slogans.de produces an annual Slogometer listing the 100 most popularly used words in German marketing campaigns. Its all-time Slogometer includes two English words – 'your' and 'you' – in the top 10 alone. 'Life', 'we', 'world', 'more', 'better', 'business', 'be' and 'on' all figure in the top 50. Endmark, meanwhile, has conducted three further studies into the use of English in German marketing activity since its initial research in 2003, the most recent of which was completed in 2013. Each study is eagerly lapped up by the German media and Endmark Managing Partner Bernd Samland is happy to admit that these days exposure rather than insight is the driving force for repeating the exercise, as the findings have been fairly consistent over the past decade: about 25% of the advertising messages published nationwide in Germany are in English or use English vocabulary, and about two-thirds of the targeted consumers do not completely understand these messages.

> *'Talking about Denglisch, we can discover two different phenomena. One is just the wrong use of English words which makes it funny for English native speakers sometimes. The funniest situation I have seen happened at the small airport of Graz in Austria: a small shop in the airport building offered round chocolate truffles as "Mozart's balls". This can be compared with plenty of similar mistranslations from "body bags" which some Germans consider as more attractive than the word "Rucksack" or hundreds of "Backshops" instead of bakeries.'*

Bernd Samland, Managing Partner, Endmark

Welcome to Germany, a country where 'body bags' in fashionable colours and funky designs – some plastered with the logos of famous brands, some featuring children's cartoon characters – are desirable possessions, often to be seen attractively displayed in shop windows. But if you want an ergonomically designed one that's good for your posture, you'd be out of luck at the 'backshop'! This kind of day-to-day misapprehension, where a word has vastly different meanings to different audiences, is often harmless and can certainly raise a smile. However, it's another ballgame when a key part of a marketing message is misunderstood by its target audience.

> *'The second phenomenon is the wrong translation of more or less correct English. For example, "Welcome to the Beck's experience" (beer advertising) has been translated by a majority as "Welcome to the Beck's experiment"; or "Drive the Change" (Renault) as "Take a chance" or "Drive with the (coin) change". This can turn out as a big problem. After our last survey Ford Germany changed its claim from "Feel the difference" to German " Eine Idee weiter" ("One idea ahead∕*

*further"), because the word "difference" had been mixed up
with "differential" and others; and when a TV journalist asked
sales people at a Ford dealer what "Feel the difference" means,
no one could give an appropriate answer.'*
Bernd Samland, Managing Partner, Endmark

Why then, given the drawbacks, should English continue to figure so prominently in German advertising? This is not necessarily a simple question to answer. Samland believes there are three factors at work. First, 'the ignorance of some mostly American or Japanese global players' about exactly how well Germans understand English. Second, an uneasy relationship that some Germans still have with their own language that is a throwback to the way it was abused for propaganda purposes in the Nazi era. And third, 'because Germans just love English, and they love it that much that they permanently invent new English words like "handy" for mobile phone or "pullunder" for a pullover without sleeves.'

However, as we have already seen, bringing English into the marketing equation is not always a wonderful idea. In the case of chemist and housewares retailer Schlecker, doing so was to precipitate a PR disaster of huge proportions. Schlecker, which at its peak employed 52,000 workers and was the largest drugstore chain in Europe with annual sales of €7bn, had been struggling with hefty financial losses for several years. In 2011, the company attempted to get its business back on track with the help of some serious rebranding, introducing a revamped logo, fresh store interior design and new Denglisch slogan: 'For You. *Vor Ort*' (roughly speaking, 'For you, locally/near you'). This not only mixed German with English but did so ungrammatically. The slogan was devised by the Düsseldorf office of international ad agency Grey, which also created a series of TV commercials for the new campaign, and its linguistic mix and liberties with German grammar were intended to be a talking point. In this, it inarguably succeeded. Unfortunately, very few people were talking it up. When German marketing magazine *Horizont* conducted an online poll of its readers, an overwhelming 77% classified the slogan as terrible. As a further 10% of respondents were 'don't knows', possibly flummoxed by the inelegant Denglisch concoction, plainly it was only a small minority who felt it was any good. This was not at all the sort of reception to a marketing makeover that a company in financial difficulties would want.

While this was bad enough, things were about to get a whole lot worse. A member of a German language preservation society contacted Schlecker to complain about the Denglisch slogan. He received a response from company spokesman Florian Baum that was dynamite. In his reply, Baum said that 'this slogan is not directed at the maybe 5% of the population that are well-educated and that you and I belong to. Please also consider the poorly and not so well-educated people. The slogan is for those 95%.' What inference could be drawn from this explanation other than that Schlecker believed most of its customers were stupid? The condescending and derogatory nature of Baum's remarks made it inevitable that they would be spread virally at great speed. On social media, there were calls for a business with such little respect for its customers to be shut down. Schlecker then contrived to make an awkward situation worse still by criticising some of the commentators on its official blog and pedantically pointing out that 'medium educational level' was not to be confused with 'stupid', as some of the comments had asserted. Needless to say, this fanned the flames of the crisis and made it an even more appetising choice of subject for the media. News outlet *The Local* reported the gaffe under the headline 'Schlecker man insults customers' intelligence', while *Die Welt* wrote that the company was the retail equivalent of the political party FDP, which had endured a catastrophic collapse in public support, and described it as 'embarrassing'.

Just how big a crisis this was for Schlecker becomes apparent if you Google the phrase 'Schlecker shitstorm'. Appropriately, in February 2012 a panel of German experts voted 'shitstorm' the biggest English contribution to the German language in 2011. 'Shitstorm fills a gap in the German vocabulary that has become apparent through changes in the culture of public debate,' the Anglicism of the Year jury said in a statement explaining its decision. Together with other hot topics such as the Greek financial crisis and the resignation in a PhD plagiarism furore of German Defence Minister Baron Karl-Theodor zu Guttenberg (cruelly nicknamed zu Googleberg), the Schlecker scandal played its part in allowing a vulgar but fabulously evocative new word to take root in German culture. How strange, though, that Schlecker's derisory Denglisch should help a far more robust English expression become familiar to German tongues. As for the Schlecker business, after embarrassment came the fall. In 2012 it filed for bankruptcy. For Schlecker it was *das Ende*.

Given the hegemony of English on the global stage, there's not really an equivalent of Denglisch in reverse (although an exception that proves the rule is Audi's *'Vorsprung durch Technik'*, all-conquering internationally, thanks to Sir John Hegarty's gut instinct for a great tagline). If there were, I would make the case for it to be called 'Engman' – which would doubtless irritate those people who have inherited the word as a surname.

What can be seen, though, is the gratuitous use by some brands of the umlaut, those dual dots atop a vowel, to bestow a wholly artificial Germanic or Scandinavian provenance. Among the perpetrators of such glyph grabbing are Häagen-Dazs ice cream, Gü desserts, FrütStix frozen fruit bars, Scünci hair accessories and Hibü directories. It's easy to see why new brands take such linguistic liberties – the umlaut not only gives graphic designers more leeway for expression and originality when creating a logo, it also alludes to a heritage of some kind, which may suggest to consumers that a brand is far more reassuringly established than is actually the case. Consumers are often wise to such tricks, but as long as they are not being made fools of, appear comfortable with the artifice and may appreciate the playfulness – for instance, Gü, with its allusion to 'goo', and, indeed, the French word *goût* (meaning taste), is undeniably a great name for a range of sticky puddings. There's also a raucous precedent for this umlaut fetish in the music industry. For a decade or so, beginning in the early 1970s, a wave of new heavy metal bands used umlauts in their names, often as a showy expression of resounding gothic intensity, to the extent that the diacritical mark is also known by the slang term 'rock dots'. Blue Öyster Cult, Motörhead, Mötley Crüe and Queensrÿche are among the leading exponents of the metal umlaut – which sounds as if it should be a traditional typesetting term. Here, from within an unsubtle musical genre in which the volume is always cranked up to 11, bands have set an example that brands have followed. Perhaps this is not so much a case of lost in translation as found in music.

An accent on accuracy – Mitsubishi ideas are a non-starter

Adrian Wheeler knows plenty about cross-border communication, having been in charge of the 28-office EMEA (Europe, Middle East and Africa) network of PR group GCI, where he advised many major clients on their international marketing campaigns. Wheeler ascended to that position after building up his own PR agency called Sterling, then selling it to GCI in the 1980s. Not long after the sale, Wheeler experienced the most personally embarrassing instance of cross-cultural misunderstanding of his illustrious career.

'We took a call from Mitsubishi, who wanted us to present our auto-industry credentials in connection with the launch of a new model – the Stallion. As was our habit, we went a step further and prepared some preliminary creative ideas: "Beyond the Mustang", and so on. The Mitsubishi team arrived and started by giving us a quick briefing on the new car. The first slide chilled our blood.

'It said: **The New Mitsubishi Starion.**

'Nearly all our presentation – research, market positioning, media perceptions, concepts – was useless. We mumbled our way through a threadbare account of our car-marketing credentials. The Mitsubishi team were very polite, but they didn't call us back.'

Adrian Wheeler, GCI

Wheeler can laugh about it now, although at the time he was mortified.

Tips and lessons

- Don't rely on Google Translate or other free online tools to create local language content. Always use a professional translation service and ask a native speaker to check the results.

- When creating a new brand, avoid names that sound ridiculous or offensive in other languages – and be mindful of common slang.
- Be sensitive to the taboos of other cultures and religions.
- Make sure you don't confuse one nationality or cultural group with another.
- Know your history!

Chapter 11

Unwise refinement and marketing U-turns

Strategic fiascos, ill-fated tinkering and terrible reformulations

In 2012, Johnson & Johnson pledged to remove all 'chemicals of concern' from its toiletries and cosmetics within three years. This followed allegations that products such as its No More Tears baby shampoo contained trace elements of potentially carcinogenic substances and mounting pressure for a boycott spearheaded by the Campaign for Safe Cosmetics. PepsiCo likewise caved in to consumer pressure regarding a controversial ingredient in its Gatorade sports drink. It announced in 2013 that it would stop using brominated vegetable oil – which is banned in Japan and the EU, and has been patented as a flame retardant! – after a teenage girl from Mississippi got over 200,000 signatures on a petition calling for its removal that she launched on Change.org. While recipe alterations of this sort are clearly for the better, there have been occasions when reformulating a product has made things a whole lot worse.

New Coke – when the world's biggest brand lost its nerve

A lack of self-confidence is not usually a trait associated with Coca-Cola. The soft drink created by Atlanta pharmacist John S. Pemberton in 1886 grew through decades of smart marketing into the world's first truly global brand and to this day its trademark remains the most widely recognised on the planet. This, remember, is a brand so influential that it shaped the modern image of Father Christmas: the jovial, bearded, portly Santa in white-trimmed red costume whom we can so easily and affectionately call to mind was dreamed up for Coca-Cola by illustrator Haddon Sundblom and began appearing in press advertising campaigns in 1931. Until Coca-Cola brought its consumer marketing might to bear, Santa had been rendered in a variety of inconsistent guises. Once the giant from Atlanta got to work – by the mid-1920s it was already selling six million Cokes a day – its representation of Santa was propelled by momentum as strong as that of a magic sleigh into becoming the real thing. For the next half century, with bottling plants proliferating internationally, the rise of Coca-Cola seemed unstoppable. This was a brand that was being expertly woven into popular culture; as its 1963 slogan triumphantly asserted, 'Things Go Better with Coke'.

However, by the 1980s and with its centenary in sight, Coca-Cola was no longer having things entirely its own way. Rival cola brand Pepsi had been steadily chipping away at Coke's dominance in the USA, reducing Coke's share in its biggest market for 15 consecutive years. Plainly, this was no blip. Executives at Coca-Cola were genuinely concerned that their iconic soft drink would eventually be outsold by the challenger brand. It looked like the sweet carbonated bubble might burst.

There was fierce internal debate as to how Coke should respond to the Pepsi threat. Major change did not come easily to a company that had made few strategic deviations while developing Coke into a mega-brand. The fight-back began in 1982 with the successful launch of Diet Coke. Although it seems hard to believe now, given how well established as a massive brand in its own right Diet Coke has become, at the time its development was mooted some inside Coca-Cola opposed the new product because they feared the line extension might detract from Coke, which had been carefully nurtured through generations on the basis of its uniformity. When the sky didn't fall in following Diet Coke's launch, a new mentality took root at the company. Emboldened executives unshackled themselves from strategic conservatism and began to consider radical change, thinking what had previously been unthinkable. Adopting a new ethos of marketing permissiveness was to lead them down the path to what is by common consent one of the greatest marketing blunders of all time.

Coke was rattled by the introduction of the Pepsi Challenge in 1975. In this huge field marketing initiative, Pepsi conducted blind tastings at shopping malls and other public spaces across the country. To the consternation of Coke executives, time after time Pepsi did far better than Coke in these taste tests, and Pepsi hyped up that fact during the late 1970s and early 1980s. Secret taste tests run by Coke achieved similar results. Additionally, Pepsi was making great inroads in building its appeal among a youth audience, for example by airing big-budget TV commercials starring some of the world's most famous pop and TV stars. Mind you, there were some hiccups. In January 1984 Michael Jackson was rushed to hospital in Los Angeles with second-degree burns to the scalp when filming a Pepsi commercial became a horrifying, agonising thriller: while performing a version of his hit song *Billie Jean*, with lyrics reworked for Pepsi, the superstar singer's hair was set on fire when pyrotechnics malfunctioned. Oww! Advertising production setbacks aside, however, Pepsi was definitely on the up.

Frightened by Pepsi's success in building an audience for the future by courting the younger generation, having failed to make much headway with price promotions and concerned that its rival had a strong taste advantage, Coke executives reached the momentous conclusion that the way to re-energise the brand was not to take its advertising in a new direction but to reformulate its recipe. It's incredible when you stop to think about it: the plan was to change the ingredients of the world's most popular soft drink! After taste tests involving nearly 200,000 consumers, a new, sweeter recipe, with a taste closer to that of Pepsi, was ready for the market. The originator was becoming an imitative me-too. On 23rd April 1985, New Coke, as it came to be known, was launched amid much fanfare. It was not received anywhere near as well as Coke had hoped.

Pepsi made mischief by running newspaper ads claiming the change in recipe was proof Coke had lost the cola war and aired an 'attack' TV commercial featuring three weather-beaten old-timers on a porch. One of the old men is annoyed and saddened that without asking his permission 'they changed my Coke'. By the end of the spot he has switched allegiance and is happily chugging down a Pepsi. As well as aiming the barb that Coke was high-handed in changing product composition without seeking the opinions of its loyal consumers, the Pepsi commercial was clever in its portrayal of oldies in dirty denim and plaid shirts. This sent a message it took pleasure in promoting – that Coke was a drink for an older demographic. The message was blatantly reinforced by the advertising's tagline: 'The choice of a new generation'.

But it was the reaction of American consumers that really mattered, and here Coke met with a vehemence it hadn't bargained for. People were flabbergasted that Coke had tinkered with the make-up of a brand that meant so much to them; outraged that it had touched a piece of thirst-quenching culture many believed should have been unassailable. Complaints came thick and fast. Soon the Coca-Cola consumer helpline was fielding 1,500 calls a day. Vitriolic letters poured in too, many marked for the attention of Coca-Cola CEO Roberto Goizueta. One that found its way to his desk was addressed, 'Chief Dodo, The Coca-Cola Company'. Another person wrote to Goizueta requesting his autograph, sarcastically expressing the view that in years to come the signature of 'one of the dumbest executives in American business history' would be worth a fortune.

Protest groups with names such as Old Cola Drinkers of America and the Society for the Preservation of the Real Thing sprang up, with the former claiming to have signed up a hundred thousand people determined to bring back the original Coke. At a protest in downtown Atlanta, demonstrators carried placards with slogans such as 'Our children will never know refreshment' and 'We want the real thing'. One man was so determined to put off the day when he would have no more of the 'real thing' to drink that he drove to a bottler in San Antonio, Texas and bought $1,000-worth of Coca-Cola. Others panic bought in bulk from retailers while old Coke was still to be found on shelves, stockpiling bottles and cans by the hundred in basements. Meanwhile, on talk shows and elsewhere in the media, Coke's actions were mocked. Suddenly the public had a renewed appreciation of Coke's heritage and a more acute understanding of how passionately connected to it they felt.

Within two weeks of the launch Coke's top executives bowed to the inevitable. Having just announced the demise of old Coke, they now had to find a sensible way of bringing it back. Coke's Chief Marketing Officer Sergio Zyman was put in charge of the project. As it happened, Zyman was due to give a speech in Europe. It occurred to him that there, away from the furore and the spotlight in the USA, might be a good place to set the wheels in motion for a speedy resurrection. Zyman summoned a small group of packaging and brand strategy experts to meet him in Monte Carlo. In an interview with *Advertising Age*, Zyman recalled: 'As we looked at the can we said, "We've got to overdo it. We've got to say to consumers this is the original." We tried Coca-Cola Original, Coca-Cola No. 1, just plain Coke. I actually still have a lot of the mockups. But Classic was the one that was the best. It said we're not fooling around. This is it.'

So it was that in July 1985, a mere 79 days after it had supposedly been discontinued for good, old Coke came back from the dead as Coca-Cola Classic. The about-turn was such a big deal that ABC news anchorman Peter Jennings interrupted an episode of soap opera *General Hospital* to bring the story to the nation. Coke was front-page news. In two days, the company's hotline received 31,600 phone calls. People were thrilled to see the return of the Coke they loved.

At first, Coca-Cola Classic was sold alongside Coca-Cola ('New Coke') but differentiated via separate advertising campaigns. Coca-Cola Classic was marketed under the slogan 'Red, White and You', emotively alluding to the star-spangled banner in a way that left no doubt that it was positioned to be as essential a part of American life as the US flag. New Coke, meanwhile, went head-to-head with Pepsi in appealing to a young demographic with the tagline 'Catch the Wave'. But it was Coca-Cola Classic that was truly riding the wave, swept along by a new public appreciation. Back from the dead, it was more popular than ever. Sales of New Coke flagged, and its second-class status in relation to the revived original Coke was underlined when in 1992 it was rebranded as Coca-Cola II. Interest in it dwindled even further in the following years, with retailers and consumers largely apathetic about its existence and bottlers peeved at the complexity of dealing with a secondary product when they could see little rationale for its continuation. It was withdrawn from the market altogether in 2002. Later that year, the word 'Classic' was scaled down in size on Coca-Cola Classic packaging, and then removed completely in 2009. Coke was back to being just good old Coke.

Conspiracy theorists have suggested that the introduction of New Coke at the expense of the original recipe was a brilliant, elaborate ploy with the goal all along having been to revive the fortunes of a product that seemed tired as it approached its 100th anniversary – cynically using absence to make the heart grow fonder. In reality, Coca-Cola was nowhere near as cunning. Spooked by Pepsi's perceived taste advantage, Coca-Cola temporarily lost faith in the product on which its global business had been built. The TV commercial for New Coke, in which comedian Bill Cosby insists that Coke has been improved and is 'better than ever', gives the lie to the notion that the whole thing was an incredibly sophisticated marketing bluff. Make no mistake, this was an epic blunder; even if it did turn out well for Coca-Cola in the end. Once the scale of their misjudgement became clear and the king of fizzy drinks was granted a reprieve, Coca-Cola executives had to scramble unceremoniously to cobble together a new strategy that embraced both Coke I and Coke II.

Today, Interbrand values Coca-Cola as a brand at nearly $80bn. It sells in almost unimaginable quantities; billions of units worldwide per week. People still love it. So, how to account for the anomaly of Pepsi consistently trouncing Coke in blind tastings?

The answer lies in the way blind tastings tend to be conducted. In his book *Blink: The Power of Thinking without Thinking*, Malcolm Gladwell explores the nature of rapid decision making that often happens subconsciously in the human brain. Talking with researchers from the food and beverage industry, Gladwell found that taste tests often had shortcomings. For example, blind 'sip tests' such as the Pepsi Challenge, in which someone might only try one or two mouthfuls, are skewed towards sweeter drinks – people instinctively respond to the sweetness, regularly picking the sweeter over the less sweet. But a home-use test, in which consumers have the time and leeway to imbibe far greater volumes of a drink, may produce the opposite result as people are more likely to find sweetness cloying if they consume a product in substantially larger quantities. The success of the Pepsi Challenge as a marketing exercise had frightened Coke into over-estimating the importance of the sip test. Moreover, as Gladwell also notes, once all branding is stripped away, there is an even greater drawback to regarding sip test results as an indicator of likely purchasing intent. Product taste is only one factor in the buying decision. Packaging and brand appeal are of incredible importance. This chimes with the 'sensation transference' theory of psychologist and pioneering marketing expert Louis Cheskin, which holds that consumers will transfer their impressions of the packaging or branding of a product to the product itself. Yet Coke had for the most part overlooked the huge advantage it enjoyed due to its massive familiarity and many decades as an emotive market leader. The company wasn't dumb enough to make the same mistake twice. With the return of the real thing, it made sure it played to its strengths.

As a final footnote to the whole affair, I should point out that New Coke wasn't the first change to the famously secret formula of the drink. Up until 1903, Coca-Cola contained small amounts of cocaine and was widely promoted as a cure for nervous afflictions. At that period, cocaine had not been criminalised. However, a massive rise in use of the drug during the 1890s and its increasing association with crime in the eyes of the public led to growing calls for prohibition. Following an article in the *New York Tribune* that advocated legal action against the company, Coca-Cola quietly tweaked its recipe, introducing spent coca leaves from which the drug had already been extracted. When watching Coke's 21st-century 'Holidays Are Coming' commercials with their joyfully welcomed giant red trucks, it's amusing to call to mind that in the early days of the brand its delivery vehicles were nicknamed 'dope wagons' and were possibly even more eagerly awaited by Americans longing for their carbonated sugary fix.

JC Penney alienates customers with pricing strategy switch

Long-time CEO Myron (Mike) Ullman was jettisoned by the board at JC Penney in the belief that the department store group needed a new lease of life in tough market circumstances. In his place in 2011 they installed Ron Johnson, the former head of retail at Apple, a highly rated executive credited with brilliantly reinventing the store environment for the iKing of the consumer-tech sector. The man behind the Genius Bar and other impressive ideas that made a visit to an Apple Store an immersive brand experience as much as a shopping trip didn't come cheap: on joining, Johnson was awarded $52.7m in stock and regularly commuted from his California home to JCP headquarters in Texas by private jet. But in a demonstration of self-belief that he was the leader to revive the fortunes of JCP, he also invested $50m of his own money in his new employer.

When Johnson unveiled his turnaround strategy in January 2012 in a presentation called 'In Praise of Fresh Air', he made it clear that he was fundamentally reimagining every aspect of the company's business. In addition to relatively superficial changes such as a new logo (see page 125) and bringing in celebrity Ellen DeGeneres as brand partner, this included a sweeping modernisation of the store experience together with the introduction of new brands and the rejuvenation of some existing brands long popular with customers. The idea was to inject a little of Apple's retail magic into stores to increase their allure. Although a shake-up to the shopping environment of this magnitude was expensive, it was a necessity if JCP, which has been around for over a century, was to deepen its appeal and relevance to younger shoppers.

Yet despite the scale of this undertaking, the most radical aspect of Johnson's blueprint for transformation was the implementation of a new 'Fair & Square' pricing strategy. In the past, JCP had relied heavily on coupons and abundant in-store sales offering hefty discounts. At a stroke, Johnson was ditching all of that in favour of a version of the 'everyday low prices' (EDLP) model that has swept Wal-Mart into such a dominant position. However, despite Wal-Mart's shining example, very few retailers have managed to make a resounding success of EDLP and it is a particularly hard trick to pull off for established retailers that previously pursued a different strategy. By moving to the Fair & Square EDLP approach, JCP would be able to cut its advertising and in-store promotional costs. But what Johnson failed to take into account was how badly this change would be received by JCP's traditional customers. One reason for this was that there was little insight to hand as to the likely fall-out from such significant change – because JCP didn't conduct much market research while working on its plans. Steeped in the Apple mentality, which as a product innovator and shaper of consumer tastes prefers to lead rather than follow, Johnson wasn't a huge fan of customer research. He was also of the view that there was little point in a staggered roll-out as quick results were vital.

So the transformation proceeded at full speed, rapidly alienating many customers who expected coupons and markdowns. The company gave up $4bn in sales in 18 months, and made devastating financial losses. Its stock fell by 75%. JCP was flirting with insolvency.

> 'The older, less affluent, coupon shopper that was the bread and butter customer for Penney left. My guess is that if Ron could have continued his strategy long enough it would have worked; but the company would have been out of business before that happened. He told us it was a three-year to five-year programme, but he failed to realise how much damage he would have to take to get to the other side of that five-year period. I loved Ron's vision, but the day he presented the vision I told all of my clients that the stock was going to fall like a stone on the back of sales and profits falling like a stone because he could not hold his old customers in the kind of transition he envisioned.'
>
> Jan Rogers Kniffen, US retail analyst

After presiding over a sharp fall in sales for every quarter of his tenure, Johnson was fired in April 2013 – to be replaced by ... his predecessor,

Ullman. There was much more to this U-turn than personalities. Ullman immediately moved away from the Fair & Square pricing strategy and gave the go-ahead for TV ads that apologised for some of the changes instigated by Johnson. 'We learned a very simple thing,' said the conciliatory female voiceover, 'to listen to you, to hear what you need, to make your life more beautiful. Come back to JC Penney. We heard you. Now we'd love to see you.' JCP also shored up its finances with a $1.75bn loan from Goldman Sachs. Johnson, so impressive at Apple, seemed unable to relate to JCP's customers, who looked to the store for coupons and discounts and were not minded to consider it a cool place to hang out.

Mars upsets vegetarians

According to the *National Diet and Nutrition Survey* by the Department of Health and the Food Standards Agency, 2% of the UK population are vegetarians. In May 2007, Mars, owner of chocolate brands such as Twix, Snickers and Maltesers, in addition to the eponymous Mars bar, announced a change to the ingredients it sourced for its confectionery. Whereas in the past these popular chocolate treats had been suitable for vegetarians, Mars revealed that it intended to introduce rennet into the production process. Rennet is an enzyme extracted from the stomach lining of calves, which is used to create whey. At a stroke, by altering the formulation of its chocolate snacks, Mars was excluding a sizeable market of one in every 50 people from consuming products many had hitherto relished. Unsurprisingly, vegetarian fans of the products were outraged that Mars seemed to be arbitrarily turning its back on them.

A food manufacturer making a move of this kind would risk a backlash in any market, but by taking this step in the UK Mars was laying itself open to huge amounts of opprobrium. British consumers are known for having a sweet tooth and have a noted fondness for what the confectionery trade calls countlines: chocolate products, often in bar form and frequently containing fillings such as biscuit, nuts and caramel, that are bought for individual consumption. Research by Datamonitor, published in April 2006, identified British consumers as Europe's most voracious chocoholics, munching an average of 10kg a year each, nearly five times as much as the 2.2kg consumed by Italians. Moreover, in the UK, countlines are by far the most popular form of chocolate, while in Germany, boxed chocolates are more popular. As Mars was a leading player in the most popular chocolate category, its decision to change the ingredients in its countlines was certain to have a direct impact on many of those UK consumers who shunned animal products.

The Vegetarian Society – established in the UK in 1847 and the oldest vegetarian organisation in the world – mobilised its members to oppose the move. Within a week of Mars announcing its decision, over 6,000 people had emailed or called the company's switchboard to complain – more than 12 times the amount of customer contact received in a typical week. In Parliament, 40 MPs signed a petition voicing their disapproval. Mars was under concerted pressure. A week after making the announcement it backtracked, conceding it had become very clear, very quickly that it had made a mistake. Mars Chocolate UK President Fiona Dawson signed an open letter, published as an ad in several national newspapers, in which she apologised, writing: 'The customer is our boss. Therefore we listen to you and your feedback.'

In reformulating its products so that they were no longer vegetarian-friendly, Mars was perceived to be discriminating against people on the basis of their lifestyle choices and beliefs. While that may not have been its intention, as a major food company it was foolish to think that the small change it made to its recipes was an insignificant one. Meat eaters might misguidedly take the view that objecting to the use of rennet is just veggies being finicky – 'Hey, it's not like Mars was throwing lumps of ground beef and offal into the Twix mix!' But for anyone who has chosen, on a point of principle, not to eat products that contain ingredients taken from dead animals, it makes the world of difference.

'The Mars blunder was a huge story for the Vegetarian Society and what was most interesting for us was that the story wasn't just about what ingredients they use, it was about whether or not people's dietary choices are worthy of respect. I describe it as a blunder because where they really went wrong was in a quote given to [leading food industry trade magazine]

The Grocer, implying that the change to non-vegetarian whey would only be of concern to a small minority of very strict vegetarians. The thing about a massive international brand is that its own weight gives any story about it huge momentum. In the end, Mars didn't make the planned change and their big rival, Cadbury's, started labelling which of their chocolate bars are suitable for vegetarians. The industry, the media and the public realised that the details really do matter and now, when big brands make a change, they often talk to us first.'

Liz O'Neill, Head of Communications, Vegetarian Society

For Mars, it was a humbling lesson in customer power. Once it made the climbdown, no long-term harm was done. However, as the next story shows, product reformulation can have far nastier consequences.

The Planta disease – product reformulation brings death and distrust

In 2013, Unilever caved in to consumer pressure 18 months after introducing a reformulated version of its Flora spread to the UK market at a cost of £29m. The multinational food company had revamped Flora to be both healthier and tastier, but many shoppers considered the product less palatable than before, and sales plunged by 12%. When market research confirmed taste was the problem, with 70% of customers saying they would welcome back the original formula, an embarrassing about-turn became unavoidable. The original formula was reintroduced in packs bearing the slightly humiliating wording, 'back to the taste you love'.

Yet this debacle is utterly insignificant when set alongside the terrible events of August 1960, when Unilever introduced a reformulated version of its margarine Planta to the Netherlands. On its pack, a red label bore the word 'renewed' and consumers were promised, 'you can taste the improvement'. Previously, Planta had been at a disadvantage compared to rival margarines on the market because it was not as easy to spread, and when used in frying and baking it spattered. Now, with the inclusion of a new emulsifier – an essential element in many food products that binds oil and water together and prevents them from separating – those problems had been solved. But in solving those problems for its customers, Unilever created new ones that were far more serious.

The reformulated margarine precipitated a massive public health crisis in the Netherlands affecting over 100,000 people, some severely. More than four hundred people were hospitalised and four died, two likely as a direct result of consuming Planta, while with the other two fatalities consumption of the product was thought to be a contributory factor. By the end of what came to be known as the Planta disease epidemic, Unilever had paid out huge sums in compensation and its corporate reputation had been dragged through the mud amid allegations that it had been deliberately misleading. The bitter irony for Unilever was that it found itself in this invidious position not because it had recklessly cut corners or through unbridled corporate greed, but because it had taken an ethical stance over its food ingredients.

It's only now, more than half a century on from the terrible outbreak of Planta disease, that the full story can be told. And the reason it can be told in detail is down to the curiosity and persistence of one man, Arnold Bosman, a public health expert in Stockholm who specialises in epidemiology. Although based in Sweden, Bosman is a Dutch national and early in his career he was mentored by an official who led the investigation into the Planta outbreak. As a qualified medical doctor, Bosman was of course fascinated to learn about the clinical aspects of the disease that had rocked the Netherlands before he was born. Out of the blue in that summer of 1960, doctors had been swamped by patients complaining of a new skin disease that looked a bit like measles. Symptoms ranged from red rashes, sores, itchiness and nausea at the mild end of the spectrum up to far more dangerous signs of infection such as high fever and ulcerated skin. Yet despite the scale of the crisis, in-depth information as to how Planta disease transpired and the manner in which the epidemic was subsequently handled by Unilever and the Dutch authorities was frustratingly thin on the ground.

A key part of Bosman's job is to share best practice with public health officials across Europe in the battle against infectious diseases. Despite the historic nature of the Planta affair, Bosman was convinced that plenty of valuable lessons could still be learned from it and he set out to develop a useful case study on it for his students. At first he was thwarted by the shortage of information in the public domain. It was a subject Unilever didn't want to revisit and there was little in the way of official government information that was easily accessible. Undeterred, Bosman dug deeper. Under Dutch law, there is a closed period of 50 years for files relating to public figures. Reports held under lock and key for decades are made available after half a century under freedom of information rules. Bosman visited the Dutch National Archives in The Hague and retrieved the personal archive of one of the great figures in the country's post-war history – Willem Drees, Prime Minister of the Netherlands from 1948 to 1958. Two years after the end of his premiership, this political heavyweight was chosen to chair the internal investigation committee at Unilever that was granted access to all the relevant participants in and documents relating to the Planta disaster. These documents, together with a copy of the formal internal report produced by the committee, which was never released by Unilever, were now in Bosman's hands. Finally, a proper account of events can be shared – by Bosman with his students, and here in the following paragraphs.

To put the story in context, we have to begin by looking at Europe as it was in the early 1950s. A post-war rise in living standards triggered a consumer boom at the same time as European countries began working more closely together on economic matters by taking the first steps towards the creation of the Common Market, the precursor to the EU. This set of circumstances convinced the executives at Unilever that there was a golden opportunity to scale up its food business internationally, with margarine to the forefront. Yet at the same time Unilever was mindful that in committing to hugely increasing the size of its food business it would have to address implications for consumer health. Responsibly, the company invested millions in setting up two scientific food safety laboratories in Europe and recruited leading toxicologists and biologists to work within them. At that time, all margarines used Palsgaard emulsion oil (PEO), the world's first commercial emulsifier, which had revolutionised the margarine industry following its introduction in 1917. But when scientists at Unilever's labs tested PEO on rats in 1955, to their disquiet they found evidence that it was carcinogenic. Unilever shared this information with the authorities in Germany and the Netherlands and enquired whether any food safety regulation could be implemented, but received no practical reply. This was a very different age, a time before robust food standards came into place.

To its enormous credit, Unilever acted unilaterally over its concerns about PEO, removing the emulsifier from its products. But in taking this responsible step, the company was putting itself at a disadvantage to its competitors, who continued using PEO and reaped the benefits of convenience in the eyes of the consumer because their margarines did not spatter during the cooking process. 'From that moment, the race was on,' says Bosman. 'There was a lot of pressure on the research and development laboratories to come up with a safe alternative.'

Several alternatives to PEO were investigated in parallel, with tests on rats and pigs followed by small-scale human taste trials among lab personnel. An emulsifier called ME-18 proved to be the most promising one – it spread well and was considered favourably by those who ate it. There were no obvious drawbacks. Excited by its potential, Unilever marketers began pushing for its introduction. The scientists on the other hand wanted to test for longer. With no regulation to guide the way, differences of opinion led to simmering tensions between the two camps. 'In 1958 the German branch of Unilever decided to go for it,' Bosman reveals. 'There are minutes of those internal scientific meetings showing fierce opposition from toxicologists saying, "it is not wise, we have just tested it for half a year and we need more tests." That was more or less ignored and they put it on the market.'

Unilever reformulated two of its existing margarine brands in West Germany – Rama and Sanella – to include ME-18. Consumers enthusiastically welcomed the 'improved' products, but the products had to be withdrawn from the market before the end of the year because tightened national food hygiene laws requiring more stringent testing of chemical additives came into force. The introduction of the margarines containing ME-18 coincided with the outbreak of a mysterious skin disease, the spread of which had experts baffled as it remained confined within West German borders. When the margarines were taken off the market in November 1958, the disease disappeared as quickly as it had arrived. A handful of doctors working in practices scattered across the country suspected there might be a connection, but when they raised their concerns they were ridiculed and dismissed as cranks by more 'eminent' colleagues who considered such a theory ludicrously fanciful. It is an appreciation of this type of scenario that Bosman considers immensely valuable in disease control to this day. 'From a public health perspective, for me this is a very important lesson. You need to try to detach yourself from dogmas, to take every observation seriously and never to trust a person just because his or her title is Professor So-and-So. We're still running into that kind of problem today; when a professor says something, the value of that is perceived as being so much higher than some doctor in a village.'

Yet with the products containing ME-18 now off the market, and any link between the emulsifier and the skin disease outbreak widely discounted as being tenuous and speculative, outside interest in establishing a connection quickly died down. Unilever continued conducting toxicology tests on ME-18:

> 'All the rats had survived. There was some scar tissue on the rats that they couldn't explain but the way they did the tests was they didn't feed it to the rats, they just injected it into their stomachs, which is not what people do with margarine. So if you get some scar tissue, nobody knew how to interpret that. There was a lot of uncertainty there but at least they were not seeing the terrible things they saw with the previous one, the PEO. There was no cancer. The people in the laboratory who tested it were fine. There was even one of the laboratory guys at Unilever in Germany who, because of the suspicions of the ME-18, drank 100ml of it in raw emulsifier form and stayed healthy. This was the level of confidence people internally had.'

> Arnold Bosman

Unilever also sought input from a committee of dermatology experts. However, at a time when there were no international standards or guidelines for this kind of work, the usefulness of their input was fairly limited. This was an era when, as Bosman describes it with a lovely turn of phrase, clinicians undertook this sort of assignment to earn some extra pocket money. Not the kind of set-up, in other words, to provide an effective fail-safe. With no concrete evidence to indicate that ME-18 could be harmful, Unilever's food scientists came under pressure once again from marketers to give the emulsifier the go-ahead. Only this time it was Unilever in the Netherlands that wanted it for its margarine brand, Planta.

When Planta Red (as the reformulated margarine is often referred to, because of its red label) was launched, a skin disease epidemic broke out in the Netherlands. As in West Germany two years earlier, medical professionals were nonplussed. At Rotterdam's municipal health authority, on day one of the outbreak the phones were ringing off the hook. GPs kept calling in to report patients with symptoms of an unexplained skin disease. Speculation was rife. Some wondered whether it might be an extreme reaction to the spraying of crops with pesticides. But one possible explanation caught the attention of epidemiologist Joop Huisman. A GP reported that a mother had brought her 11-year-old son Robbie Ouwerkerk into the surgery because of a skin rash. The mother explained that while Robbie, later nicknamed Robbie-Planta, had eaten the newly reformulated margarine, other members of the family had consumed butter instead and were completely fine. Might Planta Red be the cause of the skin complaint? she wondered. Enlisting the help of dermatologist Henk Doeglas, Huisman dashed across Rotterdam to see around forty patients who had been struck by the disease. All were asked if they had eaten Planta Red; all had indeed done so. As the product had a market share of only 5%, the conclusion was irrefutable. The margarine must in some way be responsible for the epidemic. Rotterdam public health officials got in touch with Unilever immediately. 'On the first day of the outbreak, the public health service contacted Unilever and shared their data,' says Bosman. 'On the same day, Unilever said "Okay. We're not only going to stop the production, we're going to recall all the batches that are on the market," which for 1960 was a really huge action.'

Although this was a period before email and mobile phones, Unilever mobilised very quickly. However, the company's internal minutes paint a picture of panicked executives discovering to their horror that something major had been overlooked. Desperately checking around the company internationally in search of more information, Dutch executives got hold of one of their production development directors who was visiting Sweden. When questioned, he revealed that he — together with executives high up in Unilever West Germany — had known about the suspected association between ME-18 and skin disease in West Germany, but had not shared this information with the board in the Netherlands because it was considered to have been a hoax. The realisation dawned on the Dutch board that they had a really big crisis on their hands.

Initially, Unilever received plaudits for its response. It was quick to offer compensation to people affected by the disease and the Dutch public seemed impressed by the company's commitment to the product recall, as affected batches were tracked down. Moreover, Unilever played a prominent role working with the Ministry of Social Affairs and Health as part of the crisis response team set up to deal with the emergency — although some of the government representatives on the team expressed doubts as to whether a multinational corporation with sensitive business interests to protect could be trusted to be entirely open and frank. These misgivings flared up into downright hostility when it emerged that ME-18 had found its way into another of Unilever's margarine brands, Blue Band. When Unilever directors had ordered the plant to cease production of Planta Red they did not clarify what should be done with the bulk mix that was already in the machines. Not fully aware what the problem was, the team at the production facility used the left-over bulk to make some Blue Band. It was a genuine and terribly ill-timed communications blunder, but some ministry officials weren't prepared to buy that as an explanation and accused Unilever of secrecy and duplicity.

'When it transpired that Blue Band was also causing disease,' says Bosman, 'the Ministry said "ah, you see — they were holding that back, they didn't want to share that with us and now you see what's happening." So that debate happened in public. Unilever was accused of hiding the facts and trying to sell dirty butter with new wrappings.' Until it could prove it was contamination-free, all Unilever margarine was removed from the Dutch market. The company's share price fell and it endured a spate of negative publicity in the media, which soon connected Planta disease with the epidemic in West Germany a couple of years earlier. Given that Unilever had started the search for a new emulsifier because of worries about the safety of PEO, its executives were exasperated and aggrieved to be the subject of vitriolic criticism – which explains why the company is still reticent to discuss the affair with leading epidemiologists like Bosman, even so long after the event and well into the 21st century.

All of which is a great shame, as Bosman has a clear appreciation of Unilever's point of view. 'If something like this were to happen today, from my position as a public health doctor I would rather deal with a company like Unilever because to me it seems that they understand quality and work towards the same goal in terms of having safe products for consumers.' Unilever proved adept at rebuilding its reputation in the wake of the scandal. It formed an agreement with the Dutch National Association of Medical Doctors, which it publicised to the association's membership, under which people affected by the outbreak would be compensated by Unilever if doctors made a declaration stating they had observed symptoms of the disease in the patient. Corporate law books still cite this type of compensation mechanism as one of the best moves a corporation can make to repair consumer trust.

Acting on the conclusions of its six-month internal investigation, Unilever tightened up its food development approval procedures and restructured to improve the way it shared scientific information across borders. Planta disease may have occurred a long time ago, but in an age when food contamination crises come thick and fast, there's still plenty to be learned from it.

> 'All the new generations need to go through these historic lessons to see what happened in the past but also to make their own conclusions about how it could translate to a modern situation. What if it were to happen to me tomorrow? If I'm in a small region or at the centre at a health protection agency, what do I do? Do I call the executive director of Company X to join my crisis team or not? Do I make him an ally or declare him the enemy?'
>
> Arnold Bosman

Planta was never reintroduced to the Dutch market, but the margarine brand is still available in several other countries including neighbouring Belgium. Unilever has recovered from the Planta affair to such an extent that it enjoys an enviable corporate reputation – a study on professional networking site LinkedIn released in October 2012 ranked it as the fifth most desirable company to work for in the world. It spends a billion euros a year on research and development and employs over six thousand people in R&D roles across 20 countries. More than most, Unilever has an appreciation of what the consequences can be if product formulation goes wrong.

Too well groomed in the makeover - the rejuvenation of Captain Birdseye and Barbie's Ken

It took a polar bear to finish off the long-lived, white-bearded mariner with a gruff, kid-pleasing talent for using nautical jargon to promote seafood. Captain Birdseye – or Captain Iglo as he was known in some other markets – first appeared in commercials for frozen fish fingers back in 1967. Dressed in a merchant sailor's uniform, he looked like a Santa of the seas holding down a summer job as ship's entertainment officer. After a short period of shore leave in the early 1970s, the affable, snowy-haired brand mascot was brought back on board to sell cod in even greater quantities. He made such an impact with British families that in a 1993 poll the fictitious fish-flogger was voted the second most recognised sea captain behind explorer James Cook. But when John Hewer, who portrayed the character for 30 years, chose to retire in 1998, Birds Eye seized the chance for a mascot makeover. Out went the Captain Birdseye of old with facial hair whiter than bleached sailcloth; in came a swarthy and handsome young Captain with designer stubble who was clearly intended to be more of a maritime action hero. There was even a short-lived cartoon version of the youthfully regenerated Captain with his pet pelican, Pedro. Yet just like a plastic surgeon having an off day at work, consumers found the attempt to engineer youthfulness unappealing. As far as the public was concerned, familiarity had taught them what Captain Birdseye should look like ... and he should always be a weather-beaten ancient mariner.

Once brand characters become well established, there's often resistance to radical change: versatile actor though he is, Sir Ian McKellen would make a terrible Milky Bar Kid; putting Tony the Leopard on a pack of Frosties would provoke roars of disapproval; and Lindsay Lohan as the Jolly Green Giant? I think not! So Birds Eye brought in a new, older actor, a doppelgänger for Hewer. Its brand icon was once more a salty old seadog, beard as white as sea spume, just the way the public liked it. A young whippersnapper could never hope to do the job of the old ship's master. When the Captain was finally consigned to the deep in 2010, it was a laconic polar bear puppet named Clarence, named after frozen food innovator and business founder Clarence Birdseye (whose ashes, incidentally, were scattered at sea), that took his place − rather more convincingly than a youngster dressing up in his clothes.

However, for the ultimate overboard makeover look no further than toy maker Mattel and its demonstration in 1993 that it had a queer eye for the little plastic guy. Earring Magic Ken, an edition of Barbie's male companion doll, looked like he had been extravagantly styled with America's gay nightlife scene in mind. Resplendent in a sleeveless lilac PVC jacket with matching figure-hugging mesh T-shirt, this Ken was no rugged GI Joe. His hair had been prettified with blond highlights and he was obviously no stranger to the cosmetics counter. Here at last was a Ken who really knew how to accessorise. In addition to his solitary earring, Barbie's camp friend wore a necklace from which hung a circular piece of jewellery − which a number of commentators in the media took great pleasure in referring to as a 'cock ring'. These sexually charged adornments were popularly worn on neck chains in the gay club scene of the time. Given that the core target market for the Barbie brand is girls aged three and upwards, this was an unexpected fashion direction for Mattel to take.

When Earring Magic Ken came out − as it were − gay men rushed to snap up the doll as a kitsch keepsake. Although sales were pleasingly brisk, Mattel found itself uncomfortably mired in controversy. On the one hand, it did not want to risk alienating conservative Middle America with a doll that was increasingly being referred to as Gay Ken. On the other, it was also drawing criticism from some high-profile members of the US gay community. In a piece for Seattle newspaper the *Stranger*,

Dan Savage wrote: 'Queer Ken is the high-water mark of, depending on your point of view, either queer infiltration into popular culture or the thoughtless appropriation of queer culture by heterosexuals.' This was not at all the sort of debate Mattel had intended to be part of when it set out to give Ken a trendier look to impress the children of the nineties. Earring Magic Ken was hastily withdrawn from the market. These days, if Barbie's male friends are into the gay club scene, they're rather more discreet about it.

Tips and lessons

- Research customer opinion before making any significant changes to major products or brand strategy.
- But remember that research, especially if its focus is narrow, doesn't have all the answers – so keep a bigger picture in mind.
- Introduce reformulated products only once thorough testing confirms that the changes are safe and beneficial.
- Always be clear on what you stand for.
- Changes that are disadvantageous to loyal customers will likely trigger a backlash.

Conclusion

The heightened risks of the social media age

The spotlight is on brands as never before. They are signifiers of our social identity – aspirational, ubiquitous. They help us make up our minds about what to buy and play a role in how we judge others. Great brands, for better and for worse, have made the world a more homogenous place. Arguably, they have become more solidly entrenched than ever in our lives. The red Coke can sits proudly on shelves across the globe, an enduring symbol of marketing success long after the red flag of the Soviet Union has been carted away to the museum equivalent of the gulag. But while an ideological war has largely been won, allowing strong brands to further prosper internationally, they are not immune from harm.

People expect ever more quality, content and experiences from brands. They have a sense of ownership that comes not only from spending their hard-earned cash but by investing in an emotional connection. That is a wonderful thing for marketers when all is going well. It's a very different story if consumers feel disappointed or aggrieved. The readiness with which people will take to social media to attack brands they feel are in the wrong has been proven time and again. It is the new normal. Had Twitter and Facebook existed at the time of the Edsel launch, Ford would undoubtedly have been swamped by a tide of social media criticism. If the Persil Power debacle were to be repeated now, there would be pictures of tattered clothes all over Instagram and barbed Vines at the brand's expense.

Marketers can still make the same kind of mistakes they always could, which is why learning how to avoid fundamental errors, such as those that were responsible for turning the Hoover free flights promotion into an abject fiasco, remains of utmost importance. History should never be dismissed; it has much to teach us. But, as the examples in this book demonstrate over and over again, the social media age has fundamentally altered the nature of marketing. Brands are now held instantly accountable in the court of public opinion. A situation born of a moment's thoughtlessness can rapidly escalate to the point where immense damage can be inflicted on brand reputation. Social media is an omnipresent factor in the marketing disasters of recent years. It is either where an issue caught fire in the first place or where a problem became more inflamed. How brands behave when coming under pressure via social media is a recurring theme of *Great Brand Blunders*. In a messy, frenetic online environment, populated by the opinionated and the occasional beastly troll, it is the brands that were open, straightforward, responsive and treated their audience with respect that coped best when problems struck. Others, who took a beating for their blunders, have rung the changes to avoid a repeat of such damaging assaults. Exploring how they responded and how they have changed gives us an idea as to whether our own intentions are wise or unwise.

The chances of putting a foot wrong in marketing have never been higher. Absorbing the lessons scattered abundantly through the previous pages will undoubtedly reduce the risk of that happening to you. As this book shows, blundering need not be fatal. Many of the world's greatest brands have made mistakes, only to bounce back stronger than ever. Shame lies not in failing, but in failing to learn from failure.

Acknowledgements

Writing a book like this is in many ways a collaborative effort and would not be possible without the assistance of numerous talented, intelligent and knowledgeable people. I am hugely indebted to everyone who shared their time and expertise in helping me research and complete this work.

For a start, I'd like to put on the record my thanks to everybody I have quoted in these pages. Their insight, candour and – for those who have revisited awkward moments in their careers – professional bravery are admirable and enlightening. In a book in which I often poke fun, I hope everyone involved will also feel that I have always tried to be fair. My appreciation goes out to: Matt Anderson, Pete Blackshaw, Arnold Bosman, Michael Choo, Harry Cichy, Gus Desbarats, Richard Edelman, Mark Kimber, Bettina Klinken, Allan Leighton, Rob Manuel, Paul Nieuwenhuis, Liz O'Neill, Jan Rogers Kniffen, Bernd Samland, Laetitia Sorribes, Simon Talbot, Keith Wells, Rainer Westermann, Adrian Wheeler and Jamie Woolley.

Additionally, countless people have helped behind the scenes, providing valuable leads, sage advice and access to essential information, resources and useful contacts. In particular I'd like to thank: Boris Barth, Kathryn Bishop, Stef Brown, Stephen Cooles (afraid I'll have to save Pen Island for another book), Michael Fineman, Ginny Gray, Mirjam Gulmans, James Herring, Robin Hicks, Pavel Melnikov, Trevor Morris, Silvy Peeters, Sherif Shafie, Alejandro Trípoli and Johnny Wilson.

My hearty appreciation goes to Jon Finch for commissioning me to write this book, for his great support and enthusiasm in helping this project take shape and for a convivial lunch in Banbury. I'm grateful to Hugh Brune for his encouragement, eye for detail and perceptive advice on structure and navigability, which have made for a better book.

To anyone I have missed out, please accept my profound apologies – and if possible, allow yourself a rueful smile at the irony: this is, after all, a book about blunders, oversights, ineptitude and undesirable outcomes.

Thanks also to my children for the many 'creatively constructive' distractions they have provided during the long hours spent writing this book, with a special mention for my daughter Abbie, whose assistance in breaking a bone in my left little finger as we wrestled for a ball in an over-enthusiastic back garden game of piggy-in-the-middle improved my typing no end at a point in time when my deadline for delivering this manuscript loomed large. Way to go, Abbie!

Index